tony adams

ADDICTED

tony adams

ADDICTED

the sports book of the year with **ian ridley**

HarperCollins*Publishers*

HarperCollins*Publishers*
1 London Bridge Street
London SE1 9GF

www.harpercollins.co.uk

First published by Willow,
an imprint of HarperCollins*Publishers* 1998
This edition published 2017

A catalogue record of this book is available
from the British Library

ISBN 978-0-00-826874-9

Printed and bound by CPI Group (UK) Ltd, Croydon, CR0 4YY

Photographic acknowledgements
All photographs courtesy of the author with the following exceptions:
Action Images plate section page 3, 9b, 10b, 18tl, 20bl, 21b, 21t, 22b, 22t;
Allsport 4tl, 4b, 5b, 6t, 7t, 7cr, 10t, 10c, 13t, 16b, 17t, 20br, 23t, 23c, 24cl, 24cr,
24b; Colorsport 4c, 6cr, 7b, 9t, 11t, 12b, 14t, 14b, 15t, 16t, 18b; Empics 5t, 6b,
15b, 17b, 23b; Express Newspapers 8bl; Mirror Syndication 5c, 7cl, 12t, 13b,
15c, 20t; PA News 8br.

Contents

Contents

Acknowledgements

Thanks to the following:

To Arsenal Football Club for fifteen years of employment.

To Jerome Anderson and Jeff Weston who suggested I needed to tell my story.

To Eddie Bell, Chairman of HarperCollins*Publishers*, for your sincerity.

To Ian Ridley, my friend and writer for eighteen months of self-discovery and enlightenment. I am indebted to you for shining your light on my life, and bringing my book into being.

To Steve and Mandy Jacobs for the encouragement to keep going.

To James for helping me to find the courage to rid myself of the wreckage of the past and to be free to live in the present.

Finally, to Bill W, without whose help I would still be drinking.

Love and Peace

Tony Adams,
Putney, London, August 1998

ONE

The End

I just knew what would happen. Not that Gareth Southgate would fail to score with his penalty, but that if he did miss, and if the Germans then scored with their next one, I was going to get drunk. I had not had a drink all the way through Euro '96, which, for a man coming to realise he was an alcoholic, took some doing. But then, I had been consumed by my first addiction – football. And as soon as that was taken away from me, I just knew what would happen. It was as if I had no choice.

It had been the pattern of both my career and my life: get drunk to deal with the deep disappointments, get drunk to deal with the joyous moments of achievement – and there had been many of both. Booze acted for me as an anaesthetic to avoid intense feelings, bad or good, and right now on this balmy summer night of Wednesday 26 June 1996, with the England team I was captaining just having lost 6–5 on penalties to Germany in the semi-final of the European Championships at Wembley, was as bad as it got. I needed to numb the pain. And so I would drink. For the next seven weeks. I would drink until the pain would be numbed no more.

We had not actually planned for this. For penalties, yes, but not going beyond the first five that had failed to separate the teams after the 1–1 draw in 120 minutes of play. I was standing in the centre circle congratulating those who had already scored – Alan Shearer, David Platt, Stuart Pearce, Paul Gascoigne and Teddy Sheringham. I have never been a great penalty-taker myself, and although I would have taken one if others had declined, as had happened with Arsenal in a European Cup Winners' Cup semi-final against Sampdoria the previous year, I was in no rush to volunteer. Gareth, bravely, fatefully, was.

When Andreas Möller smashed in a shot that gave David Seaman no chance of repeating his goalkeeping heroics of earlier in the tournament, I managed to observe the professional stiff-upper-lip rituals that had been instilled in me since making my debut for Arsenal three weeks past my 17th birthday. I shook hands with the opposition. I went to commiserate with everyone else, especially Gareth who was virtually in tears. It may be no bad thing thinking of others, but at that time it was my way of masking what I was feeling and just added to the emotional damage I would later see that I was inflicting on myself. Then came the lap of honour, more a walk round the stadium to acknowledge the astonishing 'Three Lions' atmosphere Wembley had created and to thank the nation for the life-enhancing euphoria of the previous three weeks. For me, there was now only one way of filling the emptiness without it.

Back in the dressing room – the away one, with the Germans having been allocated the home – I sat with head bowed just inside the door and to the right, in the allotted spot for No. 5, between Paul Ince, No. 4, and Gareth, No. 6. When I looked up to scan the scene of silence, my eyes panned around the big red and white tiles with that 'W' logo on them until they reached a makeshift bar in a corner. In a booth there, were sandwiches, oranges and water. And cans of Carling Black Label. I sauntered over and took one. It barely touched the sides. By the time I was into the second, the anger was setting in and I was slagging off the Germans. 'Them again. Penalties in 1990, penalties again now,' I said to Bryan Robson, once a playing colleague, now an England coach, who was sitting alongside me.

We had worked so hard, come through our group against Switzerland, Scotland and Holland and beaten Spain on penalties in the quarter-final. And tonight we had outplayed Germany. It had been a long time since we had done that. Maybe for the twenty minutes between Alan Shearer scoring our goal and Stefan Kuntz's reply, Germany were in the game, but apart from that we had taken them to the cleaners. And I'd had one of my best games for England as well. A toe length of Gazza's, when the ball brushed his lunging studs with the goal at his mercy, or a better finish by Darren Anderton, who had hit the post, and we'd have been in the final against the Czech Republic. And we'd have won that. No danger. Oh, what the hell. Have another drink.

I don't remember much about the coach journey back to Burnham Beeches, the team hotel near Slough. Everyone was wrapped in their own cocoon of disappointment and deflation. It was done. It was finished. All I wanted to do was get out of it. In more ways than one. Back at Burnham, there seemed to be a lot of fans and hotel staff around, applauding us. We were being treated like heroes. I hated that. I didn't feel like one. We were out and although we had emerged with a lot of credit, Tony Adams had always been a winner. Anything else hurt. As far as I was concerned, we might as well have gone out in the first round. That was always my philosophy. On the other hand, I knew we had done our best, we were unlucky and hadn't let ourselves down. A million conflicting thoughts were going through my head, as they do with a drunk in pain. And a drunk in pain has only one aim.

I think I made sense to a few people for the first four or five pints of Guinness. That was usually my drink, and luckily they always did a lovely pint of it at Burnham. I thanked Terry Venables and his assistant Don Howe, my coach at Arsenal 14 years ago now, whom I had always so admired, for their work. It was sincere, if a bit garbled, because I genuinely believed they had brought English football out of a dark age and set us on the right path. Apart from that, I can't remember what I said or to whom. Because soon after that came the oblivion I was seeking.

I woke up in my room, kit and clothes strewn everywhere. That set of questions familiar to any drunk started to penetrate my brain. Where am I? What happened? What did I say? Have I embarrassed myself, as I have done so many times in the past? How do I get home? Then the question particular to me that morning. Did we win? Oh shit, we lost. There was only one way I knew to deal with all that and everything else going on in my head. I had to get drunk again.

Most people had left when I made it downstairs to the lobby at around 10 am, all my belongings gathered up in a great big holdall. The place was now quiet and eerie and lonely. Only Gareth Southgate and Stuart Pearce seemed to be left. 'Not just the one?' I asked but I couldn't convince them to join me in a pint. Why are they more interested in getting home to their families and friends, I wondered. What's so great about reality? My reality stank. I was ready for a bender.

It seemed to me that I had done pretty well so far this year after everything that had happened. That February, my wife Jane had entered a treatment centre in Wiltshire for a drug problem. There, in the April, she had come to decide that she wanted to leave me and the rejection focused my mind for a while, so for 21 days I didn't touch a drop. I ticked them off on a calendar. Not that visiting her at a place where there were also alcoholics as well as drug addicts did much for me. I was in denial about my own drinking, sometimes feeling superior to everyone in there, sometimes inferior because they were doing something about their problem. I would meet with Jane's drug counsellors and leave seething with rage because I thought they were trying to belittle me; me, Tony Adams, captain of Arsenal and England. Back home, I would weep with all the self-pity and frustration. On recommendation, though, I had also started to see a counsellor, called James, thinking it would help me to understand Jane. In fact, though I barely knew it, I was making a start on understanding myself.

I certainly knew that once I started drinking, I had to carry on until I was drunk – and beyond. So I decided that the only way for me to be sure I was going to make the Euro '96 squad, and function properly through the Championships, was to stay away from drink altogether. I had a good drink in early May to celebrate the end of the club football season, but I knew that as soon as I met up with England it would have to stop. Even on the trip to China – where I proved I was fit enough to play despite a knee injury – and Hong Kong, where Terry let the boys have a last night out, I kept my resolve. While the players were being photographed enjoying themselves in the China Jump Club and its dentist chair, something for which they were subsequently heavily criticized, I was shutting myself away in my hotel room, knowing how I would have ended up had I gone with them. It was dawning on me that I couldn't beat the booze. After my 21-day dry period had ended a couple of months earlier, I knew when I made up my mind to have another a drink that I would go on a bender. It would not be just to enjoy a couple of pints.

I felt the same way on the Cathay Pacific flight home that was to occupy so much of the nation's attention in the run-up to Euro '96. All sorts of mayhem was apparently going on somewhere down the plane, with a couple of small TV screens being broken as a result of spirits too high, but I just sat at the front minding my own business. Again the realisation was getting through to me that if I started drinking, I would have been in amongst them at the back, doing some damage of my own.

But now the tournament was over there was nothing to stop me, I thought, as I stood here alone at the bar at Burnham Beeches. I deserved this drink, this session that I knew would develop. I had no choice in the matter, again. Why was that? As yet, though I was getting stirrings that I might be suffering from the illness of alcoholism, I had no real insight into its insidious nature and though I had shown that I could stop for short periods, I had no idea how to stay off the booze permanently. Didn't want to know. Who wants to be an alcoholic?

I had put that old mask on as I wished Gareth and Stuart all the best with their clubs for the coming season. Underneath it, the real me was crumbling, wondering what to do with my loneliness. It suddenly occurred to me that I had forgotten to get all the autographs of my team-mates that Jane had asked for. I'd have to tell her I left them on the coach, or something. If she wanted to see me any more, that is. It was yet another reason why I couldn't face up to realities, which included looking after my children Clare, Oliver and Amber, then aged eleven, four and eighteen months. Where to now, though? Only one place.

I was always assured of sympathy and company at my local, The Chequers, at Emerson Park in Hornchurch. Sometimes I would ring round people, old mates, to see who was coming out to play, just like a kid does with football. Today, sorry for myself, I just wanted to wallow alone in my own thoughts and feelings. After the eight-week term I had served five years earlier in Chelmsford Prison, I was well warned against drink-driving, and I knew I would be over the limit from the night before, so one of the security staff from Burnham Beeches drove me over to Essex. Bill, the landlord at The Chequers, was a lovely guy and welcomed me with open arms. He put my England kit bag behind the bar for me.

I would often walk in there, look along the row of beer pumps and say, 'What do I feel like today?' It was almost like a kid at the Pick 'n' Mix sweet counter in Woolworths. If it was a warm day, I might start with a chilled lager or two. Today I was on the Guinness. About two pints an hour was the standard consumption, though mostly it was hard to tell as I kept my glass topped up. If oblivion was the aim, then it would be three pints. Today I was pushing up towards three.

I watched them all come and go as I habitually did: the printers on the early shift at lunchtime, then the plumbers and builders in mid-afternoon. They came and went after a couple, though. I stayed and stayed, until the fancy took me to the Greyhound in Bethnal Green, East London, owned by a mate of mine. There the memories dim – a game of pool, probably; a club later that night. Where did I spend the night? It was Friday afternoon when I got back to the empty house that Jane had by now left to go and live in London with the kids. The phone rang. It was the FA. Did

I, as captain, want to go to the Final and pick up the Fair Play Award that England had won? 'No, thank you,' was my answer. I couldn't tell them I was too frightened to go back to Wembley with all these raw memories still hurting me. I would much rather go on the piss to blot it all out. Terry Venables went in the end. I half-watched the game on the Sunday night. I was right. We would have thrashed the Czechs if we had only beaten those Germans ...

When I had my football, I was all right, in control, focused. All my self-worth was in what I did, not what I was. In that state, I would look in the mirror and say to myself, 'Right. Remember how you are now. Let's try and keep it.' On other days, when I was drinking, I would look in the mirror and just wonder, 'Why can't you stop this, now?' I was all over the place, feeling worthless. All my pats on the back came from being Tony the footballer. Tony the person did not like himself and as the summer drained away, so did the fight and the spirit in him.

Now and then, I would go home for an hour or two between benders to run a couple of errands, but mostly I was staying anywhere, and everywhere, around London with friends and acquaintances. I left Clare, Oliver and Amber with my mother-in-law Barbara at her home in Muswell Hill, North London, or with nannies and baby-sitters when it was my turn to have them. One week, I was feeling so guilty about neglecting my kids that I thought I ought to take them on holiday. So, one day, careful to stay off the drink as I guarded the remaining standards I had left, I drove for five hours down to the Carlyon Bay hotel in Cornwall.

Though my motives were good, the holiday was actually a bad idea as I was in no mental state to look after them. The booze was too big for me, dominating my every thought. As soon as we arrived, I settled them into the room, got them to sleep as swiftly as I could, and, I'm sad to say, went down to the bar. I didn't want to leave the hotel as I couldn't be sure that I would make it back if I had a drink inside me. Later, I discovered the hotel had a babysitting service. In the bar, I would just befriend anyone, to cover up my feelings of isolation, buying them all drinks. On another night, I just shut myself in the room with the kids and a bottle of wine.

After only four days of this, I drove through the night back to Barbara's in Muswell Hill, where the kids were probably better off. I think they were bored and I just couldn't give them any attention. We came back because Oliver was starting a new school, but as good a reason for me was that I could be alone again to drink unhindered. I had the perfect excuse, too. Jane was now out of treatment and beginning to work a programme of recovery, getting in touch with how she really felt about things. Her rejection hurt and angered me. Perhaps she felt my drinking would interfere with her staying off drugs. I wrote two letters to her, one saying I admired what she was doing, one angry with her for leaving me. A rough draft of the second one would end up in the *News of the World*, retrieved by someone from a skip outside my house.

Gradually I was losing everything, it seemed, and the drink was winning. I thought it was the one thing keeping me going, but in fact it was making things worse. I was also getting into some bad scrapes. One Sunday afternoon I went into a club in Covent Garden with a couple of drinking buddies and a fight broke out around us. When you are a drunk, you seem to attract trouble. One of my mates had his nose smeared around his face and I just dived in. The next thing I knew, I was being thrown out and police were asking me a load of questions. It was the usual drunken stuff, they decided, and having sobered up a little, I was released. Then on the Monday, I would be at the door of my local five minutes before opening time, banging on it to get in. Who does that on a Monday morning? Only an alcoholic, I was beginning to realise. There I would be, at the bar on my own. There I was, a well-known sportsman, feeling alone and desperate for that first drink of the day.

Meanwhile the knee trouble that came close to keeping me out of Euro '96 was still a worry and Arsenal were sending me frequently to see doctors and to be tested. Every time I did a test I was either hungover or drunk, and I can't imagine what the results said. Quite often, I would have to be up in Harley Street for 11 am, which was great. After the examination, I was free and off the leash in the middle of London. It could be a couple of days before I got home again, full of apologies to my mother-in-law who had been left looking after my children.

The medics decided I needed another operation, which I underwent on 16 July in a private hospital in Whitechapel, East London, that Arsenal used. When I had my first knee operation in February in the middle of the football season, I was working towards getting fit for Euro '96. Now that drug was withdrawn as it was the close season and I felt very alone. I was beginning to get a glimpse of my drink problem, having been seeing a counsellor for around six months, and being forced to sit and look at myself was very painful. I was getting desperate. I wanted to stop drinking, but I didn't know how to. I thought I needed to drink. Wouldn't you, if you had all this pain and disappointment in your life?

As I sat at home with my leg in one of those casts into which they pump an air pocket, and was thus forced out of the pub routine, I began to get a bit of self-respect back, just for odd periods. I became obsessive about drawing and painting. When I was in jail, I drew Disney characters to keep myself occupied. Now I sketched things like the Teenage Mutant Ninja Turtles as well as Lady and the Tramp and Baloo from *The Jungle Book* for my children. I found it hard to concentrate, though, with a hundred things racing through my mind. Was my marriage really over? How could I play football in this state? I was in that horrible place of being without a drink and not wanting to be, but sensing that I *needed* to be.

Some days I couldn't manage it and would struggle out on crutches for a session. One day when I was in a pub in the West End, a fight broke out and I smashed a crutch over someone's head. The argument was none of my business, really, but I had to stick my nose in anyway, thinking I was helping. The poor bloke got thrown out and I was the hero. But I was the one off my trolley. Actually, I didn't remember much about it.

It was another of those incidents when I was in blackout – that state of still functioning but not being aware what I was doing, which happened to me a lot during my drinking – and about which I was put in the full picture the following day. I was taking the anger and frustration I was feeling about myself out on other people.

By the time I got back to work at the Arsenal training ground at London Colney, near St Albans in Hertfordshire, just to do some light running to test the knee, the first-team squad had gone to Florence for a pre-season friendly. Now my emotional pain took on a new intensity with the physical effort required adding to my mental torture. I was losing weight and had dropped to around 13 stone, about half a stone below my optimum, because I was not eating properly. But then, I wasn't doing anything properly. If I could just get the marriage back ... If I could get back to playing football. Just pull yourself together. Get a grip. Do better. I was trying to run my life like a football match. I've lost today. Shit. Try to do better next time.

Most of the time I was shattered as I dashed from one place to another, through what felt like traffic jam after traffic jam. I was on a rollercoaster with the drinking, slowing and under control some days because I could just have a few glasses of wine at home in the evening, then hurtling through a three-day bender. By now Jane had been 'clean', as recovering addicts call it, for over four months and was well settled in Fulham, West London. Some nights I would go over and look after the kids while she went to her self-help group meeting.

I was jealous of her recovery. I wanted to recover, too, and was angry with her for, as I saw it, taking no interest in me. In reality, she probably could not afford to let me and my sickness intrude in her life. And I was sick. While at her house, out of old habit I would search to see if she had any drugs stashed away. You would never catch me with any of that rubbish, I used to tell myself. At least I'm no druggie. But I *was*. For alcohol. I would also look for anything she might have written about me while she was in treatment. I found one passage in a diary in which I was described as dominant. I was furious.

The confusion in me about whether my drinking was a friend or enemy heightened because sometimes I could pass my local on my way back from Jane's – even though it was agony – congratulating myself in the process. Then on other nights I could not stay out of there. Some days I would be taking care of myself and my children, on others I would be relying on nannies or my local cab company to get them to school and fetch me Indian takeaways or some shopping. I would visit the counsellor, feel more hopeful about myself, then go on another deflating bender.

Nowhere was my confusion more evident than in my dealings with the Arsenal vice-chairman David Dein and the managing director Ken Friar around this time. I was negotiating a new contract with them and not happy with what they were offering. Counselling was beginning to teach me about honesty, so I came out and said the things that were on my mind. I had always signed my contracts with a minimum of fuss because I had always wanted to play for Arsenal – and several times I had heard of approaches from Manchester United but had not been interested – but in my resentful state, I was beginning to feel taken for granted. For the first time I took an agent, Jerome Anderson, into negotiations, just as back-up. 'I have always done a good job for you,' I said, 'and I know what I am worth. You've always got me cheaply. Don't make me leave it to an agent to sort this out. Just pay me what I am worth.' It was ironic that I was in no fit state to play football, but my point held good and they could see it. I got that good contract.

I'm not quite sure what my motives were, though. I thought that if I could just get some more money, Jane might come back to me. To go with the house in Hornchurch, I had also taken a flat in Hampstead, thinking it might impress her. But whatever was my thinking over the contract, I felt elated as I drove home from Highbury, not only at having secured a good financial deal but also at having stood up for myself. A counsellor might have described me as being assertive rather than aggressive.

This insight had come to me without a drink and I knew that I didn't need to have a drink to get this good feeling, so I decided not to buy a bottle of champagne. But so pleased was I at being so self-disciplined, as I saw it, that I went out to the local and got drunk. I could not work out that logic. But then alcoholism, I was beginning to find out, is not logical. Later I would hear that it is cunning, baffling and powerful and, with hindsight, in that incident I could see it. A couple of days later at training, I was telling all the boys that I had cracked this drinking business. But it was me who was about to crack.

My own turmoil was being matched by what was going on at Arsenal, although I had hardly been a part of it all summer. Bruce Rioch was preparing for his second season as manager, but all had not been well. He had been unable to sign the players he wanted and had been involved in a personality clash with Ian Wright. Paul Merson was also encountering some problems in his own recovery from his addictions of gambling, alcoholism and drugs. All the while, I, as Arsenal captain, was not there for Bruce, and I felt sorry for him. He had been good to me. He was a decent, approachable man. But I had found out at my meeting with David Dein and Ken Friar that he would not be with the club much longer. Indeed, the end for Bruce came shortly after a pre-season friendly at Ipswich when he apparently told the boys that he 'felt like Marje Proops' trying to deal with all their problems. I was out of sight and out of mind, but I was contributing to those problems by lying to him about my whereabouts and state of fitness.

The day before the season started, I was supposed to go to training at London Colney, then travel with Gary Lewin, our physiotherapist, to the hospital in Whitechapel to have my knee examined and, hopefully – for Arsenal at least – receive the all-clear to start full training. Instead I was in a hotel room at the Holiday Inn in Kensington.

I had set out on a bender with a friend on the Wednesday and stayed at his place that night. I can't remember where we went, but I have a vague memory of drinking a bottle of peach schnapps, getting drunk very quickly and feeling panicky. The following evening we set out for the Chelsea area, which I was getting to know since Jane had moved to nearby Fulham and I had been travelling over to see her. We started in a restaurant called Barbarella's in the King's Road where, full of champagne, lager and big-headedness, I booked a table for 20 for the Saturday night. I told the owners that I would bring the Arsenal team down after our first game against West Ham, a match in which I would be taking no part.

This may all sound glamorous: the England football captain, hotels and clubs in the most fashionable area of London. It was far from it. The dying stages of active alcoholism are not pretty; more usually they are filthy, miserable and degrading, as it was to be as this night wore on. It serves no one, least of all me, to cover up the reality. Only by being honest with myself and others about the facts and feelings surrounding my drinking over those 24 hours was I eventually able to make any progress and lift myself out of the humiliation that period was to bring.

I had done some crazy things in the drinking that had coursed through my life and my career. There had been all the public episodes, like crashing my car and going to jail, like falling down nightclub steps and having 29 stitches inserted in my head. Then there was the stuff I had managed to keep private: running up a bill for £5,800 in a nightclub springs to mind; smashing bottles over my head as a party piece; frequently wetting the bed. This night, when crazy turned to sordid, though, was the one that did for me.

After taking in a strip club, I picked up a girl for the night and took her back to the Holiday Inn. My next memory is of the daylight coming through the curtain the next morning, having sex with the girl but looking at my watch to read 7 am and wondering where I could get a drink at this time of day. That was the grip which booze had on me, and showed just how sick I was. She was just another fix to try and make me feel better and, like the booze, no longer was it working the way it had done in the past. No longer, either, was I concerned with the feelings of another human being. There was no pleasure in anything, only need. I just wanted to have her and for her to leave, so that I could get back to my drinking. There was nothing left to drink in the room. Cans and miniature bottles from the now-empty minibar littered the floor.

I managed somehow to make my way to my mate Pete's pub in Bethnal Green, The Greyhound. I knew he would give me a drink and as the first Budweiser slipped down, I could feel the ice-cold relief. Now, at about 9.30 am, I was beginning to come round, beginning to get enough courage to face the day. After a while, I remembered my hospital appointment. I told Pete to wait, that I would be back, but that I had to get to Whitechapel first. When I got there, the surgeon with whom I had the appointment, John King, asked me to ring Gary Lewin, who had been waiting at London Colney and trying to get hold of me, wondering where I was. I don't know what John must have thought of me. He didn't say anything, but I was unshaven and must have stank of booze.

After the appointment, I dashed back to Bethnal Green for another drink and persuaded Pete to come with me to Emerson Park for a session. After a few at The Chequers, he decided in mid-afternoon that he had better get back to get his own pub ready for a busy Friday night. I was left on my own. With no conversation to hide them, feelings of desolation and impending doom built up in me. I put a song on the juke box, 'Black Coffee in Bed' by Squeeze, but it depressed me with its lyrics about being left by a woman and about 'tears on my pillow.' I decided to go home.

There, I got undressed, lay down on the bed and tried to rest, but in my agitated state, I just could not be alone with myself. The words of this song were haunting me. The drink had stopped working; I needed another one. Amid the filthy state that was now my house, the first clothes that came to hand were a pair of jeans that I had soiled a couple of days before. They were now dry and seemed in a reasonable enough condition, so I put them on. I wasn't too worried about the stains. A shower or wash did not occur to me. At 4 pm I left the house, not knowing where I was going. Instinct took me to a local social club that was closing but where I knew that the steward, Jack, would let me have a drink. I ordered a pint of Guinness.

It was five o'clock, I noticed, when Jack came over to the table in the corner where I was sitting alone with an empty glass.

'You want another one, Tone?' he asked.

'That's the last thing I need, Jack,' I answered.

'You all right, Tone?'

'No, I'm not,' I said and I started to cry.

The booze had finally done me in. My 'friend' had turned on me and kicked me in the bollocks. I was trying to run away from all the problems piling up on me but staying in the same miserable place.

I don't know how or why it happened then, but I know what happened. At that moment, 5 pm on Friday 16 August 1996, I took – I hope, God willing – my last drink of alcohol. For so long I had done my best to avoid the conclusion, but I could no longer. I was, I am, an alcoholic. I was at that point they call the rock bottom. I was sick and tired of being sick and tired. I just wanted to stop drinking. I had asked many times to do that, but at that time I felt I was asking from the bottom of my heart. And I felt I was beaten. My soul was screaming out for help.

I got up and left the social club, still crying as I walked down the street. There were tears in my eyes as I bought some fish and chips. Back home, between sobs, I ate my first meal all day but couldn't finish it. Then I got into a T-shirt and shorts and crawled into bed. There, curled up in the foetal position, I sweated, and sweated, and sweated. All night the water poured out of every pore of my body. The words of 'Black Coffee In Bed' kept going through my head, driving me mad. I hallucinated. I had never believed in *delirium tremens* or withdrawals, but now I did. And I thought those withdrawals I got in the old days were bad enough, the old days when I would go into training on a Monday morning, put a plastic bag over my torso and under my shirt, and run round the pitch until I had sweated the beer out of my system ready for a Wednesday game.

Shaking, I got out of bed on the Saturday to report to Highbury, in line with the club rule that injured players must attend matches as spectators where possible, but after wishing the boys luck against West Ham, I left before kick-off and went back home, went back to bed. Over the next 36 hours or so, I alternated between hot sweats and cold shivers, getting up only for small portions of nourishment: cereal, toast, soup, scrambled eggs, the things that comfort you as a sick child. Dehydrated, I drank jugs of water. And I wept as I had never wept before, the pain of a dozen drinking years that I had somehow mixed with being a professional footballer oozing out. At times my body demanded a drink but I ignored it, though I'm not sure how.

On the Monday morning I got myself together enough to

make it to training at London Colney. I just could not spend another day on my own in that condition. What had been an athlete's 29-year-old body a couple of months ago felt like a 60-year-old man's as I stumbled across the car park, where – and it was surely meant to be – I bumped into Steve Jacobs, a friend of Paul Merson's who had been helping him with his recovery from his addictions. 'I've got a drink problem and I need to go to a meeting of Alcoholics Anonymous,' I blurted out. It still moves me to think about the moment. Long may I remember it. It was the first time in my life that I had asked another person for help.

Out of the humiliation had come some humility. And a twinge of relief. I had stopped fighting, finally stopped hitting myself on the head with the hammer. Until that moment I had always thought I could master by myself any problem that life had thrown at me. I was Tony Adams of Arsenal and England. I was strong. I was a leader. I had tremendous willpower. I was a go-getter, with six major trophies in English football – in fact, the whole range of League, FA Cup and League Cup, as well as a European competition – to his credit. Prison had told me I was a survivor. But I had run into something too powerful for me. Alone, I realised, I could not master what had become my drug of choice.

That Monday morning a shaft of optimism came to me from somewhere, though. If I could bring myself to devote as much energy and enthusiasm to staying off the booze as I had to my football, then I had a chance. I had, after all, always been a winner in football. And football had always been my first drug from as early as I could remember.

TWO

The Beginning

I was born in the best year of all for English football, on 10 October 1966 in fact, in Romford, Essex and christened Tony Alexander Adams; Tony, because my mum Caroline simply liked the name – and she gets annoyed if people call me Anthony – and Alexander after my dad.

Alex Adams was well known in footballing circles in Essex and he was certainly my first and probably most significant influence. My earliest memory is of standing on the touchline watching him play, usually either drowning or freezing. There was one time he was playing over at Hackney Marshes and I was the only person on the touchline. It was so cold, but I just couldn't or wouldn't leave because even then, at the age of six, I loved being around the game. At the final whistle, he bundled me under his arm and rushed to the showers to 'defrost' me.

Dad played to a good standard and even had a few youth team games and one in the reserves for West Ham, but his proudest moment was playing for the Army during his national service. Unfortunately he had to have a kidney removed in his mid twenties and was told it would be too dangerous for him to carry on. After recuperating, he did start playing again, though, but not until the age of 29 and it was not at such a high level. He was a centre-half who loved going up for corners. You copy your dad, don't you? You always want to be like him and to please him. Or else you rebel, and I was no rebel.

Mum and Dad were East Enders and both grew up in the Stepney area of London. Mum moved from house to house during the War due to the bombing, her education suffering as a result. Dad was part of a family of six, five boys and a girl. I believe they were never really close, so I think he resolved that his own family was going to be. There was, and is, a lot to be said for that.

Besides the football, my main memories of Dad are how hard he worked to provide for his family and how unfortunate he was with his health, enduring ulcers, pleurisy and shingles before having the kidney removed, all to be followed by a heart attack when I was 11. In many ways he was a workaholic. An asphalter by trade, he became a lorry driver and a roofer before moving into sales for an asphalt company. At one time when he was unable to work, Mum took on a wool shop in nearby Plaistow and they lived in a flat above.

With my sisters Denise and Sandra, ten and five years older than me respectively, Mum and Dad had moved out to Dagenham, to No. 6 Foxlands Road, when I was born. Coming from a one-bedroom flat to a three-bedroom semi with a garage was paradise for them. Then, after Dad's heart attack, I remember going with Mum to look at a house all on one level in Rainham and costing £16,000. It is where they still live, though much changed and modernised. In the early days I can remember endlessly cutting down trees in the overgrown garden with Mum and I don't think she has stopped since, making curtains, knocking rooms down, adding to them. My old bedroom has been a lounge, a kitchen and is now a bedroom again.

We were always an outdoor family, a 'doing' family, and I wanted to be up and playing football right from six years of age. My primary school, Hunter's Hall in Dagenham, did not really provide football for youngsters that age, so I pestered my mum to take me over to the Romford Juniors club. I was a big lad even then and soon found myself playing for the Under-9 team. When I reached that age, Dad could see that I was pretty keen and he decided to take the FA coaching badge. 'If I'm going to teach you, I'd better teach you properly,' he said. And he did. He had me kicking balls up against a wall of the house for hours on end, having drawn three circles on it – one point for the big one, three for the middle and five for the small circle. Mind you, I didn't need much encouraging. Sometimes, when I wrecked his roses or disturbed his Sunday afternoon kip, I think he regretted it.

Dad stopped playing and formed a Sunday morning team, Dagenham United, for whom I played in defence, along with Steve Potts, who would go on to have a good professional career with West Ham. I think we got him on a free transfer from the Cubs. Believe it or not, seeing as he is now 5ft 7in and I am 6ft 3in, we were about equal height in those days and very little got past us, with Steve usually clearing up after me. We were undefeated for the five years that the club was in existence and won the Essex Cup every season during that time. One season, we scored 151 goals and conceded none.

Because the team were so successful, we attracted lots of scouts from professional clubs to watch us and I became aware of them at about the age of 11, my first year at Eastbrook Comprehensive in Dagenham, when I was playing for my borough, Barking and Dagenham, as well as the Essex County team. I was captain of all of them. I did suffer my first injury setback at that time, though. My two sisters had both attended the school and I had got to know a lot of the older kids. In fact, I was about as tall as a lot of the 16-year-olds and somehow was persuaded to play in a rugby match between the teachers and the sixth form. Breaking my arm put my football back a few weeks, as well as ending my rugby career. I decided it was far too dangerous a game.

I enjoyed other sports, mainly cricket and basketball, at which Steve Potts, who was born in the United States, was outstanding. I also ran cross-country and high-jumped and sprinted for the school but I was so focused on my football during my secondary school period that little else mattered. I had next to no interest in academic subjects at that time of my life and on days I didn't like the look of, I could convince Mum and Dad I had a stomach ache, only to be in the park with a ball by the afternoon. Of course, I never missed PE days.

By now it was becoming clear that I had a chance of making it as a professional footballer, which was all I wanted. Everyone was telling me I was good and, to be honest, I knew I was. Before the football really kicked in, I had always felt inadequate and a loner; I could be lonely in a crowd. I had never been able to resist the mass kickabouts in the park, though, even if it took some courage for me to ask to play. I don't know why, because I did know that once the game started, everyone would respect me and would want this shy, timid kid on their side. Once I was in a football environment, I was the main man. Later on, 'equal' sides consisted of me picking three players against 20 on the other team, though even then sometimes I was told to go in goal because they thought I was too good in the outfield. Just give me a good goalkeeper, a striker who could nick a goal and tell the other defender just to kick it away, a bit like I would come to do with Steve Bould, my partner in central defence for 10 years with Arsenal. In fact, it all sounds a bit like Arsenal at times.

I remember in my early teens praying to be a professional, just wishing really, but it was to stand me in good stead, even if in those days my idea of a God was a warped one of a figure who could just make my dreams come true. That emerged from an incident that probably spurred me on in my early career more than anything.

At the age of 13, I had made it into the last 30 for the following season's England Under-15 Schoolboys side and there was to be a trial at Lilleshall National Sports Centre in Shropshire to decide on the last 22. The day before, the eight London boys selected travelled up together on the train from Euston. They included Steve Potts, Dennis Wise, Michael Thomas, John Moncur and myself, all of whom went on to professional careers. That night I remember praying to be in the England team.

I had this strange feeling about the trial match that took place. At previous trials, all the people in charge had been so friendly towards me. Now there was a strange, frosty atmosphere. Nobody spoke to me. I was handed a No. 13 shirt and was told to stand behind the goal, out of the way. It was the same for five other London boys. We were discarded. They had found an easy way to whittle the squad down.

We were told that we had been seen misbehaving on the train journey the previous day by an education officer travelling independently and who had reported us. There had been some minor, high-spirited scuffling among a few of the lads, which involved some coffee being thrown and a bit of bad language by one or two. Dennis Wise also had his ear bitten. I had certainly not been a part of any of it, though. I was sitting in the corner, trying to mind my own business, but because I stood out as tall for my age, I was one of those pointed out. It all felt so unjust and left me fuming. God had not answered my prayer. The rejection – a feeling which I would come to recognise as a huge motivating force in my life – was intensely painful to me at that age. 'Right,' I remember saying to myself then. 'I'm going to do it my way from now on.' I was going to redouble my efforts to become a pro.

My determination was apparent in a game I played against that England Schoolboys side later on. In those days, there was an annual match between London and the full national team, and at Goodison Park, Liverpool we beat them 3–1. It gave me a tremendous amount of pleasure. After an inquest, following representations by my teachers and education district, I was reinstated for the following year's England Under-16 team along with other boys whose families had also complained about the incident on the train. But the real moment had gone. The Under-15 team get to play big showcase matches at Wembley – in my year, against West Germany and Scotland – and I had missed them. I so desperately wanted to play at Wembley and thought my chance had gone forever.

Despite the disciplinary action by the English Schools Football Association, I was attracting plenty of interest from professional clubs as a result of playing for my district on Saturdays and for Dagenham United on Sundays. I went for a look around most of the London clubs – Tottenham and West Ham, Orient and Fulham, who quite impressed me – and I played in trial games for all but Spurs. I was also spotted by Manchester United and invited up for a trial, but I was an Essex boy who couldn't see himself moving away from the area. Actually, in later life I got quite worried about moving to Putney and south of the River Thames.

And of course, Arsenal, in the shape of a scout called Steve Rowley, had made contact and invited me over to take a look around the club and discuss joining them. With my Dad I duly went over to Highbury one night where I was met by Tommy Coleman, who had just become the assistant youth team manager. 'Steve Rowley sent me,' I said, but Tommy hadn't heard of Steve, who had himself not been with the club that long. I was just about to leave with Dad when Steve appeared and asked me to wait while he sorted the situation out.

Soon I was led into a room where there was Terry Burton, the youth team manager who later became Joe Kinnear's assistant at Wimbledon, along with five boys. They were David Rocastle, Martin Hayes, Martin Keown, Michael Thomas and Gus Caesar. 'That was a good day at the office,' Terry has since said to me, recalling that roomful. He put us through a session of defensive work and I thought, 'Yes, this is for me,' and knew I wanted to come to Highbury.

It was purely for coaching reasons. When I had visited West Ham, there were 30 or 40 boys in the gym under the eye of the coach Paul Brush and it was too much for me to handle. Everyone was running around like little kids, and that was not for me. I thought I was beyond that. As a footballer, I was growing up fast. My Dad knew that I would learn my trade best at Arsenal. 'If you're going to be a good bricklayer, you go to the best bricklayer to learn,' my Dad said. He had always admired people who did their job well, no matter what it was. Sometimes he would annoy me, sitting in the car after a game telling me what I had done wrong and what I could do better, but it was good grooming for what I was to experience when my game was being analysed by all and sundry in later life. He gave me pride in my performance. 'What are you lazing around for?' he would shout at me if I wasn't working hard enough on my game. He encouraged me to be a go-getter and keep improving.

I signed for Arsenal on schoolboy forms as soon as I could, on my 14th birthday. My Dad drove me over to London Colney, where the chief scout Steve Burtenshaw introduced me to the first-team manager Terry Neill. The dressing rooms were busy with players coming and going and Steve couldn't find anywhere quiet for me to sign the contract. Eventually he did – the toilets. Thus was concluded my first signing, and one that at the time probably did not mean that much to Arsenal, but I think it was to prove significant to their history over the next two decades. The humble beginnings didn't bother me. The important thing to me was that I had taken the first step towards becoming a professional footballer.

Nowadays you hear all sorts of stories of young players being enticed to clubs, though the rules of recruitment are supposed to be very strict, and all sorts of rewards and presents being offered to parents. There was no need for that with me. Money never came into it. When I travelled up to Highbury for training, I was entitled to claim for expenses but I never did. Mum and Dad subsidised me and the club. I wanted to play for Arsenal, wanted to learn my trade at a place I thought was offering the best apprenticeship. I threw everything else out of the window and became single-minded. Dagenham United came to an end and I cut back the schools football I was playing, to just the district team. On Sundays I would play for an Arsenal junior team over at Chigwell.

On Mondays and Thursdays I would travel to Highbury for coaching with Terry Burton, taking a train to Liverpool Street, then the Circle followed by Piccadilly Line underground to Arsenal station – an hour and a half each way. There used to be a big indoor hall behind the old South Stand where we used to train, the surface a terrible combination of red cinder and grit that just would not be washed off. I can remember we used to have biology at school every Friday morning and one week I had to take my socks off so my feet could be measured as part of an experiment. 'Adams doesn't wash his feet, sir!' some kid pointed out to my embarrassment.

Terry was brilliant and I learned so much from him, working incessantly on the basics of my trade, such as clearing the ball and positioning. I'm not sure young players get such a good grounding these days. He would put you in the area of the pitch where you played and work you until what you were doing became second nature. All the drills reflected what you would be doing in a game. You would have to deal with balls chipped up to centre forwards you were marking, balls driven into your 'channel'. I can still hear all the instructions being shouted to me. 'Come short for that one, Tone, knock it back to me. Left foot now, 20 balls. Come in from that angle, now this angle. Different heights now. OK, headers now.' As Gary Player once said, 'The harder I practised, the luckier I got.' When you have got small numbers – and there were usually about 10 in our sessions – you could do such intense work.

I loved it. Lots of kids just want to play a game but I wanted to practise. That also came from my Dad. When I was seven, he would be throwing balls up for me to head clear. I never got tired of it. I only got bored when there wasn't a football around. I can look back now and see how addicted to the game I was becoming. Not that I would have changed anything. I was getting on and getting success.

Nothing distracted me, either. I can remember there was quite a pretty girl who used to walk past our house now and then, sometimes when I was in the front garden keeping the ball up. I had to see how many headers I could do. I set myself a target of 10 and did that; then 100 and I did that too. When she walked by, I didn't even take my eye off the ball. Girls were scary things, anyway. I hated sitting next to them at school. You didn't know where you were with them. With football, you did. I also got an early glimpse of what celebrity status might bring. As a clumsy 12 and 13-year-old none of the girls would look twice at me. When I signed for Arsenal, suddenly the best-looking girl in the school became interested. The only person I was interested in impressing, though, was Terry Burton.

Now it had not really hit me how awe-inspiring it could be walking into Arsenal, what with the club's tradition. I might, in fact, have felt that more strongly at my local club, West Ham. In the first place, professional footballers did not seem so remote to me, as I had a cousin who was a pro, Dad's sister Renee's son Steve MacKenzie, five years older than me, who started at Crystal Palace and was sold to Manchester City for £250,000 as the country's most expensive teenage footballer. In fact, he would face Arsenal when playing for Charlton Athletic on Boxing Day 1988, with me up against him, and score twice. He also scored for City with a great volley in the FA Cup Final replay of 1981 which they lost to Spurs, when I was in the crowd courtesy of his tickets.

I had also never been a great watcher of football, except of my Dad's team, and never really had heroes, because I was always playing. Dad didn't really bring me up with tales of Bobby Moore, though I was to come to know about his talents and appreciate them all on videotape later on, and my early memories of professional players centre on the World Cup of 1974, watching Franz Beckenbauer, Johan Neeskens and Rudi Krol. I really liked Poland, because they had a good back four, and especially the big centre half Jerzy Gorgon. Even at that age ... It was only really when I got into the profession that I became aware of players I admired: Billy Bonds and Alvin Martin at West Ham, David O'Leary at Arsenal.

In a way, it was a good thing as I was not overwhelmed by anyone or anything at Highbury. I just wanted to get in there and show everyone how good I was. And I wanted to sign for two years, not just on a short-term contract, because I wanted to make a commitment to learn. Also, I was sure that over that period of time they could not fail to see my ability. Anyone can screw up on one day or in one game, but not over two years. I was confident, and probably brash – on the field, at least.

The full-time apprentices must have wondered who the hell this schoolkid was. When I came to play for the youth team, I would be verbally pushing and pulling team-mates around, bossing them about – 'Oi you, come here!' I would shout, among other things. When a high ball came in, I would shout 'TA's up'. I think some of them were resentful and poked fun at me, but I didn't care. I was going places. Some of them mimicked my 'TA's up' call, but they were the ones who weren't going to make it. That was my attitude. And I began to realise that I was being fast-tracked in the club. 'Keep working him. This boy's got it, but he needs extending,' Steve Burtenshaw told Terry Burton in front of me once.

I was still only 15 when I was first picked for Arsenal's

youth team, in the August of 1982, a 3–1 defeat at Colchester. Then, later that month, still three months short of my 16th birthday, came elevation to the reserves. I heard only the day before that I would be playing. Terry Burton phoned my Dad to tell him I had been picked to play against Manchester United at their training ground in Salford, The Cliff. Word came through to me at school from Dad and I was very proud. Though I was elated, I kept it all inside me. I did not want to brag in front of schoolmates, to get carried away. Though I was confident in my ability, I was not a cocky kid. My philosophy was that if you've got it, you don't need to flaunt it. Quiet determination was my style.

On the coach up to Manchester, I can remember thinking that only a few months before I had been playing for Barking and Dagenham against Thurrock, and now I was close to the big time. I didn't feel entirely comfortable in the company of people who were full-time professionals, a tough crew such as Colin Hill and Danny O'Shea, but I probably felt more comfortable than I did at school. It was a football environment and I knew what I was doing in that. I don't even remember being overawed when I saw that the man I was marking was Frank Stapleton, once of Arsenal himself. I must have got on his nerves, like some kids do with me now, as I was all over him in my enthusiasm. We drew 1–1 but I can't remember if I played well. Sure, I analysed it with Dad and Terry and they put me right.

I think Arsenal were seeing if I would sink or swim, and I was a swimmer. I found myself again in the reserves when the Football Combination season started, playing in front of Pat Jennings, who was then 36. John Devine, Colin Hill and Brian McDermott, all two or three years older than me, were also in the team and I went on to make 14 reserve appearances that season. The only game that really sticks in my mind was against Spurs when I was up against Mark Falco, who used to intimidate me then. In fact, he smashed my nose. It was the second time, as the same thing had happened in a trial match for Arsenal juniors when I was 13. I have also dislocated my nose six times in my career and Gary Lewin has put it back a couple of times. He says the body is naturally anaesthetised in the first 10 minutes afterwards ... not that it felt like it.

Mostly that season, though, it was the youth team, with Martin Keown my partner in the back four, and I made my debut in the Southern Junior Floodlit Cup against Crystal Palace and played my first South-East Counties League match, both in the September. The latter was a 1–1 draw against Orient, David Rocastle also in the team. In the December I scored my first youth team goal, in a 2–1 win at Charlton. I don't remember it. I was a defender and goals have never given me the same buzz as they do a striker, except for the odd one in big games. Results and performances were always more memorable to me.

I signed as an apprentice in the April of 1983, this time in the luxury of Terry Neill's office, and my first pay packet was £104 for the month. My season ticket from Rainham was costing me £150. I would be up at 6 am and catching a bus to Dagenham East station, and from there taking the tube to Highbury. We would have to pack the kit for training, which the kids don't have to do any more, before travelling out to London Colney, doing the jobs there, fitting in our own training, then getting back to Highbury at 4 pm where we would do the cleaning up until 6 pm. I was getting home at about 7.30 pm every night.

After we had done all our jobs on a Friday, Terry Neill would inspect the dressing rooms to make sure they were spotless, which they are certainly not these days. Kids today, eh? Terry would even run his finger along the top of the mirror to see if there was any dust – and it would be my fault if there was because, as the tallest, I always had to clean the highest points and objects. But I was the lucky one. It was to transpire the next season that I signed as a full-time professional so, to the disgust of contemporaries like Martin Keown, I only had to do menial work for six months.

That spring of 1983 I was chosen for the England Under-17 team for a tournament in Cannes, joining such as Teddy Sheringham, then of Millwall, and Gary Porter of Watford. We beat China 5–1, drew 0–0 and 1–1 with the Soviet Union and Qatar respectively and lost 2–0 to France. A few months later it was the England Under-16 team in Hungary, for which I still qualified by virtue of the age limit being established at the beginning of that season, playing with Tim Flowers, John Beresford, Steve Potts and Dale Gordon. I was delighted to be going; it got me out of my final exams at school. They let me go, I think, on condition I went back to sit them but I never did. I remember scoring three goals in the tournament, twice in a 4–4 draw with Yugoslavia and once in a 4–0 win over Greece.

The next season, I think a lot of people thought I would play mostly for the Arsenal reserves again, but, in all honesty, I didn't think I was that far away from the first team. At the beginning of November, the club was playing in a testimonial for Micky Droy, the Chelsea centre half, at Stamford Bridge and I was included. I don't remember too much about it, except doing reasonably well and thinking what a massive guy Micky was. It is strange how you see people when you are 17. I suppose I must seem big to kids now, but Micky really was a giant.

That Saturday, the first team were at home to

Sunderland and when it became known that David O'Leary had a knee injury, I thought I might have half a chance. We always used to train at Highbury on a Friday then go into the gym for a five-a-side game before Terry Neill and Don Howe would pin the first team, reserves and youth team lists on the board. I was a bit worried as I worked my way up from the bottom through the youths and reserves and was not in either of those teams, but soon my fears were allayed. I was to make my first-team debut. That morning I had been cleaning out the baths as Terry told the press, and they all wanted pictures of me with a scrubbing brush. I think one of the papers the next day had the headline 'ORDER OF THE BATH' over a shot of me and another said 'IN AT THE DEEP END', which was pretty accurate. The papers that Saturday, 5 November 1983, also told me that I would be the second youngest player in Arsenal's history to make his debut, after Gerry Ward, who was 16 years and 321 days when he played against Huddersfield in 1953.

I was incredibly nervous – in fact, I think I told the press later I was still shaking with nerves an hour after the game – as I sat there watching everyone go through their pre-match routines. Everyone has their own way of handling their fear, and later I would envy players like Michael Thomas, who could drop off to sleep before a match, and Viv Anderson and Steve Williams who would scan the fixture list for their £10 bet on forecasting the results. Kenny Sansom, who was to become a good pal and who had seen it all before, was the joker and did his best to loosen me up in the dressing room – by winding me up and flapping, trying to make me laugh. 'You nervous, son?' he would ask. 'Don't worry. If the ball comes to you, you know what to do, don't you? Yes, that's right. Panic … and for eff's sake don't give it to me.' He was a funny guy, Kenny.

Somehow I managed to take the field with my shirt the right way round and with the No. 5 on my back, unlike my shorts, which were back to front. Playing alongside Chris Whyte, I did not make the best of starts. In only the second minute Colin Hill threw the ball inside from the right-back position to me and instead of whacking it upfield, I thought I would show everyone what a good player I was. Before I could do that, Colin West had robbed me and chipped Pat Jennings from 20 yards to put us a goal down. It's funny how you get away with things as a young player. Later, it was Colin Hill who got the telling-off for throwing the ball infield. At half-time, Kenny told me it might be as well if I put my shorts on the right way round.

I was determined not to let the bad start get to me and although Sunderland beat us 2–1, I think I did enough to show people I had something about me. I could have gone into my shell after conceding the goal but I knew I had to stand tall and not let it affect me – something, I believe, that has been a hallmark of my career. I ran around and gave it my all, won a few tackles, headed a few balls and even stuck a loose ball in the Sunderland net, though it was disallowed for some offence. My efforts restored my confidence and I was pleased that I hadn't just thrown in the towel. Now I had made my mark. I took my driving test two days later and the examiner recognised me and declared himself an Arsenal supporter. 'This has got nothing to do with who you play for,' he said at the end, 'but you've passed.' I was just delighted and grabbed the certificate from him.

David O'Leary recovered to play in the next game, a League Cup tie against Tottenham, but I was back within a month, playing against West Bromwich Albion alongside Tommy Caton. It was a real physical lesson for me. I was 11 stone and up against muscular 15 stone athletes in Cyrille Regis and Garry Thompson. They just knocked me to bits, Regis giving me a black eye, as we lost 1–0. Even so, I was furious when Terry dropped me for the next game, at West Ham, a match against my local team in which I really wanted to play. In hindsight, he was probably right to shield me as I had had a torrid time against West Brom but it showed the kind of confident player I was even then. Older pros may have resented the way I shouted during games, telling them where to run and who to mark, but I didn't worry too much. I reckoned I had the talent to back it up and I think I had some respect. For me, it was about respect and not necessarily affection.

The team lost 1–3 at Upton Park and after also being beaten by Walsall in the League Cup, Terry Neill paid the penalty for the team's struggles, which were, let's face it, the reason why such a young player like me was getting his chance. I can't say it affected me greatly that Christmas when he was sacked and Don Howe took over. Don was to make Terry Burton his assistant, and for me the pair were to be a great double act, both football men, both the sort of experts on the training ground that I needed at that stage of my career.

Don signed me as a full professional on a three-year contract that January of 1984, and there was no arguing or negotiation about the contract. There was just me and my Dad in Don's office at Highbury and we all just knew how much I wanted to play for Arsenal. I think Don felt the same way about the club. He always called them *the* Arsenal. Money never came into it, for either of us, I think. 'I don't know how long I'll be here as manager,' he said to me, 'but I want to make sure that you are here a long time.'

Don held me back that season, giving me only one more

first-team appearance, against Notts County, which ended prematurely after a clash with Trevor Christie and with me in Moorfields Eye Hospital, unable to see out of one eye, though thankfully it was nothing serious and healed quickly. Mostly I was back in the reserves, now coached by Tommy Coleman, and the youth team. It was a busy time. I scored twice for the reserves in a 2–2 draw with Birmingham in the April and another in a 4–1 win over Crystal Palace in the May during my 28 games for a team which won the Football Combination.

I was still available to the youth team and a side that included Michael Thomas, David Rocastle and Martin Hayes won the Southern Junior Floodlit Cup and reached the semi-finals of the FA Youth Cup before going out to Stoke City 6–2 on aggregate. Steve Bould was then a Stoke first-teamer and has since told me that he came to watch, having heard about this bright young pretender Tony Adams. He left, he said, unimpressed.

In addition, there was a UEFA Under-16 tournament, in which I made seven England appearances running through that season, and I scored twice in a run to the semi-final and a third place. The coach Charles Hughes went on to become director of coaching for the FA and came in for a lot of criticism for his ideas about direct football, but I actually took to many of them. We worked a lot on regaining possession in the front third of the pitch – pressing, they call it these days – and using the POMO, the Position Of Maximum Opportunity at the far post. He showed how goals came in moves of three passes or fewer and we worked hard on set pieces and the quality of delivery from crosses and corners, which I naturally enjoyed. Some didn't. I can remember Tottenham's John Moncur, who just liked to pass the ball, wondering what all this rubbish was about. Looking back, some of it was a bit over the top, like practising shooting to miss on the far side so that we could work on the POMO concept. Just sticking the ball in the net would surely have been better.

But I wanted to play for England and I wanted to learn. Even with all these games I was playing, I was often training in the afternoons as well. One day I told Terry Burton that I didn't feel like it. 'What if this was a Saturday and you didn't feel like it?' he asked. 'You've still got to go out there and earn your dough.' The penny dropped. This was now my job. I remember saying to Terry the next day, 'Come on Terry, let's go and learn my job.' Mind you, sometimes I found it hard to see it as my job. One afternoon, I was advised to go home and get some sleep but I remember thinking 'but I've got double geography this afternoon'. Old habits die hard.

I was obsessed with it all and working hard at it. I slept games and dreamt games, and woke up thinking about them, replaying moments. I would check out my position in my mind when a goal had been scored against us, constantly thinking about how I could do better. I hardly had a life outside the game and didn't really want one. I was Tony Adams the footballer and that was what was on my passport. It still is. I had even bought a new computer and started to store information about opponents on it. So, for example, for Garry Thompson I had: 'Right-footed. Strong in the air,' along with an assessment of how I played him and how he played against me. It was all because Pat Rice had told me that when he played right-back in the Arsenal Double team of 1971, he used to keep notes on all the wingers he came up against.

My profession was also emblazoned on my car. 'Footballers make the best lovers,' said a tongue-in-cheek sticker on my Mark IV Ford Cortina, which I loved to bits with its Grand Prix S-tyres and tiny steering wheel. Sad, really – the sticker, not the car. Not that I was taking much interest in girls, as I thought they would get in the way of my career. I also felt very shy around them. Often I would act as chauffeur for my mates on Friday nights when they went beering and birding and I would drop them off at their homes, doing wheel spins around the streets.

The car had a Clarion sound system and amplifier with Pioneer speakers for my other great love, music. When the mod revival began in the late 70s at school I had bought a Parka coat and Hush Puppies and thought I looked really smart. It always appealed to me more than the rocker and greaser stuff. Then, in the early 80s I was a soul boy, into jazz funk, which was not very fashionable out in Essex, but I found some kindred spirits among the London boys when I came to Arsenal, especially Michael Thomas. We used to pore over *Melody Maker* together.

Don Howe still did not want to rush me and the next two seasons were quite frustrating for me. I felt I was ready to play more often than I did and I must have been a pain in the neck at times to some of the older players. It was not that I was arrogant, just confident in my ability, and I got away with my aggressive style of play because I think senior pros recognised that I was a serious professional already. I know David O'Leary was to say later that I helped extend his career. All of a sudden, there was this precocious teenager pushing him for his place and he could no longer cruise but had to put new energy into his game.

In 1984/85, he and Tommy Caton proved difficult to dislodge and I did not get a first-team opportunity until the end of October when I came on as a substitute for Stewart Robson in a League Cup tie at Oxford, which we lost 3–2.

I did not like losing and made my feelings known. I was particularly disgusted with Pat Jennings, by this time 39, whom I felt was to blame for a couple of the goals. Two nights later I came on for Graham Rix in a live televised game at Old Trafford where we lost to Manchester United 4–2 and the commentators were wondering who was this young lad bossing people about. Family and friends told me how well I had done and it all fuelled my ego. I must have come as a real culture shock to Pat and David O'Leary, two laid-back Irishmen.

My first win bonus came in my fifth League match, when we beat Queens Park Rangers in the November of that season, and it began a run of nine consecutive appearances due to injuries. I also won more England youth caps and made my first Under-21 appearance, a 3–2 win over the Republic of Ireland at Portsmouth, alongside Chris Fairclough in defence. I went with them, too, to Finland for a 3–1 defeat, appearing in a team that also included David Seaman, Des Walker and Kerry Dixon. Frustratingly, though, Arsenal first-team appearances were only sporadic.

It was a similar story at the beginning of the 1985/86 season with David O'Leary and Tommy Caton still the first-choice pair. Don was under a lot of pressure to get results and he believed, I think, that experience was more likely to get them. He also confessed later that he wondered at one point how well I would be able to distribute the ball. In turn, I was getting impatient with Combination games, such as a 12–0 win over Charlton Athletic, and matters worsened when I fractured a bone in my right foot against Chelsea reserves which kept me out for two months. Looking back, it was the first occasion when I remember alcohol being important to me and I recall being drunk for several periods in that time.

It was not until March that I got back in the first team for a match at home to Coventry City. I was delighted with the 3–0 win and thought everyone else would be. I was in the bath afterwards next to Don Howe and could not understand why he was so quiet. I was soon to find out; it was Don's last game as manager. We had gone out of the League Cup to Aston Villa in the February, the FA Cup to Luton in the fifth round in March and were treading water a bit in the League. There had been talk of Terry Venables coming in and I think Don felt himself undermined. Though he had not picked me as often as I would have liked, I was sorry to see him go and I respected his knowledge of the game.

With David O'Leary injured, I kept my place through the last nine games of the season under the caretaker management of Steve Burtenshaw. Things seemed to be looking up and when a new manager arrived that summer, it was to prove one of the most significant events not only in my own career but in the entire history of Arsenal Football Club.

THREE

Titled

The news was released on 14 May 1986. George Graham, a member of Arsenal's Double-winning team of 15 years before – the last time the club won the title – was to be our new manager. He was still well known in London football circles, having been manager of Millwall for the past few seasons. He had the nickname of 'Stroller' because people always said he was an elegant rather than energetic player, but on the very first day in the first week of July that we turned up for pre-season training at Trent Park in Cockfosters at the northern end of the Piccadilly Line, it was made clear that strolling would certainly not be tolerated.

George delivered a short and sharp first talk. 'A lot of you boys know me from outside,' he said and several of the senior pros had socialised with him, in playing golf and the like, but it was obvious there was to be no more of that. 'I don't mind if you call me George by mistake at first, but I want to be known as boss,' he said. And he was. We ran and ran for the first couple of days. Then we ran some more, the boss poised with his clipboard, and I felt immediately that there was a seriousness and a new intensity to the club.

He made it clear from the start that he was going to instil his way of playing right through the club, from schoolboys up to the first team. It was going to be based on strong defence, closing the opposition down and winning back the ball high up in the field. His aim was that we would be a resilient side, a closing-down side. After that first week of physical torture, we went back to London Colney where all the hard tactical work was to begin. We worked on the shape of the team, the organization, teamwork and unity. We spent a lot of time on throw-ins and corners, everyone having to know their place, in more ways than one. It all came as quite a shock for some of the senior pros, among them Charlie Nicholas, then the darling of the North Bank, who loved his skills with the ball. Charlie was never going to fit into such a physical regime.

None of it, though, worried a young player like me desperate to become the No. 1 centre-back in the club, although even I was wary with George right from the off. It was a bit like being back at school, and I got very worried about being late for training. I would be a nervous wreck if there was a hold-up on the motorway on the way in from Essex. I think George liked to foster an atmosphere of creative tension.

He would have had to have been blind not to notice that I was ready for the first team, even if I say it myself. He had had good feedback from Don Howe and Terry Neill, I think, and he was later to say that he had been impressed with me when I was an England Under-16 player at Lilleshall taking part in a demonstration while he was taking his FA coaching badge. George has always liked impressionable young players willing to work, over some of the older ones who were less 'teachable'. Within a couple of months of George's arrival, Paul Mariner and Tony Woodcock were on their way. David O'Leary was always a very shrewd professional, though, and knuckled down. George's intentions might have been gauged from his first signing Perry Groves, a quick wing player from Colchester – no star, but someone who would fit into his system. My cause was helped, meanwhile, by Martin Keown failing to agree terms for a new contract and consequently moving on to Aston Villa.

The 1986/87 season was to prove the one in which I really made it. I was the club's only ever-present player in 42 League and four FA Cup games, as well as all nine ties in the Littlewoods Cup, which we went on to win. I also scored six League goals, which only Niall Quinn and Martin Hayes bettered. I won two Young Player of the Month awards in September and February and went on to be Young Player of the Year. I also made my England debut, against Spain in Madrid in the February. To cap it all – and what a proud achievement – I was booked only twice.

In pre-season friendlies, Tommy Caton would often come on as a substitute for me but I was always destined to start the season. In fact poor Tommy, who sadly died of a heart attack soon after the end of his playing days and whose funeral I attended, did not figure at all in early season and George sold him to Oxford in the January. Mostly my partner was David O'Leary.

I scored my first goal for the first team in the third game, a 2–1 defeat at Liverpool, where I drove home a downward header by Viv Anderson. Being the kind of person I was at that time, one who could often find a cloud to every silver lining, I was disappointed that it wasn't against Bruce Grobbelaar but his deputy Mike Hooper. The move was something Viv and I worked on together, and we had a competition to see who could score the most that season, not that laying them on for each other stopped us scoring ourselves. In the end we contributed 13 – Viv contributing seven – which wasn't bad.

More disappointing for me that day was being at fault for Ian Rush's winner. I was still a little in awe of him and, looking back, at that stage of my development, my concentration would often be good for 60 minutes before it lapsed. It is part of being a young player, being punished for that one moment where the mind wanders. These days, with the presence and aura I believe I have built up, I can go out on the pitch and feel comfortable all the time. Ninety minutes was hard work in those days. But I was getting mentally and physically stronger. A year or two earlier, I had also played against Rush and he had scored a hat-trick, after I felt I had done well for half an hour. So at least my concentration span was getting better.

What I also remember about that day was Kenny Dalglish winding me early on with an arm across the solar plexus. It was the sort of professional stroke that older players used to pull; Paul Mariner did at Arsenal. Also, you give the defender a push to spring off him and send him backwards and all of a sudden you've got 10 yards of space instead of five. That was another useful learning experience, although it didn't feel it at the time. I only weighed about 12 stone and Dalglish put me out of the game for about five minutes.

I also scored against Sheffield Wednesday in the next match at the beginning of September to become Arsenal's leading scorer, and it took the strikers until the end of October to overtake me. I had also opened my account at international level, scoring in an England Under-21 1–1 draw against Sweden in Ostersund, the Swedish scorer being Anders Limpar, who was to come and join us at Arsenal. It was also my first game as an England Under-21 captain and another honour to add to the list; every team I had played for had made me captain. To be honest, my attitude in those days was that I would be offended if they didn't. The manager, Dave Sexton, was a quiet, thoughtful man and I think he wanted someone louder to get the team going. Mind you, I had been doing that anyway.

It was a proud moment but not nearly as proud as in the February when, at the age of 20 years and four months, I became the youngest central defender since Bobby Moore to play for the full England team and my whole family flew out to Madrid to see me play against Spain. It was clearly something special, especially when Gary Lineker, then a Barcelona player, scored all four goals in the 4–2 win. To me, international honours have always been something of a bonus for the hours of work day in, day out at Arsenal. As such, I have always seen my England career as separate from my club football, and something that sits more appropriately in a place and space all of its own elsewhere, like my alcoholism, as I attempt to make sense of it and place it into the perspective of my career.

When I made my England debut, Arsenal were going through a difficult patch, still in transitional phase under George. At Christmas, we had looked as if we might be Championship contenders but we were also doing well in the Littlewoods Cup and became somewhat sidetracked. As our prospects of reaching Wembley increased with each win – over Huddersfield, Manchester City, Charlton and Nottingham Forest – so our league form deteriorated, even if our final position of fourth was our best since 1980/81.

The semi-final of the Littlewoods Cup pitted us against our North London rivals Tottenham and the tie proved to be an epic. In those days, Spurs were the talented flair team with their almost continental 4–5–1 formation under David Pleat that had Glenn Hoddle and Chris Waddle playing just behind Clive Allen, who was having an amazing 49-goal season. They came into that tie having scored 22 goals in six games in the competition. We were taking shape as George Graham's Arsenal, rugged and determined, the more so in adversity, when we were underdogs. That semi-final saw it all.

Everyone thought we were out of it when we lost the first leg at Highbury 1–0 and it looked even bleaker for us when we fell another goal behind at White Hart Lane, Clive Allen scoring both. Nowadays, I think I would handle him easily, but at that time I was still learning. Spurs looked at that point as if they thought they were going to cruise it but the proper Arsenal came through. Viv pulled one back and Niall Quinn, ever the battler, scored an amazing winner. That made it 2–2 on aggregate, so we had to go to a replay, also at White Hart Lane.

Once again we went a goal behind, and once again we battled back. Clive Allen took his tally in the competition to 12 before substitute Ian Allinson equalised and David Rocastle made himself into an Arsenal legend with the winner. After that, a new Arsenal fanzine had as its title *One-Nil Down, Two-One Up*, which, as it turned out, would be appropriate also for the Final. After that glorious semi-final win I can remember drinking champagne in Camden Palais and singing unrepeatable songs about Spurs that I learned in the youth team.

We were very solid in defence, with David O'Leary experiencing a new lease of life alongside me, and Viv Anderson and Kenny Sansom, as captain, either side – the best in their position in the country. We worked diligently with George on the training ground at moving together as a unit and it was this back four which laid the foundation for their successors and the club's success of the next eight years. George did indeed instil in us the old arms-raised offside appeal and if a forward was not clever enough to time his run properly, he deserved to be offside in our opinion. We would tell the linesmen so, both with our arms aloft and verbally. 'Work on your linesman,' George would tell Viv and Kenny. 'They go to sleep.' Not with our two full-backs, they didn't. 'Oi!' or 'Yes!' Viv and Kenny would bawl loudly, and quite often after this short, sharp shock, the linesman would raise his flag as if it was triggered.

In midfield Paul Davis and Steve Williams were getting stuck in, grafting and closing people down, but when it came to winning the league championship we were a little inexperienced, with David Rocastle, Niall Quinn and Martin Hayes – though he had a great season in scoring 24 goals, 12 of them penalties – all a bit too young to be able to produce the consistency of performance needed to sustain a title challenge. Had Alan Smith arrived earlier, it might have been different. George had paid Leicester £750,000 for him in the March, but part of the deal was that he stayed with them until the end of the season. In Cup competition and one-off matches we could still fly, though. The team was just so full of energy and enthusiasm.

On the morning of the Littlewoods Final, I can remember Paul Davis filming us all around the hotel with his video camera and providing a running commentary. Looking back, to some of the older players it was among their few moments of success, but I simply saw it as the beginning of what would become the norm – winning trophies for Arsenal. It may have been naivety or the brashness of youth, but it didn't occur to me to savour this moment. I felt confident that there would be plenty more.

That said, I was very nervous and excited and I still see it as one of the most special days of my career. It was my first visit to Wembley as a player, after all, the only other time having been as part of one of those guided tours, when I was 11. I recall they put on some taped crowd noise. That day against Liverpool, there was no need. I can't remember it being louder since. Then, the capacity was 96,000 and I was just staggered by all the red and white as I emerged from the tunnel. Our fans were at that tunnel end, which makes a big difference as it gives you such an initial lift. I looked for my family but just couldn't see them up in the stand.

Liverpool at that time may have been coming towards the end of their dominance of the English game but they were still deadly, especially with Rush and Dalglish up front. They were probably the first English team to play the split centre-forward system, with Dalglish dropping off and posing serious problems of positioning for the opposing central defender.

Before I knew it, Rush had laid the ball off to Steve McMahon and turned and spun me. By the time I reacted, he had scored. The strange thing was that even though I had been caught by a sucker punch, I still had this feeling that we were going to win the game. Some days you just know you are going to succeed whatever happens, and I stressed this in team talks down the years on big occasions. Conversely, there are days when you sense defeat but you try to ignore that feeling, or at least don't convey it to the team.

I was buzzing with nervous energy after Liverpool scored, but luckily the older pros kept me focused. We went upfield and I got in a shot which hit the post. I should have scored, but Charlie Nicholas did and we had equalised. In the second half, he followed my script and grabbed a winner. Perry Groves went skipping down the line, past Gary Gillespie, and it just had to be Charlie on the end of it. There were lucky bounces all over the place as the ball pinballed into the net to confirm my feeling that it was our day: 1–0 down, 2–1 up again. I was elated and relieved because my still-growing body was suffering from cramp in the calves and I don't think I could have endured extra time. When you're out on the pitch, Wembley feels as big as everyone says it looks.

Now Liverpool had become used to winning trophies and this defeat may not have meant too much to them. But for me, as a youngster winning his first, the experience was all of a sudden enormous and I was jumping about like a madman, not at all worried what I looked like to opponents trudging off wondering what all the fuss was about. The casual approach I had had in the morning, when I was trying to view it like any other game, handling it well, not showing any weakness, had quickly worn off. Later, when Arsenal would win other, bigger trophies I would be restrained, just acknowledging that I had done my job well, but for now I was a scatty kid going up the Wembley steps to get my medal wearing a fan's flat cap, yelling 'We've won!' and singing songs in the dressing room afterwards. Now I understood what all this stuff about underdogs and team spirit was about. You could cause upsets on that alone.

I also loved this feeling of having proved everyone wrong. Alan Hansen, Mark Lawrenson – Gillespie, too, for that matter – were players I admired greatly. First I had to go out and play on the same pitch as these people. Then I had scored at Anfield. Now I had beaten them. It really used to get on my nerves when Hansen and Lawrenson were passing the ball about and getting all this praise. I knew I was capable of all that. Sometimes I thought they should just have kicked the ball clear, like I did and was instructed to do. Later, I reckoned I would come to pass the ball as well as they ever did, and perhaps there is a kid out there now looking at the way I play and admiring the confidence I feel I came to acquire in my game.

After the match we went to an Italian restaurant in Winchmore Hill, North London, then on to the Professional Footballers' Association's awards dinner and dance at the Grosvenor Hotel. I left my girlfriend at the time, Anne, at the restaurant; I just wanted to be out on the town with the boys. Looking back, I can see now that I was beginning to behave selfishly when I was drinking, but at the time I didn't care. I wanted the drink, the euphoria, the excitement. And my ego was huge.

We drank champagne in the car on the way to the dinner, Kenny Sansom going through his Lieutenant Columbo and Norman Wisdom impressions, and we were in fits of laughter. Subconsciously, I walked into those awards thinking I was better than a lot of people there. When it came to picking up my Young Player of the Year award, I made some sort of incoherent speech with people throwing some good-natured heckling at me. 'I'm a bit Oliver Twist at the moment,' was my excuse. 'What kind of a speech was that?' Viv Anderson quizzed. For me, it was a giggle and all part of the growing-up process.

The next season, 1987/88, was for me a season of seeds being sown. We were, at Arsenal, a nearly side, one still in the throes of transformation by George Graham. The Littlewoods Cup win strengthened his position and enabled him to make changes, safe in the knowledge that he had already secured a trophy and was unlikely to be criticized for any moves he made – that included selling the fans' favourite 'Champagne' Charlie Nicholas, who was never going to be George's tipple, to Aberdeen in the January. It was alright by me; Charlie was never going to match the work rate of the younger players and on which our system relied. It meant Paul Merson coming through more often to partner Alan Smith in attack.

An unrefuseable offer, both for player and club, also came in from Manchester United for Viv Anderson. Nigel Winterburn, strange as it may be to recall seeing that he is all left foot, took over at right-back after his signing from Wimbledon in the May. Later in the season, Steve Williams would be giving George some lip – Steve always was confident in his own opinions – and Michael Thomas came in. Steve would be sold to Luton at the end of that season. Gradually the older ones were being replaced with younger players who would do it George's way. That much would also become evident in my personal case during the season.

We began in exceptional form and between mid-September and mid-November won 10 League matches in succession. That autumn, in my sixth international appearance for England, I scored my first goal for my country, a header from Chris Waddle's corner, in an amazing 4–1 win over Yugoslavia in Belgrade, where we scored all four in the opening half an hour to qualify for the European Championship Finals of 1988 in West Germany. In the next game, against Holland at Wembley, I also scored, at both ends, in a 2–2 draw. 'Tony scored past Shilton,' the Arsenal fans sang in our next league game against Derby County.

Around Christmas, Kenny Sansom was injured and George made me captain, the youngest in Arsenal's history at 21 years and three months, for an away match at Portsmouth on New Year's Day. I was naturally delighted but considered it just a one-off honour. I was more concerned with our patchy League form that had seen us slip down the table to sixth. We really could have won the title that year if we had just shown some more cutting edge up front during the dark days of winter when we could score only seven goals in 11 games. I think we also missed Viv's inspiring influence in the dressing room.

Then, in the March, Kenny Sansom gave an interview to one of the newspapers that was none too complimentary about George. I think there was a problem about money, as well as with personalities clashing. They had known each other socially in previous times and perhaps their relationship could not survive a less equal, more disciplined environment. Also, Kenny was the type of defender who used to nick the ball away in the tackle, and I think George felt he would not be physical enough for what we were doing, though personally I believe Kenny was an adaptable player. Anyway, George, who probably used the article to his advantage, never took kindly to such public expressions of discontent and there was an argument in his office, after which I was summoned. Kenny had been stripped of the captaincy. George felt that he could hardly put his faith in someone who questioned his methods and he wanted to make me his permanent captain. 'I've thought about you being so young but I'm not bothered,' he said. 'You're ready for it.'

I can't pretend I was surprised. As well as being captain of every team I had played for, I had always heard people saying that I was a born leader. 'Thank you,' was about the most I could mumble when George told me. Partly I was embarrassed – I went immediately to see Kenny, who told me not to worry and to get on with the job – but I was not going to turn it down. Although unable really to enjoy the moment or show my pleasure, I was nevertheless very proud. As a captain I was going to be George's voice on the field. I'm sure he wanted someone who would obey instructions and pass them on, someone who would lift and motivate the team rather than be some tactical genius, and both he and I felt I could do that. I had already been bossing them around.

I was comfortable with the position and knew that I had a lot to offer. It made sense to me, it was the role for me. I was happy at that time to play the part that I think George had assigned for me and which the dispute with Kenny gave him opportunity to implement. I think George saw in me someone who would marshal the older players around me. I didn't really think about any of the nuances of being captain. I would just get out there and shout and order, which seemed to be George's general requirement.

So it was that I led the team out at Wembley again that April as once more we reached the final of the Littlewoods Cup after wins over Doncaster Rovers, Bournemouth, Stoke City, Sheffield Wednesday and Everton, conceding only one goal in the process. I had just recovered from an injury that kept me out of the only League match I missed that season, at Southampton, where some 17-year-old kid called Shearer scored a hat-trick on his full debut against a makeshift centre-back partnership of Gus Caesar and Michael Thomas as we lost 4–2. I was at home picking up the score on teletext and wondering who this Shearer was. Was it Duncan, who used to play for Chelsea? Alan Shearer, who's that?

This time at Wembley we were the favourites, with Luton Town the opposition. Again we went 1–0 down, before going 2–1 up. Then we were awarded a penalty as David Rocastle was brought down. Just as Nigel Winterburn was about to step up to take the penalty to give us a two-goal cushion, I remember looking up at the Royal Box to where the trophy was resting and thinking that I would be lifting it in 10 minutes or so. But Andy Dibble saved Nigel's kick and Luton came downfield to score. A minute from time, Brian Stein made it 3–2 to them. I could not believe it.

My reaction was, as ever, to go and get drunk and I vaguely recall ending up at Niall Quinn's house in Enfield watching Monty Python's *Life of Brian* on the video. I was angry that I had not got my hands on silverware as captain, something I desperately wanted. But I would come to see, quite quickly, that I learned more from that defeat than any of the triumphs that were to follow. I learned not to look at the prize but to concentrate on the matter in hand. I did not like the feeling of failure and it fuelled a determination to go back and succeed. Who knows, if I had achieved success then, I might not have gone on to be the same successful player and captain, and the subsequent trophies might not have come my way. At the time I probably needed a knock-back to fuel my drive once more.

Trying to beat Martin Keown and Tommy Caton for a place in the team had given me drive. They had seemed like obstacles in my way, but it was nothing personal. That's the way Arsenal was at that time; healthy rivalry and an intense atmosphere, reflected in the way Niall Quinn and I used to practise together outside of regular training. Each stage of my development had been a hurdle: feeling secure in the team rather than thinking I might get dropped, being captain of the team, getting in the England side and getting past that feeling of being out of my depth. I wouldn't be satisfied until I had done all those things. Even then I couldn't rest. These days I can see that the highs are easy and the lows are for learning. At that time, after that Wembley defeat by Luton, I just felt angry.

By the time I returned to the club the next season, the

feeling had turned to pain – if I had been capable of identifying what I was feeling properly, that is. The European Championship Finals of 1988 in West Germany proved to be a miserable experience both for me and England as we lost 1–0 to the Republic of Ireland, 3–1 to Holland and 3–1 to the Soviet Union. I felt I took a lot of unwarranted criticism that such a young player should not have to take while more experienced players kept their heads down and escaped relatively unscathed. It was particularly cruel after the game against the Dutch when Marco Van Basten scored a hat-trick. Imagine Rio Ferdinand, say, being blamed these days for England losing to a Romario hat-trick for Brazil.

More of that later but then, after all that, I was relieved to get home and back to the environment of Arsenal. For the first time in my career I had felt humiliated and inadequate, and I think lesser men and players might have gone under. I dealt with that the best way I knew how – apart from getting drunk, that was – by working hard in pre-season for Arsenal and trying to prove everybody wrong again, which seemed to be at the heart of everything I did.

It helped that I had a belief that we were on the verge of big things. In the summer, on the night of the Dutch debacle, a few of us were having a drink to drown our sorrows and to celebrate Peter Shilton's 100th cap. The ITV commentator Jim Rosenthal was with us and I was insisting to him that we would win the title the next season. In fact, I bet him £50 that we would. The feeling I had must have been like that of the Manchester United boys of the early and mid-90s. There was so much strength at the club. Now we had a good blend of experience and youthful enthusiasm, to which the boss had added with the signings of Brian

Marwood and Lee Dixon, two-thirds of the way through the previous season. Steve Bould had also arrived from Stoke that summer.

The omens were good pre-season when we won the Wembley International tournament by beating Tottenham and Bayern Munich and in October we lifted the Football League's Centenary Trophy by beating Manchester United at Villa Park. It was strange how at that time, when I was playing well and Arsenal were getting up a head of steam, my England career stalled. We had only drawn 1–1 in Saudi Arabia and although I scored our goal, I was blamed for the one we conceded despite the fact I was up for a corner at the time. That included a public admonishment by the England manager Bobby Robson, although to be fair I think he was going through his own testing time with the media. Anyway, I would be dropped after that game. I was reasonably philosophical about it; if that was the way the wind was blowing at international level, I was going to concentrate my efforts with Arsenal.

What with that result coming on top of the summer's misery, I was being considered a scapegoat for the ills of the English game. I didn't have enough pace and I couldn't bring the ball out of defence – that old argument against the English defender. I seemed to be dubbed as the archetype. One of the chants popular on the terraces at that time was the donkey 'ee-aw' braying aimed by opposing fans at defenders if they misplaced a pass or cleared the ball into touch and I was a target, along with a few others. I think I first heard it at West Ham in the beginning of October, in a game that we won 4–1, then at Derby County's old Baseball Ground the following month. It was always at its loudest at the confined stadiums where you could hear everything.

Then, the following spring – the day after April Fool's

Day, in fact – we played at Manchester United and drew 1–1, with me scoring at both ends. After the coach journey back, I stayed the night at Paul Merson's near St Albans. Paul had the *Daily Mirror* delivered and I woke up to a picture of me on its back page with a pair of donkey's ears drawn on. I was really hurt. After that it just got worse and a month later in our next away match at Middlesbrough's old Ayresome Park ground, so many carrots were thrown at me that I could have opened a fruit and veg stall. One caught me right on the ear, which was really swollen after the game.

That stung physically and emotionally. I dismissed it as all part of the job and used it to focus on my game. Publicly it motivated me, and I used to enjoy winning games away from Highbury – and we were becoming experts at digging in and winning away games – so I could get one over the opposing fans giving out the abuse. In fact, I used to say to the lads that they had chosen the right – or wrong – person to pick on because I was bigger and better than that and I could take it. Kicking the ball into touch? Well, it couldn't be in the back of my net then, could it? That was my attitude.

Privately, in all honesty, it hurt like hell and the only way I knew how to deal with that pain was to get drunk and get on with the next game; drink and football, my two saviours. I was into my routine for life. My whole way of being was to get up and train, sleep in the afternoon, maybe go out with my pals in the evening then get up and do it again. Fish and chips on a Friday night and before you know it, it's a Saturday game, to be followed by a drinking session. Wednesday, Saturday, Wednesday, Saturday. I lived for those two days, fully committed to the cause, fully determined. That way I didn't have time to dwell on the hurt. I just thought, 'Well, we're going to win the League and show them.' I was more sensitive about these things than my tough-guy image would indicate, but if I had thought about it too much, I might have gone under.

We're going to win the League. That became our quest and our mantra. We squeezed and squeezed teams, then squeezed them more. In front of John Lukic, the back four of Dixon, Bould, Adams and Winterburn – Nigel having moved to the left to replace Kenny Sansom, who was sold to Newcastle that Christmas – had taken shape. Michael Thomas and either Paul Davis or Kevin Richardson – and what a bargain buy he was from Watford for £200,000 the previous season – closed down everything in front of us while on the flanks, David Rocastle and Brian Marwood had pace to burn as they got up and down the touchline to perform defensive duties as well. We called Brian 'Snowy' because he settled so quickly after his move from Sheffield Wednesday and he, Alan Smith and Lee Dixon, who had all moved into the St Albans area, were known as 'The Three Amigos'. In his first season, Lee was outstanding, getting up the wing and putting in some telling crosses to 'Smeggy' (as I called Alan Smith because he was a Brummie, though all the other boys knew him as 'Smudger'), who would score 25 goals that season, with Paul Merson cleverly playing around him.

Sometimes, usually away from home, we would play three centre-halves, with David O'Leary coming into the defence. George was particularly proud of the fact that his team were the first to play three at the back. Mostly, though, it was the familiar 4–4–2 in which everyone knew their job so thoroughly. Every day of the week George would hammer us on the training ground. We would go through routines of one-on-one, two-on-two and even five defenders against eight attackers, working on closing down the opposition. Closing and squeezing, tackling and tackling, until it became the mentality. At Highbury, we just put teams under pressure in every area of the pitch. We have one of the smallest playing surfaces in the country and teams just could not find space to pass the ball against us. It was another reason why George wanted us to get the ball forward quickly ourselves. It was all expected to start with the strikers, and Alan Smith and Paul Merson became just as good as Rush and Dalglish at working across the back four. Teams got weary just trying to get the ball out of their own half and eventually surrendered possession.

Our start at Wimbledon back in August had made me apprehensive – for about five minutes. Bouldy was playing on the right side of defence, with me left, of the central two at the back and marking John Fashanu at a free-kick. When Fashanu peeled away to head home, I wondered what George had signed here. I think I was upset that all my old playmates were being replaced one by one: Niall Quinn by Alan Smith, Viv Anderson by Lee Dixon, and now David O'Leary by Steve Bould. 'You had the hump when I signed the Stoke boys, didn't you?' George said to me once. 'But, eh Tony, I knew what I was doing, didn't I?' And he did. Not everything George did was brilliant, as would later become evident, but mostly I had confidence in him, and certainly at this time. Before we knew it, Merse was playing a blinder at the other end, Smeggy had scored a hat-trick and we had won 5–1.

A team really only needs respect for each other rather than affection to be successful and there are several examples down the years of players within teams who detested each other. It has always been said that there were great enmities in some of the old Liverpool teams of the seventies. But this Arsenal team actually liked each other. We socialised together, half of the team grew up together – me, Merse, Rocky, Mickey Thomas – and most of the players lived near the training ground. As for me, the players called me 'Son of George', now that I was his mouthpiece. 'Been to see George?' they would say after I had come out of his office. 'Got another new contract, have we?'

We climbed to the top of the table on Boxing Day with a 3–2 win over Charlton as part of a run of seven wins and three draws in 10 games and established an eight-point lead. Naturally, Liverpool being Liverpool, they started whittling away at it. Then came the day that would stick in so many people's memories, though not, I have to confess, mine. On 15 April, we beat Newcastle 1–0 while Liverpool were playing Nottingham Forest in an FA Cup semi-final at Hillsborough. I'm sure I watched the news pictures of fenced-in fans dying on the terraces that day, but I'm astonished to say that they hardly affected me because, I'm sad to admit, that was the man I was at that time. I wouldn't have allowed it to affect me, wouldn't have cried, because I knew we still had to go to Anfield for what would be a huge match. I just wanted to play football and any other issue seemed irrelevant to my life. The way I was then, numb to anything outside of my circle in life, I lived in a self-centred world and did not think beyond that.

Later that year, for example, we would play the Argentinian side Independiente in a pre-season match in Miami. Before the game, I was asked to carry out the Argentinian flag and I agreed, until David O'Leary pointed out that there had been many British casualties during the Falklands War in the not-too-distant past and it would be disrespectful to them and their families to carry the flag.

Back home, it might also have caused a row since it was being televised live. David was right and I quickly told the organisers that I would only carry the British flag. Now I was angry with them and the Argentinians for even thinking I would do it. But I was not really capable of thinking for myself properly in those days and, besides, what did politics have to do with football anyway?

The Hillsborough disaster changed the landscape of the season completely, with our match against Liverpool now put off until Friday 26 May. While we stayed focused on things, it must have been almost impossible for the Liverpool players.

For our match against Manchester United at the beginning of April, George went with a back three of David O'Leary, Steve Bould and me to defend the wide open spaces of Old Trafford. It was the 'donkey' game in which I scored at both ends but at least the 1–1 draw was a vindication of the tactics. We stuck with it then as it brought us wins over Everton, Norwich and Middlesbrough as well as Newcastle. It all looked so good when we won 5–0 at Highbury against a wilting Norwich, who themselves had looked like title contenders earlier in the season but had been unable to sustain the challenge. With the insurance of the back three and Lee Dixon and Nigel Winterburn bombing forward on a nice sunny day, we were confident and we were buzzing. Afterwards there was a real elation in the dressing room, but no one was taking anything for granted. There was still, no doubt about it, an underlying fear that we might make a mess of it.

Then, looking nervous and feeling tired, we were beaten 2–1 at home by Derby County the following weekend. The long season of closing teams down was catching up with us. Dean Saunders turned me inside out – it has always been the small nippy strikers who have given me the most trouble – and reached his 20 goals for the season. 'You can go on and win the title, now I've got my 20,' he said to me. The prospect of that, however, was receding.

It grew dimmer when we played Wimbledon the following midweek. We went back into a 4–4–2 and, to be honest, really expected to win comfortably. They had nothing to play for and we thought they would just play out the game; they owed nothing to Liverpool, whom they had beaten in the FA Cup the previous season after having lost to them at home just a few days earlier. But neither did they owe anything to us and they have always enjoyed tearing into the Arsenal, the toffs of London. Besides, the Highbury pitch was terrible, which suited Wimbledon. It started well enough with Nigel Winterburn giving us the lead with a rare right-footed shot but they equalised through a young lad called Paul McGee, who was making his debut. The whole team ran over to congratulate him and I thought, 'Jesus Christ, what's the matter with these idiots? This is not fair. They're supposed to lie down.' I felt insulted that they were trying so hard. We didn't play well, but after falling behind we scrambled a point with Alan Smith's goal.

It was enough to take us back to the top of the table, replacing Liverpool who had beaten Queens Park Rangers the previous night, but only on goal difference and they had a game in hand. That Saturday they won the FA Cup by beating Everton 3–2 after extra-time. The following Friday they could win the Double when we went to Anfield. Highbury was now in gloom and George thought we needed to get away from football for a while, so he gave us a couple of days off.

Steve Bould, Niall Quinn, Paul Merson and I – some social quartet, that – decided to go down to Windsor for the

Monday night race meeting and took a boat along the Thames. Being single men, Quinny and I got chatting to a couple of girls and were getting along well with them until two bruisers came down from the back of the boat to inform us that the girls were their wives. We had had a few drinks and were getting a bit loud, I suppose, but eventually the scene calmed down. A few days later George called us into his office to say he had received written complaints from the two men and he told us to send written apologies and flowers to their wives, which we did.

Anyway, once at Windsor, we encountered Peter Shilton, who had a horse running. 'Only one in the race that can beat it,' he said. Naturally enough, we backed that one rather than his. Naturally enough, Shilts's horse won. The last we saw of him was him giving us the thumbs-up from the winner's enclosure. We returned the gesture as if to say, 'Yes, we were on it,' not daring to give him an inkling that we hadn't backed his horse.

After the racing, I think Merse and Bouldy made their way back home while Niall and I drunkenly made our way to a nightclub in Maidenhead where we were refused entry. From there it was on to a hotel at Heathrow to get our heads down. The next day the bender continued. Quinnie had to see his bank manager in Richmond, so we headed over there for another drinking session. Then, via a bar called O'Riordan's in Brentford where Niall insisted you could get the best Guinness in London, it was back to his place in Enfield for some more. Finally I phoned my Mum and Dad's, where I was still living, on the Wednesday. Not surprisingly, they had been worried about me.

It was an example of a young bloke taking things to extremes, though nowhere near as extreme as things would become. At that time my body could take it and it was simply my way of dealing with the Derby and Wimbledon results and putting the forthcoming Anfield ordeal out of my mind. Had I dwelt on either of those two subjects, I might well have felt fear that I did not want. No damage had really been done. I laugh now when I see the film of Nick Hornby's book about his life as an Arsenal supporter, *Fever Pitch*. There was half of North London and beyond fretting about the title race and me, the team's captain, on a bender.

It had completely by-passed me that Liverpool had beaten West Ham on the Tuesday night in their game in hand to move three points clear of us. They were top for the first time that season and now they had a better goal difference. Our task was clear: we had to win by two goals to take the title. They could afford a 1–0 defeat and still be champions. On the Wednesday I got back to work ready and raring to go for one of the biggest games in the club's history and what was to prove probably the most dramatic finale ever to an English league season.

Emotions were still raw on Merseyside after Hillsborough and I think everyone felt for Liverpool in a way they had never done before. The Red machine was human after all. Perhaps Liverpool felt the way we had done against Wimbledon: don't you dare even get on the same park as us because we are going to win the League. I'm sure it all worked in our favour. There is no doubt that Hillsborough had affected them but we were focused on what we needed to do. We were going to work and as professionals could not afford any sympathy for them.

The task was massive. Liverpool had not lost by two goals at home for three years and they were unbeaten in 18 league games since New Year's Day. Arsenal had not won at Anfield in their previous seven visits. But there was a change in mood. Now everyone thought it was Liverpool's title, as opposed to a few weeks earlier when it was considered to be ours. We preferred to be in this latest position. There was something about this Arsenal which liked doing things the hard way. I certainly did. Tony Adams had been proving people wrong for five years. If we had gone up there needing a draw rather than a win, we might not have been in the same determined frame of mind.

There was a lot of talk among the betting boys in the team on the coach going up about the odds for the game. They could not understand why we were something like 8–1 to win the title and 16–1 to win the game 2–0. It didn't make sense because we had to chase the two goals and we thought we would all have a bet at those odds. But for all the mood of confidence that everyone instilled in each other, deep down I have to admit that there was some doubt as to whether we could do it. I was never going to let that show and nor was anyone else, mind.

We travelled up on the day of the match, as we usually did when George was manager, and were booked into the Atlantic Tower hotel for the afternoon. After we had had a meal and a nap, George called us all down from our rooms to a meeting in the conference suite. He was already in his usual smart blazer and Arsenal tie. It was as if to say that he was ready for the game and now it was our turn. He stood up beside a blackboard and told us exactly how we were going to do it. I can vividly remember his team talk because of the way he called it and the way the match would later pan out.

'Keep it tight. Keep it very tight,' George said. 'You know what it's like at Anfield. Don't let them settle, don't let them play, because if you do, you know they can pass it and hurt you. Pressure, pressure, pressure all over the field. Make them kick it long. We've got two 6ft 3in centre-backs who will mop it all up. I won't be too disappointed if it's still 0–0 at half-time. We can maybe get a goal early in the second half and go on from there.' Later, George would say that he actually thought we would win the game 3–0. Whether that was tongue in cheek or not, I'm not sure. Jim Rosenthal might as well have paid up then rather than later, on that bet he struck with me.

People prepare for games in different ways to suit their personalities. My way, when we got to the ground an hour and a half before the game, was always to take mine and other people's minds off the game, if that was what they wanted. Those who wanted to focus on the game that early could ignore me, but not many did. It was going to be a long night. There was no point in peaking emotionally too soon. I talked about other peaks. I told the lads I had had a date a few nights earlier with the Page Three girl Suzanne Mizzi and was detailing to them what she was like. It was a complete lie and I'm sure the boys realised that, but it gave them the chance to have a laugh with me and take the mickey. When I insisted, the banter became more laughable.

You would never have known we were going to play such an important match in an hour's time. You felt you could have your fun in this group. You knew they were pulling for you and you for them, so making fun of each other was in many ways a mark of the respect you had for each other. It all worked for me then, and it achieved what I wanted. It masked the way I was really feeling, the nerves and the fear.

Once back in the dressing room after the warm-up out on the field, with 10 minutes to kick-off, it was my turn to give a more serious team talk. I was a screamer, a bawler, a motivator, having taken my lead from Terry Butcher with the England team. I always copied good things and the controlled aggression of Terry's 'caged tiger' performance often seemed to work well. 'Come on, we are having this. Believe we can do it,' I said. 'We haven't worked all season to waste it now. We haven't come this far to lose. Don't come back in this dressing room at the end with any regrets.'

The buzzer sounded in our dressing room for us to take the field, but George stopped us. He always put his fingers to his mouth and issued a shrill whistle when he wanted our attention. 'Don't worry about that, just ignore it,' he said as the buzzing continued. The shouting stopped and the clatter of studs on the floor fell silent. Everyone listened. Whatever else anyone felt about George, he had total respect at this time because of the success he was bringing us. I think if he had told us that night that the way to win this match was to go and jump from the roof of the Kop we would have done it.

He always had one last-minute piece of information that he wanted to get across and for us to hold in our minds. At somewhere like Norwich, it would be something motivational like, 'Let's get the job done and get out of this country town with the points.' At other times it would be inspirational: 'It's about resilience today,' or tactical: 'Make your runs'. Tonight his theme was not to let Liverpool settle. 'Pressure them. We want a rushed game.' The shouting started again.

We passed under that old 'This Is Anfield' sign, but it didn't frighten me. I didn't feel any need to spit on it or bang my fist on it as some of the Wimbledon boys were reported to have done, because I had respect for Liverpool. Respect but not fear. I'm told Bill Shankly was once asked if he thought Anfield intimidated players and he replied: 'Only the bad ones.' Exactly. And I didn't think I was a bad one.

The noise in the tunnel soon changed to a quietness on the pitch when the game kicked off. It was almost eerie – and ideal for us. The Hillsborough effect played its part in Liverpool being subdued, but so did we. No real alarms first half. Might even have taken the lead with Bouldy's header. Rush, whom I was marking, picked up a knock and was replaced by Peter Beardsley. I remembered what George had said about not worrying if it was 0–0 at half-time. 'Don't panic if we haven't scored.' I wasn't even thinking about winning at that stage, just concentrating on playing my game and doing the right things.

At the interval George reminded us of the virtues of patience, but what struck me most was the sea of faces in the dressing room: Pat Rice, Steve Burtenshaw, every coach on the staff, reserves, youth team, the lot. It was a thing that dated back to Bertie Mee's time as manager of the Double team at Arsenal: if you are going into the lion's den, take as many friendly faces with you as you can. It was always the same for Cup Finals. George also liked to turn to them quietly to ask if they thought he had missed any little pointers. After another two penn'orth from me, just offering encouragement and reinforcing the message of staying patient, it was once more into the breach. And it was just uncanny how the game unfolded as George had envisaged it.

We had not really worked on anything special, just the usual set pieces, including free-kicks. And one of those paid off, only seven minutes into the second half. Nigel Winterburn, taking the dead-ball kicks on the left in the absence of the injured Brian Marwood, swung in a free-kick and Alan Smith ghosted in, as was his speciality, to glance it home. There was a moment of concern when a linesman's flag went up and Liverpool claimed an offside or that David O'Leary had fouled someone. Anything really. But I was confident it would stand when David went over to the linesman as all the Liverpool players gathered round the ref. Clever pro, David. We're well represented in the discussions, I thought. Dave will sort it out. The referee consulted the linesman but the goal stood. I was actually disappointed that it hadn't been me who headed it in. Later on the coach I would be telling everyone that it had been me attracting all the attention of the Liverpool defence that had created the goal. Later still, I would be claiming it as mine.

Now I could see we had a cracking chance here. And when Ray Houghton missed a good opportunity to equalize, I knew it was our time. The omens were good. But it was such a rollercoaster ride that doubt began to set in. Ten minutes from time, Michael Thomas went through and missed. That was it, we had blown it. Now I confess to becoming less composed. When John Lukic got the ball in his hands with seconds to go, I yelled at him to hoof it upfield. We had to get on with it and I also wanted some time for the defence to get out. 'Just kick it John, for eff's sake,' I screamed.

But either he didn't hear me or chose to ignore me because suddenly he's thrown the ball out to Lee Dixon. I couldn't believe it. The next thing I know, Dicko has found Smeggy, who's turned and laid it off brilliantly to Mickey. Now he's got a good bounce off Steve Nicol. Now he's through on goal. Now he's clipped it over Bruce Grobbelaar. Fantastic. Pandemonium. But wait. Liverpool have a last attack and Mickey's got the ball at his feet in our own penalty area. I thought he would hoof it. Instead, he's coolly passed the ball back to Lukey, as you were allowed to do in those days, it now seems amazing to think. Then the final whistle has gone. I ruffled the hair of John Aldridge, who had annoyed me when he did just that to Steve Chettle after the poor Nottingham Forest defender had conceded an own goal when the semi-final eventually did take place post-Hillsborough. 'That's for Steve Chettle,' I told him. George seemed the coolest man in the place. When I ran to embrace him, there was only the most formal of hugs. Then, the next thing I knew, at the age of 22, I was lifting the League trophy.

Back in the dressing room, Steve Bould and I punched out the entire ceiling of polystyrene panels in our boisterous jubilation. Liverpool, with a touch of class, kindly sent the champagne that had been chilling for them through to us. I think there were about 200 empty bottles by the time we had finished, about a couple of dozen of them having been drunk and the rest just sprayed. We just wanted to be back on the coach and back in London. Brian Marwood led the singing back down the M6. 'We call upon Georgie to sing us a song,' we demanded but he wouldn't. He just sat at the front with his own thoughts, savouring the achievement. Occasionally we would glimpse that satisfied smirk of his when he turned round to say something to somebody. Everything, in the end, had gone right for George, who needed to use only 17 players that season. We probably weren't the most talented team, but we were probably the most organised and disciplined and that was good enough for me then.

Back in North London, we all headed for a nightclub in Southgate called, appropriately, Winners. It was staggering at this time in the early hours of the morning how many Arsenal fans were still milling around hoping to catch a glimpse of us. They must have known about the nocturnal habits of some of our number. I think I ended up at Niall Quinn's again, along with Martin Hayes.

On the Saturday morning, we all took taxis back to London Colney to pick up our cars and then for me it was on to the Jack and Jenny pub in Witham near my home. I remember meeting some mates, drinking all day then all night at one of their houses. When daylight interrupted, I went home to put on a suit, then called a taxi to take me to Highbury where we were to meet to parade the trophy through the streets of Islington that Sunday in an open-topped bus.

I had lost all track of time, though, and it was still only about 7 am when I got to the steps of the main entrance in Avenell Road which houses the famous marble hall. I just sat on those steps and waited for everyone to arrive, dozing off occasionally. The groundsman Paddy Galligan got a shock when he came to open up and found me there before him. When we went on the parade, people were throwing cans of beer up to us. All contributions were gratefully received.

At that time it was all working. The drinking was no problem. I was doing my job well, we were Champions. It didn't matter that I was out of the England team. I did not know I was an alcoholic in development, nor what the price of such an intense way of life was going to be. I was just living on my talent and my instincts, doing my two-fingered best to prove everyone wrong about me and to accumulate trophies for Arsenal.

FOUR

Nicked

There is a beautiful line that opens the novel *The Go Between*. 'The past is a foreign country,' LP Hartley wrote. 'They do things differently there.' It comes into my mind as I look back on my life at the beginning of the 1990s, because the past was where I used to live.

Now, I wonder how I survived a serious car crash and subsequent conviction for drink-driving that sent me to Chelmsford Prison for just over eight weeks. Then, I just simply survived. My football was such an obsession with me that all the other events just took second place and sometimes hardly seemed significant at all. As long as I could lace up my boots and get out on the training ground or the pitch, then everything was all right.

In footballing terms, 1989/90 was a treading-water season. We almost seemed to take a season off after all the exertions of the previous, title-winning campaign. As a young team, it had drained us emotionally and physically, perhaps. Whatever it was, there was not the same intensity to us that there had been when we won the title. Come May at the end of that season, the feeling for me would certainly be the opposite of the elation of exactly a year earlier, though there would be a common denominator called alcohol.

There were high points in the football. I enjoyed scoring the goal in a 1–0 win over Tottenham at Highbury, and we did lead the First Division just before Christmas. Mostly, though, it was a series of disappointments that illustrated how fickle the game can be. I suppose the signs were there from the start as we lost the Charity Shield to Liverpool, and followed that with a 4–1 defeat by Manchester United at Old Trafford on the opening day of the season. Some place to be sent, that, as defending Champions. I had been up all night because my room-mate – and I don't want to reveal his name – had been smoking and the smell had made me feel sick, so I was not in the game when I let Steve Bruce in for a quick opening goal. After United had then got a penalty, George Graham pulled me off and sent on Gus Caesar, who was given a torrid time by Mark Hughes.

After Christmas, we faded to a weary fourth and went out of the FA Cup in the fourth round, having fallen at that stage of the League Cup as well. It was also a sadness for me that George sold my best friend Niall Quinn to Manchester City. Neither was my general mood improved by my stalling international career. I played four B-team games that season as I tried to reclaim a place in the full England squad for the 1990 World Cup Finals but come late May, along with Alan Smith and David Rocastle, I would be cut from the squad as Bobby Robson pared it down from 26 to the final 22.

So, after a club season that would have been deemed reasonable in George's later years but was at that time a great let-down, it was with some relief that I greeted the last match of the campaign. Now, before going off on an end-of-season club tour to Singapore, then linking up with England in that ultimately thwarted hope of making Italy, I could relax. As usual that involved a good drink.

I had been asked down to Canvey Island in Essex by our physio Gary Lewin to present some awards at a local football club dinner. I had a few drinks there, basking in everyone telling me what a great guy I was, then decided to go on to a nightclub nearby called King's with Brian Horne, the old Millwall goalkeeper, who had also been at the dinner, and we had a few drinks. I think it was about 5 am when the taxi rolled up back home in Rainham.

Come 10 am when I woke up, it dawned on me that I would need my car, which I had left at the venue of the awards dinner the previous night, to drive over to Heathrow later that day to meet up with the team to go to Singapore. A friend agreed to take me over to Canvey but I couldn't remember where we had left the car and it took ages to locate it. Finally we did and then decided that it might be a good idea to go over to this pub I knew in Rayleigh for a lunchtime drink. I didn't want to get too drunk because of the drive to Heathrow, but I didn't realise then that alcoholism is an uncontrollable illness; once I started, I would have great trouble in stopping. I didn't realise then, in fact, that I was suffering from alcoholism. After four or five lager tops, I was buzzing again. I was Charlie Big Potatoes. And I was all over the place. Probably all I was doing was topping up from the night before.

Soon I had been invited by someone in the pub to a party at a house in the neighbourhood and I decided that I had a few hours to spare so I tagged along, chipping in to the kitty for the crate of beer. I was torn between the drinking and going home to get changed from the shorts and flip flops I was wearing, then packing to go to Singapore – and the booze was winning. It turned into a barbecue when someone started cooking, though later in the tabloids it would be described as an orgy because someone who was at the gathering told the papers that there was a couple upstairs having sex. I was in the garden playing drunken cricket with a few blokes, complete strangers all. Now the time was getting on. I was angry all of a sudden that I had to go and work again when the season was over. I did not want to go to Singapore and was beginning to think I might not have left enough time to do what I needed to at home then drive the sixty or so miles to the airport.

In fact, I barely got 60 yards. They heard the crash at the barbecue.

We were in a residential street in Rayleigh near to a main A-road into Southend, but I barely saw that as I drove straight across it without stopping, even though it was a dual carriageway. I remember thinking, 'What's that road I've just crossed over?' as I entered another residential street and I turned to look back. It was then that I lost control of the car. I didn't know where I was going but I was doing about 75 or 80 mph.

Then, as I was still wondering where I was, the car clipped a telegraph pole, so I was told later, and shot me straight across to the other side of the road. To add insult to injury, a few weeks later the telephone company would send me a bill for the damage. Now I was completely out of control. I felt the impact of something solid, which turned out to be a brick wall at the front of someone's house. The next thing I knew, I was in their front garden, the car now stationary.

On impact, the car windscreen had shattered, which was fortunate as my head was thrown forward towards it and I felt some glass hit me. Two things had kept me alive: the seatbelt, which I rarely did up in those days but have done ever since, and the sturdiness of the 4 x 4 Ford Sierra sponsored car I was driving.

The driver's door had come off and I staggered out, picking glass out of my hair. I was shaking from head to toe. My shoulder was hurting from the whiplash – and I wonder to this day if the injuries I have had down the right side of my body playing football have something to do with the knot of muscle I still have there – but I was in one piece.

By now the lovely old couple whose front wall and garden I had just demolished had come out of their front door. They were probably shocked but were more concerned for me. 'Are you all right?' they asked. 'Would you like a drink for your nerves?' I'm sure they meant a cup of tea or something, but the first thought that went through my head was a brandy. I replied that I thought I had probably had enough, thank you.

The police arrived and breathalysed me; 134 was the reading, I think, almost four times over the limit of 35. I didn't have a leg to stand on, basically, which I think is the right phrase seeing that I was legless. I was later told that I could have refused the breathalyser at this point but it never occurred to me to; I was scared not to do what a policeman asked.

At the police station, they took a statement, in which I said that I had swerved to avoid a car reversing out of a drive. I was panicking and made it up, though I did see a car in a drive which, in my drunken state, I may have mistakenly thought was moving. I had to wait a while for another test to confirm the reading. I told them that they had better hurry up because I had a plane to catch. I was more worried about the wrath of George Graham than anything the police might charge me with. The reading usually drops the second time around but with my body still processing the alcohol, mine was even higher – 137. I was charged with reckless driving and driving with excess alcohol. I was free to go now but would be summoned to attend a trial at a later date.

By now I was getting worried about this Singapore trip. My mate who had taken me to Canvey and come on to the barbecue, had heard the crash, come to investigate and followed me down to the police station. Now he drove me home, where I grabbed a few things and put them in a suitcase, put on a pair of trousers over my shorts, shoes – without socks – and my club blazer and headed for Heathrow, courtesy again of my chauffeur.

The team was already boarding the plane when I got there. The press had got to hear about the crash, and reporters had gone to the airport to ask George and our club secretary Ken Friar about it all. It was news to them. I think they were quite amazed when I eventually turned up, with all the journalists now having left thinking I wasn't going to make it. A few of the players asked me how I was but apart from that, nobody really talked to me when I got on the plane. The press had told them what had happened and I don't think they knew what to say. I think it is fair to say George snubbed me, leaving me alone to stew. I was shocked, numb, with the shame now beginning to hit me. I felt like a naughty boy who knew he had done something wrong. I just sat and brooded. For thirteen hours. Occasionally, I would find little shards of shattered windscreen glass in my hair.

When we got to Singapore, a group of Oriental reporters were waiting for me. 'Tony Adams, you crash car!' they were shouting at me. I just ignored them and kept walking. The enormity of what I had done had begun to hit home. I was thinking that I needed to stop doing this, but I didn't know anything else. Later that night I plucked up courage to phone my Mum and Dad. I think they were worried silly about me. I had hurt them a lot, but at that time I was rarely aware of the grief I was causing other people. Given time and more alcohol I could blot it out, anyway. On that trip, I lifted a trophy when we beat South Korea 1–0, but I can't say it meant much to me.

Being omitted from the World Cup squad that summer probably did me, and perhaps even Alan Smith and David Rocastle, a power of good in Arsenal terms. I was fresh – well, as fresh as I could be, having taken myself off to Rhodes after Bobby Robson's rejection and spent a week drunk – and full of determination to prove people wrong yet again. That summer I also met Jane, who was to become my wife. She was working behind the bar in a club called Ra Ra's in Islington, one of the regular stops on my crawl around North London's drinking establishments.

George Graham spent the summer in a more business-like mood. He had recognised our limitations of the anti-climactic previous season and acted. He signed David Seaman and, to join the list of centre-backs, Andy Linighan. This despite the fact we already had, besides me, Steve Bould, David O'Leary and Colin Pates; good guys, one and all, and honest pros too of the type George tended to favour.

I just thought that it was good that we were strength-ening the squad. I never thought that anyone would be realistically challenging for my place. It was probably the one thing I wasn't insecure about in life at that time. A few people were coming to the end of their playing careers, like Brian Marwood. He had been fantastic for a couple of seasons, but he had done his bit and now George brought in Anders Limpar, the flying Swede, on the left. John Lukic, Martin Hayes and Kevin Richardson also departed.

There was a freshness to us from the outset of the season, and a steely togetherness. By the time we visited

Manchester United in October, we were in second place and what happened at Old Trafford that day spoke volumes about our character that season. George always said that he thought we were the one team in the South capable of going up North and matching the top clubs up there for commitment and attitude, and this game demonstrated it. In general, the two sides did not like each other and we were developing into the two at the top of the English tree.

The particular protagonists that day were Brian McClair and Nigel Winterburn and they had been at each other all afternoon. Eventually, it spilled over into some pushing and shoving between the two and everyone else joined in, mostly to try and calm it all down or protect their own. We were a strong side, a tough outfit and we took it personally if something was happening to one of our mates. It is very much how United would develop, with Roy Keane and Paul Ince together in the team.

You are like brothers, like family, and if someone is beating up your family you go to help. I remember being on a club trip to Cyprus one year and we had lost David Rocastle, so Colin Pates and I went out to look for him. That was the kind of concern we had for each other and in the end we found him in the corner of a bar somewhere. You talk to young players about team spirit these days and I have to admit they do find the mixed message difficult: 'You're telling us to help our mates, but then walk away from trouble? How does that work then?' they ask. There is no right answer, except in terms of self-discipline. In those days, we knew that publicly George would condemn any indiscipline, as he had to do, but privately if he felt it was in the cause, then he would not come down too hard on us.

Anyway, the so-called Old Trafford brawl was really nothing. Paul Ince came wading in and someone dragged him away. Alex Ferguson got off the bench to add his opinion from the touchline and I told him to sit down and shut up because he was making things worse. The media billed it as a 21-man brawl but at least 16 were simply trying to sort it out. You see worse incidents over on Hackney Marshes.

The FA's disciplinary commission took a dimmer view, not surprisingly, given that the media were pouring fuel on the fire. As a club we were fined £50,000 and George £10,000 individually, though how he could have prevented it I'm not sure. Worse, we were deducted two points, which at the time was really worrying with a new championship challenge materialising. At least we had won at Old Trafford, 1–0, with a goal by Anders. It showed what we were made of.

I appeared personally as Arsenal captain before the commission and they asked me why I had run fifty yards to get involved. I felt a duty, I told them, as captain to try and sort things out. They said I had made it worse and that I should have stayed away, along with everyone else, as it worsened the situation and provided the press with more grist for their mill. A 21-man brawl sounded so much worse – or better, for them – than a two-man disagreement. A few years later when I was with England, Terry Venables did some interesting work with us on flashpoints during a game, showing how to move in to a trouble spot, turn your back on the opponent and push your own man away. I told him that this could not be a Dagenham boy speaking; would he ever have turned his back in an East End fight?

I earned a recall that November to the England team, now under Graham Taylor's control, for a World Cup qualifying match against the Republic of Ireland in Dublin, a game that saw Paul Gascoigne controversially omitted.

Gazza was not ready to play that week, though, and I thought Graham was probably right, knowing what a scrap it would be on the bumpy Lansdowne Road pitch. It was precisely because it would be like an English league game that Tony Adams – you know, the defender who didn't really have the pace and couldn't bring the ball out but was a typically dependable stopper, so the label said – was recalled. I played in a three-man defence with Mark Wright and Des Walker and we drew 1–1 to vindicate Graham.

That month I was also reported to the police for giving a 'V'-sign to some Queens Park Rangers supporters during a match at Loftus Road. We had fallen 1–0 behind, conceding our first goal for more than 600 minutes, and I was getting wound up by all the 'ee-aw' donkey noises from the home fans. Unable to respond more physically, when Paul Merson equalised on the way to our 3–1 win, I just aimed the gesture at the home fans. I think they report someone at QPR every week, so sensitive are they there, and the police eventually dropped any idea of a criminal charge. The FA fined me £1,000, though it was soon to be the least of my worries.

All seemed to be going well and at the beginning of December we beat top-of-the-table Liverpool 3–0 at Highbury, with Anders Limpar having a great match, to confirm that we were definitely back as title contenders. I can now see, however, that there was an undercurrent of things going wrong personally for me, and in our next match on the horrible old plastic surface at Luton, my 200th League game for Arsenal, I was sent off for a so-called professional foul just after the new interpretation of the rule had come in. I thought Philip Don made a mistake. I did mistime the tackle but the attacker, Iain Dowie, was running away from goal.

Anyway, I didn't let it affect me and I scored in the next game, a 2–2 draw against Wimbledon at Highbury. Though it was a disappointing result, we had equalled a club record established in 1947 of 17 unbeaten matches at the start of a season, a figure we would eventually extend to 23. As Christmas approached, all was good cheer at Arsenal. Except for one filthy black cloud on my own horizon.

Wednesday 19 December 1990, at Southend Crown Court, was earmarked as the date and venue for my drink-driving case to be heard. It was also the day of the Arsenal players' Christmas party and I told the boys I would be along later. Many people wondered why I opted for a trial so close to Christmas but I had already put it off once and, besides, I thought I was going to get off. An irony was that if I had postponed it again, I later found out, I would have got off as the police officer who charged me was emigrating to Canada. Apparently the rule is that it has to be the same officer who brings the case to court.

I had hired a barrister soon after the car crash and he had told me that this was a serious offence for which I could well go to jail. My solution was to change my lawyer. I did not want to hear the truth about anything in those days, I just wanted reassurance rather than reality. It was also naivety on my part; some of the people around me who knew about these things warned me about what might happen but I simply ignored them. Nobody, least of all me, thought I was going to go down.

I stood upright in the dock, putting on the stiff-upper-lip act. Surely the judge would see that I was a nice boy? If he knew me, he certainly wouldn't convict me. 'I'm not a criminal. I'm a good person who has just done wrong,' I thought to myself. It was only when I had a drink inside me that I became different. As I often did in those days, I veered between feeling superior to everyone and inferior. I didn't feel like a well-known footballer now, just a bloke who was out of his own environment.

I had been briefed to say 'Thank you, your honour' to the judge even if he was putting me down, but then I would have done so anyway. After the charges had been read out and I pleaded guilty, I sat down in the dock next to the court warden. I can remember looking round and thinking how nice it was that everyone from the Arsenal vice-chairman, David Dein, down had come and were willing to speak on my behalf. I was most worried about my parents. It must have been horrible seeing their son going through all this. Mum couldn't face going into the witness box and I didn't want to put her through that so a statement from her was read out.

Over the next three hours, David O'Leary and Pat Jennings were among those who appeared on my behalf as character witnesses, but I think the judge, Justice Frank Lockhart, had already made up his mind about the seriousness of my offence. Who knows, if all the people at Arsenal hadn't spoken up for me, then the sentence might have been more severe. The judge would say later that the offence did seem out of character, according to the people who appeared for me.

The papers also reported him saying: 'You were out of control for 130 yards, the length of a football pitch. It is incredible that you came out of the car alive, let alone unscathed, and a merciful relief that there was nobody there to be killed or injured. You have not been to prison before, therefore I must consider if there is any alternative to prison today, but because of the serious nature of the offence, I can see no other practical alternative.'

All I really heard, though, was 'nine months' and

nothing after that, not from the judge nor my people, who were gasping with shock, apparently, in the public gallery. George Graham was the most stunned and later outside the court he said that Arsenal would appeal. The boys heard the news on the radio at their party and were also amazed.

I couldn't believe it either. I was sober in the dock and I had some good qualities. What had I done to deserve all this? There were theories that because there was a high-profile anti-drink-driving campaign going on that Christmas, I was made an example of and I do think there was some truth in that. In fact, I may have done some good. One policeman I know later said that I should have claimed some credit for the success of the campaign. Some people did in fact tell me that I made them think twice about drinking and driving during that holiday season.

'Sorry son, I've got to do this,' I heard the warden say as he gripped my arm and led me down to the cells, the words 'nine months' still echoing in my head. As mine had been the first case of the day, I was installed on my own in a long, thin and dingy cell, where I sat on a bench. 'What happened? Why nine months?' I asked the warden. He explained to me that five months on the reckless driving charge had been suspended and that I was doing four in all, with a three-month sentence for the excess alcohol to run concurrently. 'Oh, right,' I said. 'Not too bad then.' Rather than being relieved, though, in reality I was stunned. Having my driving licence suspended for two years and being fined £500 hardly seemed important.

I had to sit there in the cell waiting for all the other trials to be heard. To pass the few hours, I chatted with the warden about football and he offered me a cigarette, which I declined, and brought me a sandwich. I was also given time with Mum and Dad. They were very upset, not surprisingly, and I told them not to worry, that I would get through it all. I was genuinely concerned about them, but it also helped me to avoid thinking about how I was.

I was soon joined by the next case, who had received 18 months for causing an affray and hitting a policeman. Later, when there were four of us and it was time to be transferred to prison, I was handcuffed to this guy.

'This has really capped my day,' he said. 'I'm a Tottenham fan and I get 'cuffed to you. What a nightmare.'

He didn't seem bothered about the 18 months or his wife just having had a baby as much as his enforced travelling partner. I just wanted to hit the little toe-rag. But then, I was a criminal now as well and not really in much of a position to judge other people.

We were led outside to a white minibus where it was obvious that the usual routine for the two prison warders detailed to accompany us to Chelmsford Prison had taken on a new interest. 'Could you sign this for my son,' I was asked. I was still trying to be the nice guy and duly obliged as other pieces of paper demanding my autograph were then thrust into my hand. It had still not hit me that I was going to jail. If I had stopped to think about it, I would have been scared witless and at that time I had no emotional resources to deal with that fear. The best thing, I decided, was to treat it like an overnight stay before an away game. I had spent hundreds of hours in hotel rooms whiling away time until matches, with whoever was my room-mate, playing games, telling jokes, doing coin tricks. That's what I would do. Pretend.

In the reception area at Chelmsford, which was a bare room with just a few chairs, I felt that everyone was looking at me. A couple of the prisoners were serving tea. One warder told me that I would be all right, not to worry. I thought that another was looking down his nose at me. Both sides of the human coin were here, nice and nasty. They took my details – name, age, etc – along with my suit and put my valuables in a box.

Then I was issued with prison wear: dark blue jeans, which I later doodled on with a pen, a sky blue T-shirt, a tatty woollen pullover which was too tight, blue socks and black plimsolls. I was even given prison underwear. I wasn't really reacting to anything and had other things going on in my mind, so it didn't really bother me wearing things that someone else had worn. I treated it like kit at the football club; just another pair of shorts and socks. I was also issued with my number. I was to be prisoner No. LE1561.

It was now early evening and before being allocated a cell in the prison proper, I had to spend a night in the remand area of the wing, one of four that extend from a central control area and make up Chelmsford. One wing was for the sex offenders; the next day I would be sent to one of the others. That night, though, I was in with a mixture of everything: convicted people waiting for a cell, innocent people waiting for their trial. Before being locked up for the night, we were subjected to a prison awareness video about Aids and drugs. It didn't alarm me; I chuckled or grinned all the way through it. I was trying to remember about that overnight stay for an away game.

Except that the cell was no hotel room. It was a khazi, although there wasn't one of those. Just a bucket in the corner. The brick walls, painted in that institutional cream colour, were filthy and the bunks were basic. 'I'll take the bottom, eh mate?' I said to the bloke lumped in with me. He was only in for a couple of days for not having any insurance on his car. He said he had seen me drinking in boozers round Rainham way.

We spent the night laughing and playing cards. It wasn't a lonely night of worrying or weeping. I told him not to worry about selling his account of sharing a cell with me to the papers if he wanted to make a couple of thousand quid when he got out. He did, as did other cellmates I encouraged during my time there. 'PRISON'S A JOKE FOR ADAMS,' was the headline in one of the Sundays that week, I think. Again it was my way of dealing with it, of avoiding having to confront the fear.

Most people would recognise the cell I was allocated the next day from the Ronnie Barker comedy series *Porridge*. It was here they filmed all the interior shots. I was up the iron steps on the landing floor. Rumour had it that my cell had been the one John McVicar was once in, the one from which he escaped, through the kitchens. It was just like the remand wing. Just as spartan, just as basic: all its 12ft x 8ft contained was bunk beds and two cupboards for clothes on which you could put the radio, books and tapes for the personal stereo you were allowed. And a bucket. There was no table, chairs or sink. 'This place is a shithole,' I wrote to Jane a few days later.

On Christmas Day we were banged up for 23 hours because so many of the warders were off for the holiday period and they didn't have enough staff to cover us if we were out of our cells. There was no special Christmas lunch; certainly no crackers or paper hats. I spent most of my time listening to the radio – and the Madness song 'It Must Be Love' sticks in my mind – and writing letters. I don't recall it bothering me. It was the same on New Year's Eve. I listened to a lot of matches on the radio around that time, with Trevor Brooking's voice on the commentary, and I recall hearing Alan Smith scoring the winning goal against Manchester City on New Year's Day. Sometimes I was probably the lucky one. When England were playing Cameroon in the February, I can remember the commentators describing a freezing night and I was tucked up in a warm cell.

In the early days, I did not know how to react around other prisoners, nor they around me. Some of them wanted to be my mate, some of them wanted my autograph. I was determined not to be the big shot because I knew in this environment you could get slapped down pretty quickly by much harder men than me, men who would not take kindly to any display of arrogance. I picked up the lingo pretty quickly as well; 'screw' for warder, 'con' for prisoner, that kind of stuff.

'How's your bird?' someone asked me one day.

'Well, I'm missing her a bit,' I said.

'No, your *bird*. How you getting on with doing your time?'

There were certain things you didn't ask of people or say to them. Discussing the length of your sentence was out. If they are in for life and you're only in for a couple of months, then resentments fester. With certain people you also got the message that it was best also not to talk about what they were in for. You didn't want to know. People did discuss the concept of justice quite a lot, though. I received quite a lot of sympathy for my punishment outweighing my crime. And even the screws found some of it difficult to understand, like how a bloke who stabbed another bloke he found in bed with his wife could get the same sentence as a paedophile. I just found myself agreeing with everyone.

In all, I had three cellmates during my time. First, and for the longest period, I was in with a guy called Rob, who taught me everything he knew about institutions – and he had some knowledge to impart. He had been in detention centres, borstals, the lot, for thieving. He was a good little boxer, Rob. From Colchester. Crazy eyes. He showed me how to stick pictures up on the wall of the cell with toothpaste – just family ones, mind, it was too tacky to have naked women up, which was not very good for you, either – and that it also worked to clear up spots. He stuck batteries on the radiator overnight to get an extra bit of life out of them for the radio. Kicking them round the cell also worked for a little while as well. After Rob was Kiwi, a New Zealander naturally, and then a Brummie whose name escapes me, both in for drugs.

Rob liked to smoke dope in the cell at night, which made him giggle. The screws turned a blind eye to 'poo', as it was called, which was not too difficult to get hold of. I didn't want anything to do with it, one reason being that I was paranoid about anything illegal being found among my possessions in my cell. It was searched once, as it could be at any time, but they found nothing. In fact, I was always worried about getting caught doing anything wrong. I remember being terrified once when I was quietly using a washing machine and someone crept up behind me pretending to be a screw and said, 'What you doing then?' I didn't want to go 'down the block' to the punishment cell.

That was another reason why I didn't make any attempt to get hold of alcohol, which I didn't see much of and didn't feel I needed at this time anyway. I was offered a nip at Christmas by one of the cons, like me a low-risk category D prisoner, who had a bottle of scotch as a result of one of his trips out of prison in his job as an assistant to the screws on court duty. I turned it down. To me, there was no point in having such a small amount. I would rather have nothing.

I got into the prison routine pretty quickly. I had to. The day would begin at 7.15 am when a screw banged on your door, which he did one by one along the landing, before unlocking it. Then you would queue to take the bucket to the toilets to slop out, which was the worst job of the day. If you just had to do more than urinate during the night – and it happened to me only once, for which I could only apologise to my cellmate – you would empty the bucket out of the barred window on to the courtyard.

Slopping out done, at 7.45 am it was breakfast, which you picked up downstairs and took back to your cell: cereal, toast and, yes, porridge. The food was not bad. I tried to eat as much as I could in there because I was going to stay fit and needed plenty of energy for the work I would do.

After breakfast there would be an exercise period which was really just walking round the courtyard, talking to people. It was here that you encountered the whole range of characters. Two giant, hard lads approached me to say they were big Arsenal fans and would take care of me if ever there was any trouble. In fact, there were quite a few Arsenal punters and another, a larger-than-life character called Pat, used to bring round the refreshment trolley, so I was all right there. One guy told me he had been in prison with George Best, another said that he knew Ian Wright, still with Crystal Palace at that time, from playing football in South London. Did I know him? Plenty said that they had played against me in junior football in Essex. We had quite a few mutual acquaintances.

No disgruntled Tottenham supporter ever tried to hit me – though the barber was a Spurs fan I didn't trust, which was why I came out with quite long hair – and mostly I was treated well, probably because I kept my head down and spoke when I was spoken to. I was willing to listen to them, rather than shout off my mouth about my life, unless they asked me about it. In fact, I never witnessed any violence in there, although one day I saw a pool of blood in the showers. I didn't ask any questions. That was a bit like Arsenal, when you sometimes saw blood from an injury around the place. The difference here was the gossip about people getting a hiding. I also heard of two suicides and one attempted, where the bloke tried to hang himself but was saved by his cellmate who pressed the alarm button and got him down. The cellmate was given a couple of days off his sentence for that.

One morning in the exercise yard, I got a tap on the shoulder and was told that this Arsenal fan wanted to walk with me. He seemed a really good bloke. We talked about football and he asked if I would send him some souvenirs when I got back to Highbury. He said there was no rush and I soon found out why. Someone told me that he was serving a 'life times four' sentence for throwing petrol over two Pakistanis and setting light to them.

After exercise, it was back to the cell, where I would do some sit-ups and press-ups, before being allowed a communal leisure hour at about 10.30. Usually you could watch a video, something like *Only Fools and Horses*, or play cards or Monopoly. Lunch was at 11.30 am, a meat-and-two-veg school dinner, which you would also get, with a slight variation, at 3.30 pm, before being banged up for the night at 4.30 pm. In between the two meals you would be allowed an exercise period of an hour in the gym, doing weights or playing basketball, that kind of thing. They would unlock your door at 7 pm for a cup of tea and a biscuit, and for you to get a glass of water for the night, but after that it was a 12-hour stretch of confinement, except on Wednesday and Friday evenings when those who wanted could go to the gym to work out. I would curse when the lights went out in the cell at 11 pm if I was in the middle of reading. It took a long time for the place to settle down at night. Doors would bang open and shut. There would be coughing and shouts of 'Shut up.' You could also hear the crying of the YPs – young prisoners of 19 and under.

Most nights, a little mouse would come into our cell and Rob and I named him Mickey. He became our friend. Sometimes we would catch him and put him in a matchbox so that we could release him in the showers the next day to wind blokes up for a laugh. It was just like being back at Arsenal. You needed that bit of fun to lighten up your situation. We would always catch Mickey again and put him back in our cell so he could scuttle back off to wherever he lived.

You were not allowed to receive any extra food parcels from the outside, nor make any phone calls and there was no television, so in the evenings I would read a lot; something like Jeffrey Archer or Harold Robbins, until the sexy passages in that were doing me no good. I also liked to draw and was pretty good when given the time. Cartoon characters were my speciality. I also had an amazing amount of mail to read and reply to. It was amazing in its breadth of opinion and feeling. Of course, there was a lot of hate mail from fans of opposing teams who delighted in my fall. One postcard had a donkey on the front and said on the back: 'Having a lovely time in Spain, hope you're having a hard time in Chelmsford nick.' They were rarely signed and most of them I threw away.

I even received a scrawled, barely legible or comprehensible letter from Reggie Kray at Gartree Prison in Leicestershire where he was then in his 23rd year of maximum security. He wished me well, wrote that 'whenever you get fed up, do something positive like a few exercises,' and told me about a mate of his who went to every Arsenal home game. It was a bit chilling but when word went round among my fellow inmates about it, I received instant respect. Reggie was obviously some kind of a hero.

Virtually everyone at Arsenal wrote to me. George's letter, written on hotel notepaper the night before a game at Leeds, expressed the certainty that I would endure the ordeal without whingeing and would be back to lead the team to more trophies. 'Dear Big Nose,' Perry Groves began in the jokey style that most of my team-mates adopted and wondered if he could have my four match tickets and car park pass. David O'Leary asked if I had sorted out the Singapore match fee for the boys yet. They were probably embarrassed and did not really know what to say to me. One letter from a team-mate surprised me, though, by pointing out forcefully that I had done wrong.

From outside, Bobby Robson and England colleagues, like Bryan Robson, Peter Reid and Tony Cottee – the man who coined my nickname of 'Rodders' after the Nicholas Lyndhust character in *Only Fools and Horses*, whom I am supposed to resemble – commiserated with me. Alex Ferguson wrote: 'What I do know about footballers is that you can't leave your character in the dressing room. It goes out on the field with you and whatever you see of a footballer on the playing field is a true representation of his life. That being the case, Tony, you have no problems.'

Letters also came from the FA, where Graham Taylor said I had 'everything to play for,' while Charles Hughes wrote that 'adversity introduces a man to himself ... the great thing in life is not to ensure that we never fall but to ensure that we never fail to get up when we have fallen.' Many people wanted to come and visit me, but we were only allowed an hour on Thursdays or Sundays, which you had to apply for, and that was taken up by either Mum and Dad or Jane. I looked forward to them coming to break up the week, hearing all the family news, and we all put on a brave face for the occasion. It wasn't too bad; it wasn't like I was serving 15 years or anything. Pat would come over to our table in the big communal room with his refreshment trolley and tell Mum and Dad he was looking after me.

The two letters that surprised me most came from Paul Davis, stand-in as captain at Arsenal while I was away, and Glenn Hoddle, then an England team-mate. Paul's was extremely understanding. He had served a long suspension from football for uncharacteristically landing a punch on Southampton's Glenn Cockerill and wrote of his belief that adversity would make me a stronger, better person. It was too deep for me really at that time, like Charles Hughes's sentiments, but thought-provoking anyway. Glenn was not long into his own spiritual awakening and wrote powerfully about the demons in my soul and the drink poisoning my spirit. It seemed to me at that time the last thing I needed to hear. I was already paying my dues and taking my punishment, without having to hear all that sort of stuff. I just wanted to get this experience over with and get on with my life as it had been.

As soon as I arrived at Chelmsford, I had applied for a job as I had been told to do and a couple of weeks after Christmas I was duly assigned the plum position of gym orderly. The prison authorities were good like that and if you were, say, a plumber, they would do their best to help you keep your hand in with appropriate work ready for the outside world. The first bonus was that I got my food before everyone else at 7.30 am so that I could be down the gym ready for eight to get it in order for the various exercise hours. Often the sex offenders – the 'nonces' – would be on the early shift. I can't say being around them bothered me too much, as it did some blokes in there. Between sessions, I was allowed to use the place myself and would kick a ball about and go on a circuit of weight training.

The screws were good to me, especially a guy called Terry Cooper who had once played left-back for Lincoln City, and another called Peter, and they helped get me fit. They also let Gary Lewin from Arsenal come in occasionally to check on my fitness. One of the warders knew David Webb, then the manager of Southend, and he brought his squad into the nick one day for a training session arranged mainly for me but which a few selected prisoners were allowed to join in with. I had lots of excuses – muddy pitch, borrowed boots – but the fact is that I was less fit than them and I remember Brett Angell, the Southend centre-forward, gave me a hard time that day.

In the afternoon, I would get another couple of hours of physical exercise, playing tennis up against a wall or joining in with basketball. They also had this game where a medicine ball was thrown on to a mat among 50-odd blokes and the winner was the last one left not having been pushed off the mat and still clutching the ball. It was a real free-for-all. One day I clung on and clung on and finally won. It gave me a huge sense of achievement. There were some big blokes in there.

Although I was not allowed to join in with the prison football team because Arsenal would naturally have worried about me getting injured, I did help them by talking to them and giving them a few tips, especially before their big game against Essex Police, which was something of a grudge match, as might be imagined, and lived up to its billing. This, along with making tea for the screws at the gym, was my way of paying them back for the training I got. There were other paybacks for me, though. The goalkeeper worked in the kitchens and made sure I got extra food, while another player worked in the stores and got me some dungarees.

The job in the gym paid £3.09 – up from the 50p you got then as the basic pocket money – which allowed me to buy Mars bars and batteries for the radio. I was almost enjoying it. One day the prison governor told me that I had the option of being moved to the much easier regime of Ford Open Prison but I declined the offer. He reminded me that I had written to Jane saying that Chelmsford was 'a shithole' – a letter he had seen because all of them were vetted – so why did I want to stay? In fact, I was comfortable with the routine I was in. I was getting fit for Arsenal and I felt secure with the environment and did not want more change. Time was flying. The discipline was good for me. When the door slammed at night, I didn't feel claustrophobic but safe.

Not that I wanted to stay a minute longer than was necessary. At the beginning of February, I received a letter saying that with good behaviour, my sentence had been commuted and I was to be released on Friday the 15th, at 7.30 am. To my relief, four months had become 58 days.

When the day dawned, the press were in the know and were waiting at the front gates, where my Dad was sat in his car. He was just a decoy, though. At the back of the prison was my brother-in-law Ian and I was taken through the screws' mess to his car. I dived in and we made an unhindered getaway to Hornchurch where Jane was waiting for me in the house we had just bought. The ordeal was over.

There was no thought of getting drunk immediately, even though I knew I would sooner rather than later. I would come to see that prison did have an effect on me, but it had really done nothing to make me look at my drinking and had been no deterrent except when it came to driving when drunk. At that time, it didn't go through my head that I might stop. But then, my first drug still just held sway and I had agreed with Arsenal that I should get back in the saddle and play again as soon as possible.

The next day the first team were away at Leeds in an FA Cup replay and the reserves had a home match against Reading, switched to Highbury from Elm Park because of snow on their pitch. I was really looking forward to it. When I took the field I was amazed at the crowd of about 7,000 and the reception I got. I was back among my people and it felt good. We only drew 2–2 but I ran around like a dervish with energy, if not match fitness, to burn. At the end I yelled to the skies and clenched my fists. It was partly theatrical and partly release. The old 'Big Roar' as I used to call it, was back. 'CRY FREEDOM' was the headline in all the papers the next day. With the first team having won at Leeds, there was champagne in the dressing room and later Steve Rowley took me and Jane out to a restaurant – in Chelmsford.

I was warmly welcomed back to London Colney and training on the Monday. It was funny. In prison, all the cons had wanted to know what David Seaman and Anders Limpar were like. Now David Seaman and Anders Limpar wanted to know what Fingers Phil and Benny the Hat were like. I endured the jokes and gave back some stick. Paul Merson kindly told me that my conviction had been a dampener on the Christmas 'do' but they had had a good drink-up anyway. I asked why they had lost a game – 2–1 at Chelsea, which was to be the only league defeat of the season – while I was away.

Arsenal had been very supportive of me while I was in prison – financially, that is. They had fined me two weeks' wages but after that continued to pay me – I never told them about the £3.09 in case they stopped – despite plenty of public criticism. Now it was payback time, I felt. Besides, I wanted to be back in this superb team that was putting together a dream season. After another couple of reserve games, I came back to the first team for a tricky, muddy FA Cup fifth round tie at Shrewsbury, where we scrambled a 1–0 win.

I slotted straight back in without too much trouble, but it took me some time to contribute as much as I had before. My weight had dropped to 13 stones and I didn't feel I was 100 per cent on top of my game for a while. But I knew that other players coming back into the team had often given me a lift, so I think my return also did with them. And the way things were at Arsenal, if someone was not quite doing it, the rest of the boys would help them out. So it was for me.

My first League game back sent us to Anfield for another epic with Liverpool. We were second in the table, three points behind them and it became a turning point in the title race as we won 1–0 with Paul Merson's goal, to complete a double over them. I was not to miss another League game that season and, just a month after leaving prison, even won a recall to Graham Taylor's England side. Well, it was the return 'league' match with the Republic of Ireland, wasn't it? Call for the stopper. In the event I wasn't fully ready, my old friend Niall Quinn eluded me to score the Irish goal in another 1–1 draw and I was replaced at half-time.

A 2–1 win over Cambridge United put us into the FA Cup semi-finals, where we were drawn against Tottenham. Such was the interest in the game and the demand for tickets that the FA agreed it should be played at Wembley. It was just an astonishing day. I firmly believe that this Arsenal side should have done the Double, and was certainly good enough to do so, but that day Spurs, I have to admit, were on fire. Gazza's amazing free-kick of power and precision that beat David Seaman set them on their way and Gary Lineker also gave me a hard time as they won 3–1.

No one was going to deny us the title, though, and we won it at a canter – not that George would ever have allowed one of his sides in those days to canter. On Saturday 4 May, Liverpool lost 4–2 at Chelsea and we strengthened our position with a 0–0 draw at Sunderland. Then on the Bank Holiday Monday, Nottingham Forest beat Liverpool in the afternoon and we were able to take the field at home to Manchester United in the evening as Champions. We went on to play some inspired football to win 3–1 and avenge an out-of-character 6–2 defeat by United in the League Cup earlier in the season.

Even in our final match, at home to Coventry, George Graham would not let us ease up. 'Can't we just relax a bit?' we asked. 'Go out and look like Champions,' he said. 'Go out and be the Arsenal.' We beat them 6–1 and finished seven points clear – and that with the two-point deduction following the incident at Old Trafford earlier in the season.

There was another open-topped bus ride through Islington, with the tinnies being thrown by fans as accompaniment again, and another trip to Singapore, before which I avoided any barbecues in Rayleigh, and where we lifted that same trophy of the previous year by beating Liverpool 4–3 on penalties.

The feeling of winning the title again during that 1990/91 season could not quite compare with that first time and all its drama, but this was probably the best

Arsenal team I had played for, certainly defensively, as our record – the best for a title-winning team this century – illustrated. The back five of Seaman, Dixon, Adams, Bould and Winterburn that was to become so familiar was in harness for the first time and was practically unbreachable at times. I was the only one to miss a game – eight, when I was in jail. I had not realised David was as good as he was when he was with Queens Park Rangers, probably because I had managed to score twice against him the previous year. And Steve Bould was simply outstanding. That season I won the Supporters' Club Player of the Year award and I think it may have had something to do with sentiment and me coming out of prison, but in footballing terms, as a defender Steve was next to unpassable. Also, going forward, we hit a peak and were steamrollering teams. Anders was doing things that Brian Marwood used to do and Alan Smith won another Golden Boot award.

That summer, I went on holiday with Jane to Antigua and staying at the same complex was John Parrott, who had just won the World Snooker Championship. It was important to go back and win it again, I said to him, because people just label you lucky if you 'only' do it once. No longer were we 'Lucky Arsenal', the billing that had attached itself to us after the 1989 win at Anfield. Two titles in three years has nothing to do with luck.

The next season would see us back in the European Cup with the end of the ban on English clubs after the Heysel disaster and that would occupy a lot of our attention. The FA Cup was also becoming a crusade of mine as the last domestic honour to be won. When I was 17, I remember Don Howe talking about the average career span of a professional being eight years, which meant only eight attempts to win the Cup. Here I was, having had seven tries already. And though I was still only 24, going to prison had shown me that anything could happen. I had done time and now I wanted to make up for losing it.

FIVE

Cup Kings

Football, like the other addiction from which I was suffering but which I was still a long way from coming to accept had me in its grip, is a disease of wanting more and more, even if it is usually a healthier and more wholesome version. I had two Championship and one League Cup winners' medals but like a row of optics or beer pumps in a pub that seem to beckon someone like me, other prizes appealed and I was thirsty for them.

For sure, you are always trying to win every competition you enter, but instinctively some take priority and for me, with Arsenal being the first English representatives allowed back in the European Cup after the Heysel ban, that competition assumed major importance. We were an exceptional side at that time, I believe, but my expectation that we would do well, it turned out, was based on similar naive optimism and lack of awareness that told me a year earlier I would not be going to jail. As Manchester United have discovered, it is just so difficult trying to retain a title and win the Champions' League. And at that time, with English clubs having been out of Europe for six years, we had no experience, no real knowledge of the qualities required for the job.

I think the Highbury crowd expected us just to keep

pouring forward and rolling over foreign opposition the way we did with domestic opponents. Perhaps we did ourselves in those days. The previous season Manchester United had won the Cup Winners' Cup in their first season back in European competition following the ban, so there were a lot of people thinking that English clubs were as good as we had ever been in the days when we dominated Europe.

George received a lot of criticism early on for not strengthening the squad but the one that won the title should have been strong enough, though we would miss Steve Bould through injury for much of the season. Ten games into the campaign George did make one of the most important signings in the history of Arsenal Football Club, bringing Ian Wright to Highbury from Crystal Palace for £2.5 million, but Ian would be ineligible to play in Europe that season of 1991/92.

We began well, defeating Austria Vienna 6–1 at home with Alan Smith scoring four and although we lost the return 1–0, we were comfortably through to a second round tie, the prelude in those days to the league competition, with Benfica. Again we secured a good first-leg result, a 1–1 draw in Lisbon, but the return leg was far from the formality many people expected.

Against the Austrians, we had squeezed and battled in the familiar style that had won us the League title and they were not good enough to deal with it. The Portuguese were stronger altogether and although we took the lead through Colin Pates, they came back to hit us on the break and force extra-time. As we went looking for the winner, I missed one of the biggest sitters of my career, scuffing a shot from about two yards out. Then they broke out again to grab another. Now behind, we were chasing and we left ourselves open.

It became helter-skelter football and George hated that. Finally, one of their forwards, Isaias, nutmegged me and suddenly it was 3–1 and we were out of the competition.

There was a lot of talk about the continentals having better technique than us but we certainly had the chances to win, whether they were more gifted or not. It might have had something to do with tiredness, as we were playing twice a week, what with League Cup ties as well at that time of the season. George always used to say that teams were being punished for being successful and no help was being given to English clubs in Europe. It has changed for the better now with more accommodating kick-off times on weekends before European games and exemptions from the early rounds of the Coca-Cola Cup.

Mostly with that Benfica game, though, you just look back and realise it was one of those matches you are not supposed to win – and it was the one we most wanted to. I had put my heart and soul into the competition and I confess to feeling after our European Cup exit that the season was over, even this early in autumn. After a bad start to the league season, which had seen us draw at home to Queens Park Rangers then lose at Everton and Aston Villa, I sensed deep down we were not going to win the League, even though we had four wins in September thanks to the impetus of Ian Wright's arrival that saw him score on his debut in a League Cup tie at Leicester, then grab a hat-trick against Southampton. I missed seven games over November and December with a hernia that needed an operation and we slipped to as low as 10th before we got back to the basics of closing down and working hard to put together a 17-game unbeaten record that took us to fourth.

During that spell we put on some amazing shows, like a 7–1 win over Sheffield Wednesday when it was 1–1 with about 20 minutes to go and they had a chance to go 2–1 up before Kevin Campbell came on and seized the game. We also beat Liverpool 4–0. Ian Wright performed some outrageous scoring feats, scoring all four in a 4–2 win at home to Everton but he also went through a six-game goal drought.

I had once watched Ian in training for England, staying on to see the forwards practise their shooting after the defenders had finished their work, and been astonished by his finishing; bang, bang, in from all angles. During this barren period he was trying to chip or slide the ball home. I told him that he had been clinical and decisive before, and just to remember 'bang, bang', not to get too clever. It was something that I would remind him of whenever he later went through dry spells and usually it worked.

By that stage of the season we had gone out of the FA Cup in the third round at Wrexham. With the Welsh club having been 92nd in the Football League the previous year and us having been champions, the 2–1 defeat was a major shock in the game. With us being Arsenal, it was a major shock to us. Pride was stung. You just don't do that kind of thing with the Arsenal. And I believe it was the match that turned us into the side we were to become over the remaining seasons of George's management.

It all looked comfortable enough when Alan Smith put us ahead just before half-time. We then absolutely battered Wrexham and should have been well clear when Mickey Thomas, the old Manchester United and Wales player, drilled home a free-kick from out of nowhere eight minutes from time. Soon after, they somehow squeezed another past Dave Seaman and we were out. Even then we shouldn't have been, with Jimmy Carter having the ball in the net in the last minute but the goal being mysteriously disallowed.

An hour later we were sitting on the coach watching all those Wrexham fans banging on the windows and gloating after what had been their Cup Final. Sitting at the back, I told the boys that I would rather go out here and now than in the semi-final against Tottenham as we had done last year. I told them to remember this feeling because we didn't want it back. I told them that this is such a stupid game, such a funny competition, that we would probably win it the next season.

From a personal viewpoint, things looked up the next month when my son Oliver was born in Harold Wood hospital at eight minutes past four on a Friday afternoon, 27 February, a half-brother for Clare, my step-daughter from Jane's previous relationship. It was good timing. We had no match on the Saturday and I could go and indulge my excitement by wetting the baby's head properly. I was now serving my two-year ban from driving and getting taxis everywhere. After witnessing the birth and checking Jane was okay, I was quickly over to Hornchurch at Palm's, a bar on the A127, and drunk by 8 pm. It actually became a standing joke between Ray Parlour and me that the birth of a baby was a good excuse for a bender and we ought to go to the hospital more often and check out the new-born so we could then go out for a good drink to celebrate.

The football that year ended in anti-climax, though, when I was again omitted from an England squad for a major championship, the 1992 European Championship Finals in Sweden, with Graham Taylor preferring a whole host of centre-backs to me. Then, a few days before the tournament, Mark Wright pulled out with an injury and Graham phoned me to say he was trying to get dispensation to call me up as a late replacement. It never happened and so I went on holiday with Jane. Perhaps the rejection was, again, good for me as Arsenal were to come back strongly after the season 'off'. I was certainly keen. Jane and I were married on Saturday 11 July and I was at pre-season training the following Monday.

It was clear from very early on after his arrival that the profile of the team was changing with Ian Wright becoming more and more of a focal point. He had had a terrific year in his debut season, scoring 24 league goals in only 30 games. Coming to such a big club from Palace, well it was like his birthday, wasn't it? All goalscorers are, I think, given their first season free at a big club. Robbie Fowler scored 30 in his debut year, then came Michael Owen. It is a question, once defenders get to know your strengths and weaknesses, of doing it all over again. The good ones do, as Fowler did, and Wrighty would do too. With the talent and enthusiasm he had, he was always going to get us goals. The question was, how might the balance of the team develop?

In our opening match of the newly formed Premiership in 1992/93, against Norwich – my 250th league game – it looked none too promising as we led 2–0 at half-time, then somehow lost 4–2. By November we had regrouped well enough to win six games in a row and go to the top of the table but it was a consistency we could not sustain. It was all so amazingly topsy-turvy and unlike Arsenal. Three wins were followed by four games without one. By the beginning of January, with me serving a two-match suspension over Christmas, we had slipped to ninth.

Transition in the team was subtle, the Wright factor central. He was a quite outstanding goalscorer and his hunger for goals needed to be fed. Often we would give him the ball over the top or whipped into the penalty box and he would duly convert. I'm sure half of his goals were created by the unselfish Alan Smith, whose personal goalscoring output dropped in the way it had at Leicester where he helped Gary Lineker make his name.

It is why, I believe, we developed into a good Cup side. We had an outstanding goalkeeper, a back four which was absorbent and resilient, could keep the game tight, and a striker who could always grab you a winning goal. It was hard to reproduce every week because of the demands on a defence that is likely to crack under the pressure sometime, but a powerful formula for a one-off match. And when you are working yourself up to a pitch for a Cup occasion, it drains you of resources for League encounters.

We were short of human resources, too. George always maintained that it was difficult for him to attract the top players, especially the gifted midfield players, to the club, because of the wages structure which meant they could get better money elsewhere. That summer of 1992, he had managed to buy only John Jensen from Brondby of Denmark for £1.2 million, although in the February of this season he would re-sign Martin Keown from Everton for £2 million. In addition, the rampant '91 team was gradually being broken up; David Rocastle's serious knee injury had sapped his effectiveness and he was sold to Leeds, and Michael Thomas had departed for a better contract at Liverpool the previous Christmas. If we had tried to play like that team, we would probably have been hammered every week and been relegated. I think George deliberately sacrificed the flamboyant team to make the most of limited talent. The aim now seemed to be to do well in the Cups, keeping it tight and pinching goals.

In the League Cup, now sponsored by Coca-Cola, we first drew Millwall and managed only a 1–1 draw in the home leg. It was the same score at The Den, Kevin Campbell equalising after Lee Dixon's own goal and when it went to penalties, I just knew David Seaman would do his stuff. I think he saved four of theirs and we were through. When you have nights like that, you begin to sense that you just might be on to something. In the next round at Derby, Dave was again exceptional and pulled off a string of fine saves to enable us to take a 1–1 draw back to Highbury, where we completed the job 2–1.

The following round took us to Scarborough on a foggy night. I couldn't see from one end of the pitch to the other, but David O'Leary, who was playing in an unfamiliar central midfield role, kept on at the referee Keith Hackett to go ahead with the game, because we didn't want to have to come back. It had already been postponed once, though we had got the call early enough and had not travelled. I think the ref just gave in to David in the end. Nigel Winterburn popped in a goal and there was no way they were going to come back and score against us after that. That meant a quarter-final at home to Nottingham Forest, a match we won comfortably 2–0 with two Ian Wright goals which gave us a semi-final against his old club, Crystal Palace.

We were just too strong for them and won the first leg 3–1 at Selhurst Park, where I was furious about giving away a penalty and chased the referee to give him some loud abuse, such was the way I was at that time. A 2–0 win at Highbury completed a comfortable job. The goal that stuck most in my memory was Andy Linighan's, though it was not as important as the one he would score a couple of months later. He was enjoying a run in the team due to Steve Bould's injury and having an outstanding season. I maintained that I was creating them for him, as the decoy man at set pieces. Everyone would be looking to mark me, certainly the best header of the ball in the opposition, which was giving Andy the opportunity to get among the goals.

We were also going well in the FA Cup at the same time, and I had a good feeling when we were drawn at Yeovil Town in the third round. As I reminded the boys, the Double side of 1971 had also begun there. Then, they scored three goals; but this time so did we thanks to Ian Wright's hat trick in the 3–1 win. There followed an amazing tie against Leeds, who had been League Champions the season before.

At Highbury we were 2–0 down and I remember saying in the dressing room at half-time that we should just go for it and not worry about losing by five or six goals. Ray Parlour quickly got us a great goal back and eventually we equalised. The replay was bizarre. The script said that it should be a dour, tough game of few chances, but it just defied all our efforts to keep it tight. They scored, we scored and on it went in one of the most exciting games I have ever played in. When the final whistle went – and how the ref had enough breath left to blow, I don't know – we had won 3–2, Wrighty scoring twice. If I was getting a good feeling about the Coca-Cola Cup, the vibes from this, on top of Yeovil, were outstanding.

In the next round, we had another routine 2–0 home win over Nottingham Forest, who must have been sick of us that season, to earn a quarter-final with Ipswich Town. Even if our League form was patchy, now we were really firing in the knock-out competitions. As reward, George gave us a couple of days off and on behalf of the boys as captain and social secretary, I arranged a jolly outing to Towcester races. It was a pleasant enough day out, mostly because I could drink all day. That was never going to be enough for me, though.

When the coach got back to London, a few of us decided to go on to a pub or two. Still not having had enough after that, I made for Ra Ra's in Islington, the club where I had met Jane, for a few more. I was very drunk and in blackout. What I remember after going in there is in the form of little cameo images: shouting my mouth off, the reception of a hospital accident and emergency department, nurses talking at me and a taxi home. The full story had to be told to me later.

It seems that at the entrance to the club, I got talking to a friend of Jane's, who turned away to speak to someone else and by the time she had turned back, I was on my way down these 30-odd concrete steps which led to the club itself. I fell in a crumpled heap at the bottom, blood gushing from my forehead. In fact, there was blood everywhere. The next thing, apparently, was that someone who knew me in the club persuaded a friend of his, who was a cabbie, to take me to St Bartholomew's Hospital a couple of miles away. I remember hearing one of the blokes who took me there saying to the other, 'Don't tell them it's Tony Adams,' and they tried to give the nurses booking me in a false name so that it wouldn't get out in the papers.

I didn't recognise him at the time, not surprisingly given the state I was in, but the doctor who stitched me up was the same one who usually did the job at Arsenal on match days. He was going to give me an anaesthetic, he told me, but was worried by a possible reaction to the quantity of alcohol I had consumed and decided against it. I probably didn't need one anyway. I don't remember feeling a thing. The wound, which was by the bone of my brow, was so deep that it needed fourteen stitches on the inside and fifteen outside. Soon I was ready to go home but the nurses refused to let me, saying that I could not leave until they were certain I was all right. By now it was about 6 am. 'Don't worry about that,' I said, 'I'm fine,' and I got the two blokes who had brought me to Bart's to take me home.

Not long later I was at training explaining to George how it had all happened and justifying it by saying that it was in my own time, on my day off. I was telling him that I would be fine to train. It was like that scene from *Monty Python and the Holy Grail*, where the knight still wants to fight on though his arms and legs have been chopped off. 'You can't even head a ball,' George said to me. 'It's only a flesh wound,' I'm sure I said.

He was annoyed with me, I could tell, but would probably say he dealt with the situation coolly. It was just the fear inside me, plus the guilt and shame that the booze had created, that made him seem fearsome. My solution was to brazen it out and when I assured him that I would be fit for the FA Cup quarter-final at Ipswich in ten days' time, he came round. I think he told the press I had fallen down some stairs at home. Now I retell it, it sounds like I was in control of the situation. But really, I felt under some pressure.

It was why, come the Ipswich tie and after having missed two League games before then, that I was raring to go, desperate to impress in fact, probably fuelled by the remorse that drives an active alcoholic on but without knowing it at the time. Then, everything was just instinctive. When I opened the scoring by heading home Paul Merson's free-kick, the ball smacking off the huge plaster that was covering the wound, all the bottled-up emotion in me was released and pictures in the next day's papers captured it in the contorted face that accompanied my celebration. 'What was that all about? What kind of celebration is that?' the lads would later ask me. 'You looked like an idiot.' I didn't care.

I was exceptional on the day, no getting away from it, as we beat Ipswich 4–2 to reach the semi-finals. George told the papers that I was his Captain Marvel and that I had amazing guts to come back from what had happened to me, just having had twenty-nine stitches in my head. I think he was just happy we had won again. It also, now I consider it, enabled me to justify my behaviour and carry on the way I was. If I was that good on the pitch, I couldn't be that bad off it, could I?

And this FA Cup was looking more and more ours with each passing round, a thought that was powering me on. Again we were drawn against Tottenham in a semi-final and again the FA agreed to take it to Wembley. I saw it as the perfect opportunity for revenge for 1991. And I was sure we would get it. Those two years ago they had Gascoigne and Lineker, individuals capable of winning big games if not carrying a team through a whole league season consistently. Now they were gone and we were the ones capable of nicking the big games.

I don't think either side was particularly pretty at that time, though we were very strong defensively, and we got to the 79th minute with the game goalless. I remember our winning goal vividly. I scored it. This one, unlike many of the others, I couldn't forget. It was just too big a day and game.

We had a free-kick which Paul Merson stepped up to take, and as I ran forward I made eye contact with him to pick me out. He was an intelligent player, Paul, and knew exactly where to put the ball. What's more, he could deliver it there, too. Andy Linighan was with me at the far post. 'Take them all inside,' I told him as Paul shaped to take the kick and when Andy made a run, the Spurs defence covered it, going with him. I was left alone at the far post and Paul's kick allowed me to meet the ball perfectly and head home. Later, Teddy Sheringham told me that he got stuck in the Spurs wall when he should have been at the far post and he ended up arguing with Neil Ruddock, whom Ted thought should have then stayed with me.

So we were through to the Final and our supporters had something to crow about after having to endure the defeat of '91. Honour was satisfied in North London. We would now be playing Sheffield Wednesday, by coincidence our opponents also in the Coca-Cola Final.

Whatever our deficiencies at that time, one of our characteristics was that if we fell a goal behind, we never felt that the game was over but that if we took the lead, it almost certainly was. John Harkes put Wednesday ahead in the Coca-Cola but we always felt we could come back. We were certainly not overawed by Wednesday because we felt they had something of a makeshift team out. It turned out to be Paul Merson's game, though that would be over-shadowed by a bizarre incident that I was involved in.

First, Paul equalised with a great shot from outside the penalty area, then got to the byline on the left and crossed for Steve Morrow to score the winner with his first goal at first-team level. Later Merse, who was fighting his own battle with drink at the time, would be pictured on television miming throwing pints of beer down his neck in a gesture of celebration that would one day embarrass him. He would come to deal with it and get over it, though. As active alcoholics we did what we did, we were what we were. It was more what happened to Steve at the end of the game that was of immediate concern to me.

You do some silly things in those spontaneous moments in football when the adrenalin is flowing. When the final whistle went, Steve ran towards me, elated, with his arms outstretched and I grabbed him to congratulate him. Then I lifted him and before I knew it, he had tumbled over my shoulder, down my back and on to the Wembley turf. As I turned I saw him stretch out his arm to break his fall but it buckled on him. I knew immediately something was wrong and as Gary Lewin was tending to him, I could see by the angle of his arm that there was some serious damage. In fact, the funny bone of his arm was broken and I could see that his shoulder was dislocated. 'That's not supposed to be like that, is it?' I said to Gary.

Momentarily I forgot about it as I had to go up the 39 steps to collect the trophy, but for me what happened to Steve put a dampener on everything. The team went to a restaurant for a celebratory meal but I felt too sickened to go. I just went home. I didn't feel it would be right to be out enjoying myself. I was hurting for Steve. I was still upset for him later that week when I went to visit him in hospital with some of the boys, because quite apart from the physical pain I had caused, I felt I had spoiled his moment. I took him some consolation champagne. 'I hope I'm not remembered for the injury more than the goal,' he said to me but, trying to make light of things, I said he probably would be. 'But don't worry,' I added. 'Plenty of Wembley goalscorers are forgotten, but people will never be able to forget you. We've all got our crosses to bear. I'll probably be remembered as a donkey.'

Naturally Steve missed the FA Cup Final a month later, which was a better day for me though it still had its concerns. Before the Coca-Cola Final, we had stayed for the first time at Sopwell House, the hotel near St Albans that we were to use as our base when the dressing rooms burnt down at London Colney a few years later, and we decided we had to stay there again the night before. As the coach pulled out to drive the twenty miles to Wembley, I was worried about whether Jane would be at the match because we had begun to have a few problems between us at this time and she had not turned up at the hotel with the other wives and girlfriends. As I led out the team fifteen minutes before kick-off, what should have been the realisation of the ambition that Don Howe had fired in me with his talk of the FA Cup almost ten years ago now, was set aside as I searched the stands for Jane in my pre-occupation with whether she was at the game or not. In the end, she was.

It was not a great game, David Hirst equalising after Ian Wright had given us the lead. I don't think the media were happy that the two Cup Finals were being contested by the same two teams. And we were fast getting this tag of 'boring Arsenal' so it was all just grist to the mill, never mind Sheffield Wednesday's part in that. We didn't care because we had been undervalued, in my opinion, for the quality of our football in 1991 and we were still in the process of accumulating trophies.

Before we could do that, we had to play David O'Leary's testimonial, when we put out an almost full-strength team and 22,117 turned up to watch a 4–4 draw with Manchester United. Then came my fifth visit to Wembley in seven weeks. After the Spurs semi and the Coca-Cola Cup Final, I had also played for England in a 2–2 draw against Holland when we surrendered a 2–0 lead and damaged our World Cup qualifying chances.

Anyway, in the FA Cup Final replay, Wednesday again proved tough opponents but we felt we always had the psychological edge on them, having beaten them already in the Coca-Cola Cup. After Wrighty had again given us the lead, only for Chris Waddle this time to equalise to take the game into extra-time, I think everyone was getting ready for penalties when Andy Linighan pounced to head home the winner. I was delighted for him. He had stepped expertly into Steve Bould's boots and he was a genuine guy besides, an honest pro who loves his family. Whenever you went out with him after that, he would go through his party trick if you were in company. 'Yes, it's me,' he would say to people, with a face as deadpan as Tommy Cooper's. 'You've recognised me, haven't you? You've guessed.' The people would look a bit baffled and he would say: 'Yes, that's it, '93 Cup Final. I won it.'

Within weeks of the FA Cup euphoria came disillusionment with England. After a poor Euro '92, Graham Taylor had returned to me as a first-choice central defender and I had played in all the qualifying games to date for the World Cup of '94 but now, I have to say, I did not particularly relish two important matches, in Poland and Norway, within the space of a few days and my concerns were to prove well-founded.

I was as professional as I could be, getting myself together after the Cup celebrations, but there were things going on around me that warrant explanation in detail later when it comes to discussing my England career in depth. These things were beyond my control, and a national team I was involved in again returned in some disarray after a reasonable 1–1 draw in Poland but a seriously damaging 2–0 defeat in Norway. With a slight ankle injury, I was thankful I did not have to go on to the summer tour of the United States, against whom we lost, which also involved Germany and Brazil.

To be honest, I just wanted to be free for a few weeks of drinking before gearing up for a new season with Arsenal and a chance, after the Benfica debacle, to redeem ourselves in Europe, this time in the Cup Winners' Cup.

Goodbye to George

What a season 1993/94 was to prove, and what a reflection of my life at that time. Pre-season began in Johannesburg and saw me at one point smoking a joint, drunk, in some club at 6 am. The campaign ended with me lifting yet another Cup in wonderful Copenhagen, a trophy that would be George Graham's final one before scandal enveloped Arsenal the following season.

As might be guessed by now, our South Africa tour was for me just an extension of a summer's drinking, but we did fit in some football, which included a 2–0 defeat of Manchester United and we got back home to lose the Charity Shield to them as well, the third time for me, on penalties. Again we began the League season badly with a 3–0 home defeat by Coventry City but redeemed ourselves with a 1–0 win at Tottenham two days later, Ian Wright scoring. It was almost like a smash-and-grab Cup performance of the sort we were coming to specialise in and illustrated something that was now going on, possibly subconsciously, with the team. Only Eddie McGoldrick from Crystal Palace had been added in the summer, while dear old David O'Leary had moved on to Leeds for a swansong to his career and Colin Pates left for Brighton.

Andy Linighan had captured the mood well before the FA Cup Final against Sheffield Wednesday. He used to put on his Winston Churchill voice for such occasions, just like the Spurs game this early season, and say: 'They shall never ... never ever ... pass ... the Arse.' People laughed at him, but it was also how we all felt. There was a serious message and feeling behind it. We knew that we were defensively a resilient team – and that was to be George's word for the season. But we also knew that we couldn't keep getting up for Cup games in midweek, then doing it all over again on the Saturday. The effort took its toll.

So I think we accepted deep down and quite early on that we were not going to win the Premier League, especially as Manchester United were to prove outstanding champions that season. We conceded only 28 goals but you are never really going to win a title by scoring only 53, of which 23 came from Wrighty. We were becoming reliant on him for our goals, which was fine for the cups, particularly in Europe where we were not yet well known, but we had become predictable and lacked variety in League competition. We got as high as second in the October but it was downhill from then on, despite a four-month unbeaten run after Christmas when the games were mainly drawn, five in a row at one point.

That October also saw England and me in trouble. The 2–0 defeat by Holland in Rotterdam just three days after my 27th birthday was a bitter, virtually fatal, blow to our World Cup hopes and caused gnashing of teeth all over the country. When I got back on the Thursday, a day off, I felt I deserved a session and needed to drown my sorrows. Ray Parlour was a willing companion.

After visiting a few pubs in the Hornchurch area over lunchtime, we decided we needed some food and called in at the local Pizza Hut, mainly because you could still get a beer with your meal in mid-afternoon. We were mostly minding our own business but had to endure some abuse from a neighbouring table where a few Spurs fans were winding us up. I was getting the inevitable 'donkey' stuff. When we had finished eating, we got up to go and something snapped in me. I grabbed a nearby fire extinguisher and pulled out the pin, Ray got hold of the contraption and squirted the water at the people giving us the grief. Then we legged it.

I didn't think much more about it until a reporter knocked on my door the same night, to be followed by CID soon after. I could hardly give a 'no comment' to them. They told me that a complaint had been filed but after talking to me they decided just to give me a warning. It was going to be in the papers, though, and that Saturday morning, before a game against Manchester City in which I knew I had to play well and did as we recorded another goalless draw, I had to phone George Graham to give him my side of the story. Ray and I then had to see him at South Herts Golf Club. I was lucky. I got away with this one. Ray got the bollocking.

On the field, Arsenal had at that time a different priority, I think. The Coca-Cola and FA Cups did not carry the same attraction after we had won them once and we duly departed both in the fourth round. In the Coca-Cola Cup we fell at home to Aston Villa while in the FA Cup, after beating Millwall with my goal – and my contributions were becoming rare but beginning to assume more and more importance when goals from Ian Wright were not so frequent – we lost to Bruce Rioch's First Division Bolton Wanderers 3–1 in extra-time. Naturally enough, with George's desire to pit himself against foreign coaches and the players looking for new horizons, the Cup Winners' Cup provided the challenge.

I was suspended for the first game against the Danish team Odense, which suited me fine as I then started with a fresh slate when it came to yellow cards. We came through but not comfortably – winning 2–1 away and drawing 1–1 at home – and after that I was to be an ever-present. In the next round we were drawn against Standard Liege and really served notice of our intentions in the competition. The 3–0 home leg win was good enough but the 7–0 victory in Belgium was an amazing performance. We were without a suspended Ian Wright and had to look for goals from elsewhere. With other players rising to the occasion – Paul Merson buzzing everywhere and Alan Smith free to go for goal instead of acting as provider – goals came from throughout the team. I even contributed my first European goal.

My second one came in the quarter-final, against Torino. We secured a goalless draw in the Stadio delle Alpi, a trip that was most memorable for the best pasta I ever tasted. Ray Parlour kept sneaking up to the buffet for more and George caught him and had a go at him – first pizza and now pasta. Then at Highbury, I headed the only goal of the tie from Paul Davis's free-kick in the second half. It was the sort of training ground routine we had worked on so often. We knew that set plays would be important in Europe, with chances at a premium, and we became very good at them. Good delivery into the danger area, plenty of movement, timing of runs and solid headers of the ball were the ingredients.

We had been this way for some time, but on such high-profile European nights, it was becoming noticed more and more what sort of an attritional Arsenal this team was. For various reasons – among them an inability to buy the best talent, and a lack of youth team players coming through – we were not a great side. We knew it and George knew it. If we had tried to compete with talented players in open games, we would have been blown away, I am sure.

Our best hope lay, once again, in playing to our strengths: defence and a poached goal either on the break or from a set piece. After the gung-ho Benfica lesson of two seasons earlier, we had recognised the need for patience and did a lot to convey that message to the crowd, through press statements and programme notes. Gradually Highbury caught on and stayed supportive even if we weren't going hell for leather at the opposition all the time. George was also methodical and paid attention to every detail of our game and our opponents'. The system was based on a few good players and a lot of workers around them. Because he had brought us success – and that first League Cup was so important in this – we continued to respect and trust him. And obey.

George was a master at studying the opposition and finding their weakness. He was very thorough, he had them watched closely and took us through the videos of them. Sometimes he would put a marker on a key player, like he did in the Torino game with David Hillier on Benito Carbone, who later went to Sheffield Wednesday. A defensive midfield player might also slip into the back line to make sure we always had two on one attacker if they played three up front. Often we would play a 4–3–3 ourselves, to stretch the opposition, which could convert into a 4–5–1 when we didn't have the ball, so it was particularly hard work for the wide players, which was probably why George had fallen out by now with Anders Limpar, who was sold to Everton that March. The system wasn't always pretty, but it was always pretty effective.

Actually that Torino game was the only time George ever really asked me for a tactical opinion. That match seemed to tax him more than any other because I think he felt they were a better team than us, what with Andrea Silenzi and Enzo Francescoli then a force up front, though when we watched the videos of them, the boys would rubbish them as our way of dealing with it and not being intimidated. Except for Steve Bould, who always thought everyone was better than us. Anyway, as I got on the bus that night, George was sitting at the front and called me over to sit next to him.

'What do you think about putting David on Carbone?' he asked.

'Sounds good to me,' I said.

I think he just wanted some reassurance but it was strange to see him vulnerable for a moment.

Our opponents in the next round, Paris St Germain, were a better side than us, too, at that time and probably the best we faced in the competition. George Weah, who had scored their decisive goal in the previous round against Real Madrid, was near the peak of his game, as was David Ginola. They also had a good Brazilian in Valdo but what happened to him was typical of our success; we stuck Stevie Morrow on him and he kept him quiet. That said plenty about how everyone was performing to their limit. At the Parc des Princes, Ian Wright gave us the lead –nipping in ahead of me and nicking another of my goals from a Paul Davis free-kick – but then Ginola equalised for them, to make the final score 1–1.

We tore them to bits physically in the return at Highbury. We were all over the pitch closing them down and I think it shocked them. Typical was Lee Dixon not letting Ginola have any peace or time on the ball. It was the old-style Arsenal I had not seen for quite a while. Personally I felt on the top of my game, getting in some good tackles early on. I am always best playing on my front foot, being proactive rather than reactive, making things happen and dictating to my striker rather than the other way round. Steve Bould hit the post before Kevin Campbell finally got the goal that mattered. We hadn't outplayed PSG, hadn't outpassed them, but we had imposed ourselves on them. It was similar to Anfield in '89. We knew that if they were allowed to, the opposition could really play. We didn't allow them to.

And so to Copenhagen for a Final against the Italian side Parma, against whom no-one gave us a chance. Apart from Alan Hansen. On the flight out, I was reading a column he had written in one of the papers and he was talking about the way we play being geared to winning a game like this against the odds. With the Arsenal mentality, he added, he would not be surprised if we won the Cup. It stuck in my mind as being a good summary. You could understand why we were considered the underdogs, though. We were without Ian Wright, suspended again, and the injured John Jensen, so George assembled a midfield that included Steve Morrow and Ian Selley. Parma would play a then influential Tomas Brolin, Gianfranco Zola and Faustino Asprilla up front. It was some prospect, some challenge.

We trained in the Idraettspark the night before the game and Parma arrived for their session towards the end of ours. They looked immaculate, like superstars, and were very aloof. Only their coach, Sven-Goran Eriksson, a smart and pleasant man, spoke to some of us and shook hands. We thought that at one point their players were laughing at us. 'Look at them,' Bouldy said with contempt. If they had been a bit more friendly, they would have helped their cause but it was perfect for us. We left the stadium really wanting to bring them down to size.

It was also the kind of adversity I guess I have always thrived on and before the game I was really revved up, a man possessed. When we won the two Cups the season before, I had led the team in the warm-up routines, for all the seventeen ties we played – yes, seventeen. This season I had missed the Villa game that had seen us concede the Coca-Cola Cup so I had been keen to take over again after that. I was going round every player individually, really motivating them, spending more time with those who might have been more nervous, like Ian Selley and Steve Morrow. 'Come on,' I said. 'No regrets. This is it.' It was galvanising, Anfield-style stuff again.

I may have been over the top but it seemed to work. When the game got underway we were flying, squeezing Parma, not letting them settle. I don't think they realised what they were in for. With the amount of talent they had, they probably thought they were just going to turn up to collect the trophy. My only complaint was that Alan Smith scored his goal too early in the game and we had so long to defend it. Not that Parma found a way through too often. When they did, David Seaman was fantastic. He was playing with a pain-killing injection in his cracked ribs and there was one save I don't know how he made. But he did, and the song that our fans had adopted – 'One nil to the Arsenal', to the tune of the Pet Shop Boys' 'Go West' – was ringing round the stadium.

We had great support that night, with our fans seeming to be in every part of the stadium. We also had the neutrals on our side because of John Jensen. We were amazed what a hero he was in his home city. He wasn't much of a drinker, John, despite his nickname of Faxe after a Danish beer. Early on in his Arsenal career a few of us took him on a bender via Walthamstow greyhound stadium, where he passed out.

Anyway, the season had ended on a high note, which was staggering really, considering that it seemed to be heading nowhere early on. The previous autumn, when I had been part of that England misery in Rotterdam which cost

Graham Taylor his job, seemed such a long time ago. Now, at international level we had Terry Venables in charge and he even called up my pal Steve Bould for two end-of-season matches against Norway and Greece which the pair of us could enjoy playing in together, even if I was resentful that those two nations would be going to the World Cup instead of us when we were a much better team.

Anfield and that first title had been the most emotional achievement of my career thus far but in many ways, Copenhagen represented the most satisfying of the six trophies I had now won, because of our meagre resources but major endeavour. I'm sure George also saw it as a huge coaching achievement. At the back of my mind, though, was the concern about how long we could keep this up, so demanding and draining was this style of play becoming. Not to mention my drinking way of life.

That summer of '94 should have been a time for basking in glory and looking forward to new challenges. Instead, I was worried that it was going to be more of the football that I had not been enjoying. Naturally I enjoyed the success, and the release and excitement engendered by the big Cup games, but the grind of training and weekly League matches was becoming hard work, mentally and physically. We had been getting battered every week because there was no rest for the back four, no protection from elsewhere in the team. It was taking its toll. It was no fun. Drinking, when I got the chance between games, was helping me to cope with it all, I thought.

The problem was that we didn't have enough players of talent and there was no one really coming through the youth system, mainly because we couldn't really attract the top young players. We had been victims of our own success in a way, with kids unable to see how they might get past that back four that was in place and get into the team, so they were going to other clubs. The days of myself, David Rocastle, Michael Thomas and Paul Merson emerging were long gone.

George had bought only one proven player in Stefan Schwarz from Benfica for the beginning of the 1994/95 season, along with two goalkeepers in Vince Bartram and Lee Harper. 'I'm trying Tony, I'm bloody trying,' George would say when I asked him about major signings. 'The board won't let me have the money. The Chris Suttons won't come here.'

Bitterness was building up in the squad. As well as hearing that the wages weren't available for the top signings, players were asking for improved contracts and being refused by George. We had just won six trophies but there was no money available. As players we found it all hard to understand because those players who were coming in were getting more than those already there. What about rewarding those who had done it for you? We should have been as big a club as Liverpool and Manchester United, but we weren't doing what they were doing in their heydays of the 80s and 90s respectively – and to be fair to him, what George had been doing four years earlier – which was developing or buying players, like for like, to replace those whose best days were passing.

What happened in my testimonial that August, to mark ten years as a full-time professional with the club, only added to my feeling of flatness with the way things were at Arsenal. The club had given me a date for a benefit match, not an ideal one just before the start of the season, and I didn't really want to fork out the £50,000 and more it would have cost to bring Bayern Munich or Glasgow Rangers. I have to admit I thought the supporters would turn up, even though the opposition was a London club we played quite regularly in Crystal Palace, newly promoted to the Premiership. I was being naive.

Only 12,348 turned up, many of them from Palace. Obviously I had expected too much. Perhaps the Arsenal fans thought that I had enough money anyway, which at that time was actually not the case. Some kind souls sent me cheques through the post afterwards, saying that they had been away when the game was on. Arsenal were apologetic, and my Dad, who had done a lot of work on my behalf, was particularly upset. The club said that they would make it up to me in the future but in all honesty, having put myself through it week in, week out for ten years, I have to admit to feeling let down by them and the Highbury public.

The Premiership campaign got off to, at best, a mediocre start and in November I sustained an Achilles tendon injury, which was to keep me out for ten league games. In fact, that season I was to miss 15 of the 42 games, the most since I had become a fixture in the team more than eight years earlier. It was to be the start of a bad two-year period of injury for me. In many ways I had been lucky to get this far without a serious injury, but I don't think what was happening to me was coincidental. I had been banging away for so long on the field, and living hard off it, so something had to give.

Physically and mentally I was drained. I had been pushing my body and now it was turning round and saying 'no more.' My performances had been dipping but because I was proud – and talented, I believe – I was getting by in many games. This Achilles injury was my body telling me not to go through the pain barrier any more. I also felt that the club was losing its way, that the manager was losing his grip on the team and events. It was a miserable time – though the gloom was alleviated for a while when Terry Venables made me captain of England for the first time in the October, two days after my 28th birthday, against Romania to continue my proud record of leading every team I had played for – and it was about to get even more miserable.

I can't remember being particularly shocked when I read that December about George having received payments totalling £425,000 from the Norwegian agent Rune Hauge following the transfers of John Jensen and Pal Lydersen, a Norwegian defender signed in 1991 but who had hardly played. I was pre-occupied with my own situation: the injury, the drinking and trying to deal with things at home. Jane was having a difficult pregnancy at the time with our second child together. And when our daughter Amber was born in the early hours of the morning on Friday 26 January, I wasn't really capable of dealing with much. I missed training that day, got drunk and even got Jane to phone Arsenal the next day to say I was ill and wouldn't be able to play in the reserves game I was down for.

I also thought all the George stuff was just a lot of paper talk. Though I wasn't taking part much in first-team affairs at the time, I was more concerned about what he was going to do to arrest this slump the team was in. In the January he bought a raw John Hartson from Luton for £2 million, Chris Kiwomya from Ipswich for £1.25 million and in February Glenn Helder from Vitesse Arnhem for £2.3 million. So there was some money available. It smacked, though, of desperation and being too little, too late.

We were now half way in the table, which for Arsenal was unacceptable, had lost in the quarter-finals of the Coca-Cola Cup at Liverpool, and been dumped out of the FA Cup in the third round at home to Millwall. And for me after injury came insult. The match that saw my return to the team, against Sheffield Wednesday in early February, also saw me sent off for the second time in my career. The Achilles had healed but a broken wrist I had sustained in training had not and I was wearing a light plaster cast. Mark Bright had caught me in the face and I turned to the referee, Keith Burge, to complain and show him what Bright had done to me. As I did so, I caught Bright and he went down. 'I was only showing you what he did to me,' I said but it cut no ice and incredibly to me, I got the red card. With John Hartson also being sent off and the team losing 3–1, it seemed to sum up the state we were in. It couldn't get much worse. But it did.

The Sunday papers were full of the news that George was about to be sacked and I can remember being down at my local pub, the Chequers, talking to people about the reports. 'No,' I told them. 'I don't believe any of it. He's given the money back and the board will back him. We've been through worse scrapes than this.' The next day, Monday 20 February, it was confirmed. I got to training to find all the lads talking about it and after the usual work-out before a home game – against Nottingham Forest the next night, which I would again sit out – George's assistant Stewart Houston sat us down and said that, yes, George had gone.

Everyone was stunned, of course, but after that initial reaction I actually had mixed feelings about it all, if I am honest. A part of me was relieved. It was like when you are at school and you hear that the teacher is off and you don't have to put up with the discipline any more, the constantly being told what to do. And I knew that George's mind was elsewhere and that the team had been suffering as a result. I think he was weary of it all. He and Arsenal had run their course and I could see that, when we were playing the two legs of the European Super Cup that January against Milan. They were a great side then but George and I always felt we had a better back four than theirs. Once, it would have been a challenge to him against the world's best. Now he hardly seemed to bother with it.

George had always known how to win football matches, how to motivate players, but now it was all overtaken by the problems of buying players and negotiating their contracts. Some of the lads were coming to me, upset that Glenn Helder had come in on two and three times their wages. On the other hand, I wanted back the George I knew, the one who got us up for games, who organised us. The George of when it was good.

It was typical, in a way, that money was behind it all. George and I were very different in this area. It was very hard for me to comprehend because I had never really been money-orientated. There are those, like Peter Beardsley, who play for the love of the game and I considered myself one of them. Until long after this episode, when I was beginning to realise my worth both as a person and a player and wanted to negotiate a better contract, I had never really worried about my contracts. I just always signed them. Once when I queried something in one of them, George just said, 'Are you sure?' It was out of disbelief that I had spoken up, I think. 'Don't think the others are getting more than you,' he used to say. He always offered me a figure and I took it.

Later that week, George came back to London Colney to say goodbye. It was a short speech that lasted less than fifteen minutes. It was also quite moving and nowadays I would probably cry. Then, I choked it all back. It was more about us than him. 'Thank you for all the great times we have had here,' I remember him saying. 'You've all done really well in your careers and I'm sure there's more to come. You're still in the Cup Winners' Cup so good luck with that. Stewart's in charge now so give him the respect you gave me.' At the end there was a spontaneous round of applause and with that, he was gone.

After more than eight years, George's management of Arsenal had come to a sudden end but in a strange way it was good for me. The chairman Peter Hill-Wood spoke to me, telling me that Stewart Houston would be the caretaker-manager for the rest of the season and that he needed me, as captain, to be strong for the team. 'Make sure the team stick together. It's an important time for us,' Mr Hill-Wood said to me. It was Tony to the rescue again, I felt, and to some extent I resented it. But we had the Cup Winners' Cup run going and it was something to focus on once more. I had a cause again. I could get myself together for that.

We had been fortunate to come through the autumn's rounds. After a comfortable 6–1 aggregate win over Omonia Nicosia, we gave a sloppy home performance against Brondby of Denmark. Having won 2–1 away, we drew 2–2 at Highbury to squeak through 4–3 overall, with them being denied what could well have been a penalty in the last minute to go through on away goals. When the quarter-final against Auxerre came around in the March – the frustration of England's abandoned match against the Republic of Ireland in Dublin the previous month behind me – I was ready for the challenge.

Auxerre were a good side and the following season would go on to do the League and Cup Double in France. They held us 1–1 at Highbury and the odds, yet again, were stacked against us away from home. Stewart and I talked about it in depth the night before the away leg in his hotel room, me jealous that he could sit there and have a glass of the local Chablis. The question that went through my mind was: What would George have done? The French had a neat little playmaker called Corentin Martins and we discussed putting Martin Keown on him. We would go for the old formula: keep it tight – 'nice and resilient' in George's words – then look to hit them on the break. It was exactly what happened. It wasn't last-ditch defending but solid, composed and controlled. Steve Bould and I knew exactly what we were doing. Ian Wright got his customary goal with a brilliant shot and we clung on to it like gold.

So, we were still capable of it. There was a lot of George still in us. I have to say we were also capable of folding as well, because the old consistency and concentration could slip, as almost happened in the semi-final against Sampdoria. They had some outstanding individuals in Zenga, Vierchowod, Mihajlovic, Lombardo and Mancini but to be honest I thought we were two poor teams making mistakes. Bouldy rescued us in the first leg with two goals in the 3–2 win but again we went abroad as underdogs.

It was another exciting game but this time it wasn't controlled or planned defending. It was all off the cuff and we were fortunate. At 2–1 down, I thought it was all over, that they were through on away goals. When they made it 3–1 with a few minutes to go, nothing much had changed. Now they were through on more goals and we still needed one to force extra-time. Amazingly we got it, a bad mistake on their part letting Stefan Schwarz's powerful long-range shot find a path through their defence into the net. Extra-time resolved nothing and when we reached penalties, I always fancied our chances. We had David Seaman in goal, after all. When I scored mine, it gave us a 3–1 lead and Dave did the rest, making his third save to send us through to the Final. Amazing stuff.

We flew back that same night and after a few hours' sleep, the boys turned up at my testimonial golf day at Warley Park in Essex, which was a good excuse to celebrate and let the hair down. George came too but I was a bit embarrassed around him, until I had had a few pints, that is.

And so we were in another Final, this time against Real Zaragoza, at the Parc des Princes in Paris. When I think back, we gave our fans a good couple of seasons ... Turin, Copenhagen, Greece, Genoa, Paris. I would have liked to have been a fan, too, sometimes to see some of these places rather than just hotel rooms. Mind you, the palatial hotel we were in now at Versailles was beautiful. I recall that finally Arsenal had given in, probably due to Nigel Winterburn's constant complaining, and we were allowed to make phone calls home at the club's expense.

I remember, too, a conversation with Steve Bould, travelling to the stadium in the coach. 'Can we keep doing it, Bouldy?' I wondered. 'We can't keep nicking it, can we? Tottenham in that semi-final, Sheffield Wednesday in the final. Parma. Keeping it tight and nicking it. Sooner or later, our luck's got to run out, hasn't it?' Steve just smiled. You should always be careful what you say before a game.

Again we bounced back from adversity, John Hartson equalising after we had gone behind, but it was a cup tie too far. Expecting us to win that one was expecting too much. With time running out, Nayim got the ball wide on the right. You could see what was in his mind. He looked across our back line and saw that one of his strikers was offside so he went for it, sending a looping shot from wide on the right near the half-way line up into the night sky. A back-pedalling David Seaman could only touch the ball into the net in trying to turn it over the bar, but we attached no blame to him. He had got us here and, besides, it was a brilliant shot. Fair play. Nayim meant to do it all right. What made it worse was that he used to play for Spurs.

My reaction again was to go and get drunk and I stayed drunk on our post-season tour to China and Hong Kong. I wouldn't even have gone to see the Great Wall if I had been given the chance; that was how my priorities were at that time. About the only thing I remember from it is a scrape that Ray Parlour and I got into with a taxi driver in Hong Kong. Actually, come to think about it, I remember very little because I was in blackout, just an argument and doors banging, though I know Ray had to appear in court and pay a fine as a result of the altercation.

Later Stewart Houston would complain that the incident out in Hong Kong cost him the chance to become permanent manager, but I doubt it. I think we were always going to have a new man in charge. After all the ups, and finally the down, of the George Graham years, I think a new broom not associated with him was needed. My Far East bender was just another example of the way it was for me at this time. It seemed a fitting end to an era.

SIX

The Double Vision

Endings also mean beginnings, and the man chosen to preside over the new era at Highbury was Bruce Rioch. Both for me and the club, though, any new dawn was to be postponed. Things were getting on top of me with my drinking now seriously interfering with my football. I was just one of several problems that Bruce would have to cope with until eventually they overwhelmed him.

I don't think Stewart Houston was ever really going to get the job, even if we had won in Paris, although he was to remain as Bruce's assistant. There was a lot of talk about Bruce – Steve Bould had been on loan with him in his early days at Torquay when he had pinned a young player to the wall in a fit of anger – but really we knew very little about him.

Some days, when I was drinking and tense about how things were turning out, I wondered what the hell he was doing here. How dare this man come in and take over my club? That was one thought that went through my head. I was not even willing to give him a chance. At other times, I thought how approachable he was. During a pre-season tour of Sweden we stayed up late one night and talked about our various ideas on the game over a few beers and I thought we might be able to forge a working relationship. I think he respected what I had achieved in the game, but much of my thinking was pretty distorted at this time. Some days I would agree with him that changing to three at the back would be the best system. Other days I was just pining for it to be how it had been under George.

I didn't even feel any optimism with what were major signings in Dennis Bergkamp and David Platt during that summer of '95, even if everyone around Highbury seemed to think that we were getting things together again. My own world seemed bleak at the time and little seemed to improve it. 'Is Dennis Bergkamp really going to help us?' I wondered. My doubts seemed to be confirmed when we went up to Middlesbrough for a game later on that season and Dennis contributed little. In the showers afterwards, Bruce turned to Dennis and said: 'You're having a problem with two games a week, aren't you, Dennis? We might have to think about resting you in midweek.' Resting him? What is going on here? We are paying £7.5 million for a player who can only play now and then?

Quite often amid feeling sorry for myself, I would feel sorry for Bruce because his captain wasn't really there for him consistently in person and rarely in spirit. Sometimes I could get myself together and I scored in a 4–2 home win over Southampton, and then twice in a 3–0 win at Hartlepool in the Coca-Cola Cup. But there were plenty of down days as well, such as at The Dell in December when I was sent off for hauling down Neil Shipperley.

Bruce was trying to change us from the direct style of George into more of a passing team, and he was doing reasonably well at it – in fact he would take us to fifth in the Premiership come the end of the season, which was a big improvement – but I don't think he really had enough quality players to be able to take it the next step and challenge for the title. That got to him, I think, especially when he was unable to sign players himself. After what happened with George, the board were not going to concede control of transfers. Had he got success in his first season, like George had done, things might have been different. And Bruce did come close. Having reached the semi-finals of the Coca-Cola Cup, we took a 2–0 lead over Aston Villa in the Highbury leg, only to be pegged back to 2–2. After a goalless draw at Villa Park, we went out on away goals and they went on to win the trophy.

By then I was but a distant memory, having suffered a serious cartilage injury in the February. It was freezing cold and the pitch at London Colney was rock-hard. We all wondered what we were doing out there in those conditions. When John Hartson came ripping across me in a challenge, I knew the knee had gone badly. It was not like a hamstring pull or a muscle tear. It felt bad. It was freakish and accidental and John felt bad about it. I couldn't even struggle back to the dressing room and they had to drive a car out to the pitch to get me. I was taken to the clinic in Harrow in my kit and they operated on the knee the same day.

Bruce was very good to me during the injury, never once trying to rush me back. Although I'm sure he wasn't fully aware of what a state my private life was in – how I was drinking through this period, with Jane in treatment – he knew how important Euro '96 was to me. Before the previous Christmas, I had captained England again against Colombia and also played against Norway, Switzerland and Portugal so I felt established in Terry Venables's England team. A couple of Arsenal reserve outings and a full game in Paul Merson's testimonial that May got me back on track, at least in footballing terms, before the England tour to China and Hong Kong where my fitness was confirmed.

After the high of Euro '96, discussed elsewhere, and the low of those seven weeks of drinking that followed it, I was still not there for Bruce, who was experiencing a breakdown in his relationship with Ian Wright and having problems with Paul Merson, who was undergoing his own difficulties in his recovery from his addictions to gambling, alcohol and drugs. After the team had drawn a pre-season friendly against Ipswich, Bruce was angry with the attitude and application of the team. 'I feel like Marje Proops with all you lot,' the lads told me he said in frustration at matters other than football getting in the way. It was to be one of the last things he did say. A few days later he had left the club.

At this point, Arsenal were in as much turmoil as I was. Stewart Houston lasted barely a month in his second spell as caretaker manager before taking over at Queens Park Rangers, where Bruce joined him in a reversal of roles as his assistant. Now, as a safe pair of hands, we had Pat Rice in charge for a few games, one of which was my return to the team, at Middlesbrough, in late September. It had been six weeks since I quit drinking, two since I had told the boys in a team meeting I called on a Friday at London Colney that I was an alcoholic and it had subsequently become public. I was relieved it was all out in the open. Now I finally felt ready to go back to work.

I was really up for the game at the Riverside Stadium. It was a little like coming out of prison that time – in more ways than one – and the reception I got from the travelling Arsenal fans was amazing. Lee Dixon was injured after half an hour, so I was sent on and immediately I felt I was buzzing. Juninho didn't have a chance that day, I was round his feet, banging into him at every opportunity. No reaction to the knee or ankle injuries at all.

One of Bruce Rioch's legacies was European football

and the UEFA Cup match away to Borussia Moenchengladbach represented the next game in both my physical and mental rehabilitation. It also represented the first appearance of our new coach, whose recruitment from the Japanese club Grampus Eight had been confirmed a couple of days previously – a Frenchman by the name of Arsène Wenger. I had first been told in a bizarre phone call from the chairman on my mobile phone as I was driving through West London one day.

'Tony, Peter Hill-Wood here,' said that booming, well-spoken voice.

I actually swore and told whoever it was to stop taking the piss.

'No, Tony, it's the chairman, I'm phoning from New York,' he insisted. 'It's the chairman. I hear the shit's hit the fan. Don't worry. We've got a good guy coming. Rally the troops. See you soon.'

I can't say I was overly impressed by Monsieur Wenger's initial contribution. We had lost the home leg 3–2 to the Germans but were doing well enough over there, at one point taking a 2–1 lead. At half time, he came into the dressing room, took over from Pat Rice and changed us from the 3–5–2 that Bruce had introduced to a back four and we went on to lose the game 3–2 and the tie 6–4. I was not best pleased at being pulled off in the second half. At the end Arsène said nothing before disappearing smartly.

A lot of my old angry thinking was resurfacing: 'What does this Frenchman know about football? He wears glasses and looks more like a schoolteacher. He's not going to be as good as George. Does he even speak English properly? We could have won that game. I might never get another chance now to play in European football. How dare he.' I went up to Pat Rice and let him have my opinion.

The interesting thing was, though, that a new and different me was beginning to emerge as a result of not drinking. Another part of me, the rational part, was saying: 'Give him time. Let's have a look at him. He might be a nice guy. He might do good things. Let's stay open-minded.' And a few days later he came to me to talk about tactical changes, saying that he wanted to move to a back four. I told him calmly that we had been used to it under George and won trophies with it, but were just becoming comfortable with the three that Bruce Rioch had introduced. 'We're doing all right, we're fourth in the table. There's a time and a place for everything so why don't we wait till next season?' I said. I surprised even myself with the calmness of my argument and he agreed not to make any major changes immediately. We had established a working relationship.

I think he was pleasantly surprised with what he found. I'm sure he was concerned that all of his defenders were 30 and over, but he saw in the way that we were playing that we could still do a job and he decided to tinker only a little for that first season. I am sure he was right in his approach and by late November we even topped the Premiership for a while.

Personally, like my emotions without alcohol, my season was very up and down. After the European exit, I played the next 10 League games, which included a 3–1 win over Tottenham and a pleasurable left-footed goal on one of the ventures upfield I now felt I had been given licence to attempt, not only by Arsène Wenger but also because I was feeling adventurous as a person and player. In the next game, however, a Coca-Cola Cup tie against Liverpool at Anfield, I was booked in the first minute, and in a 2–1 win at Newcastle I was sent off for what was judged to be a professional foul on Alan Shearer, though I maintain it was a tangle of legs as we both chased the ball. Then I scored against Derby, and a month later conceded an own goal that cost us the game at Sunderland. What with losing out in the FA Cup to Leeds and George Graham, but internationally having enjoyed captaining England, now under Glenn Hoddle, in Georgia, my early recovery from alcoholism was proving rollercoaster stuff.

But even if my mind and emotions were healing, my body was taking longer. A recurrence of the ankle injury forced me to miss England's important World Cup qualifier against Italy at Wembley, which we lost 1–0, and I could not return after half-time during a home defeat by Manchester United, one of a couple of defeats in big games against them and Liverpool which saw any hopes of the title disappear. I was in and out of the team with injury – playing only 28 games in the season – which was beginning to concern me. As was my disciplinary record. On the last day of the season I was sent off for two bookings at Derby; two sendings-off in six months after only three in 12 years previously. Was I slowing up? Were the injuries taking their toll? My life was certainly beginning to take a huge turn for the better, but I could not escape the feeling that my football was being questioned.

Even after a summer off, I did not feel especially optimistic about either my own game or the team's prospects when the 1997/98 season came around. It just shows how long an English season is and how things can change dramatically.

Early on, I still had a lot of reservations about Arsène and I was hardly inspired by the players he had signed, though Patrick Vieira had proved himself promising the previous season. Only Marc Overmars had a proven reputation but he had had a serious injury. In pre-season, I can't say I was impressed by Gilles Grimandi or Emmanuel Petit from Monaco. Arsène had brought in Nicolas Anelka and Christopher Wreh, and sold John Hartson and a Highbury legend in Paul Merson to Middlesbrough, which made a lot of people worry which way the club was heading.

As a student of the athlete, Arsène thought that players probably could not go on beyond the age of 32 or 33 and he also brought in younger players to reduce the average age of the squad, like Alex Manninger, Luis Boa Morte and Alberto Mendez. I don't think he was fully aware of how good the players at the club were, though, particularly the back four.

One newcomer I did take to was Matthew Upson, just 18 and who came from Luton, because Don Howe had recommended him to the club and that was good enough for me. I was suspended for the first two games of the season and on opening day I took Matthew under my wing when we travelled to Leeds, sitting with him in the directors' box, saying things to him that Don had said to me: 'Watch Steve Bould and what he does, his positioning, where he runs.' Steve actually had an exceptional game but Gilles Grimandi gave a goal away and Ian Wright's goal was only good enough for a point. Afterwards I spoke to George Graham and was okay with that, though I sensed the unease of a few of the Arsenal directors round about.

I had done all the running in pre-season and was fine with that, but as soon as it came to twisting and turning or kicking a ball, my right ankle felt weak, as a couple of reserve games revealed. Arsène gave me longer to get myself right and the schedule was extended by another week. Finally, fed up with sitting out the first six games, I decided, on the doctors' say-so, to start taking anti-inflammatory tablets and to give it a go.

At first it felt fine. I went out to Greece for the UEFA Cup tie against PAOK Salonika and thought I played well, though it was too much like hard work again as we went down 1–0. It felt like the back four against the rest again with no one up front to hold the ball up, Dennis Bergkamp missing due to his fear of flying. My own fear was something I was dealing with quite well, now I didn't drink. In fact, I spoke to Dennis about it once when we were getting changed for training one morning but it didn't seem like he wanted any help at that time.

On our return, we won at Chelsea thanks to Nigel Winterburn's great shot and then went top when we beat West Ham 4–0 at home, a game in which I was pleased with the way I subdued John Hartson. Still, I didn't feel the team was gelling. At Everton we let slip a two-goal lead, when I thought the French boys looked like half-a-game merchants, Marc Overmars wasn't working for us and Wrighty seemed to be playing on his own but dipping in form. We were a good back four when everyone defended, but it was beginning to feel like '95 again when we were under the cosh.

A 5–0 win over Barnsley, who were a poor side at that time, hardly seemed to count and goalless draws against Crystal Palace and Aston Villa were more typical. They were followed by a 3–0 defeat at Derby, where Wrighty missed a great chance early on. We also went out of the UEFA Cup after a silly 1–1 draw against the Greeks at Highbury. We just weren't scoring goals and it was putting too much pressure on the defence; we weren't defending and attacking as a team but operating as two separate units instead. Defeats in November against Sheffield Wednesday and Liverpool, when Steve McManaman scored a magic goal, just accentuated our problems.

Amid it all, I enjoyed England's do-or-die goalless draw in Rome where we pipped Italy for the one qualifying place for France '98 from our group. It was just my sort of match, all backs to the wall and keeping it tight on a one-off basis, but even then I felt I was going through the motions a little. I did not have as much to do as some people thought, but there was no doubt it was a major result and something to be savoured.

Amid it all, too, we squeezed a 3–2 win over Manchester United at Highbury just when they were flying early season. We were 2–0 up in the space of half an hour through Nicolas Anelka and Patrick Vieira but they came back to equalise. I think Arsène got caught by surprise by Teddy Sheringham, who scored both United's goals, and the way he drops off deep to get the ball. Arsène got lucky, I thought, when Patrick got injured and Steve Bould came on as a sub, to form a back three with me and Gilles Grimandi. I thought Bouldy should have been playing from the start.

Anyway, we were much tighter and United barely got a sniff after that. Finally we grabbed what in hindsight was a very big win, even if we didn't really deserve it, with a brilliant header by David Platt from a corner. The old Arsenal was still in there somewhere and it showed that if we could just weld all the talent in the team together more consistently, we could beat the best. I remember saying in my programme notes that United were the team to beat, and that we could almost forget everyone else. If we were within three or four points of them come the second half of the season, then we had a great chance.

Not that it seemed too likely. I was getting fed up switching between a formation of two central defenders and the three. At the time, it didn't seem that we had two good ones so we needed the three. I could cope in the Manchester United game because I was doing all the old organizing and cajoling; all the things I like best. But to keep making the transition was draining me. I'm sure my views, whenever I spoke to Arsène about the two systems, were also coloured by my concerns with my ankle. By now I was getting up in the morning after games barely able to walk. My knee was aching, along with my back, and the ankle was simply painful. The whole right side of my body seemed to be giving way. In recent years I had never really had a long enough rest between seasons to recover and now I was paying the price. When I was fit and right, I could adapt easily to any system. In this state, I was finding fault in everything.

After the defeat at home to Liverpool, I felt I wanted some answers about our indifferent form but nothing was being said. We came in on the Monday and then had two days off, which surprised me. I consulted Steve Bould, who had missed the game but had watched it, and he pointed out that Michael Owen had gone past me on my right side a couple of times. I said a few things to Pat Rice and he in turn suggested a team meeting on the Thursday. Arsène agreed and after training we assembled at 1pm in a conference room at Sopwell House.

Arsène began by saying that the team wasn't working hard enough and that there didn't look to be enough desire in the side. Often players go quiet in team meetings and that was what happened now. I felt I had to speak up.

'That really hurts, boss,' I said. 'If you are saying that about me, I feel it is unfair criticism. If I'm not good enough, or injured, then drop me but don't say I've got no desire because I have always given my best.'

Then Bouldy weighed in with a few observations, about the defence not getting enough protection, and David Platt also had his say. I took up the theme. 'Look, we have always based our strategy on defence from the front and we're not doing that. I don't feel I can get tight on my centre-forward if they are going to put the ball in behind me.' Wrighty wasn't making his runs, Dennis was doing it only in fits and starts and Patrick and Emmanuel were not shielding us properly. Patrick, I felt, was young and arrogant and was going around kicking people. He needed to be calmed down a bit but wasn't getting enough guidance. He was dribbling too much instead of keeping the moves flowing. 'Manu' just could not last for 90 minutes; he was not used to the sustained pace of the English game and Premiership teams fighting to the end even when behind. 'Five against the rest again,' I said.

We cleared the air a little and some of the criticisms were rectified on the Saturday when we went to Newcastle and won 1–0. Marc Overmars, for example, worked really hard on the left flank to give us some protection. It wasn't a confident or flowing performance, though. I sensed we were just papering over cracks.

Then came a 3–1 defeat at home to Blackburn the following Saturday, a miserable day all round, not least for Ian Wright. Wrighty had not long beaten Cliff Bastin's 178 goals for the club with a hat-trick against Bolton, after which he had gone to the window of the dressing room overlooking Avenell Road to acknowledge the fans. Now, with him struggling for form, a few were shouting up less celebratory things and he opened a window in the bathroom to shout back down. Someone duly complained to the police.

This game was more about me, though. I had to concede

that two of the goals stemmed from my mistakes and now I had to look more closely at my own part in the team's travails. Wrighty's reaction was extrovert, mine was introvert. I just sat with myself and felt bad.

The next day I looked in on the Arsenal web site on the Internet and was horrified by the comments. 'Tony's playing rubbish,' it said. 'It would be such a shame if he were to end like this.' I felt really angry. What was all this? Even if it does end like this, they have had good value from me. 'They're a fickle lot, these fans,' I thought. Coupled with a remark I overheard, when Don Howe told Pat Rice that he didn't think I looked right, that I wasn't pushing and pulling and organizing and jumping and screaming, I felt really down.

I had played 13 games in a row but I hadn't been right. The ankle, the knee, the back were all aching. I still believed that all my criticisms of the team and certain individuals were valid, but now it was time to examine my own role in things and whether I could go on. I asked for a meeting with Arsène, and on the Thursday after the Blackburn defeat, which saw us 13 points behind Manchester United, we spent three hours drinking cappuccinos and talking as the December afternoon darkened outside.

I gave him my version of events, why the team was struggling, even that he needed to work more with players to put right their faults. He just replied that they were professionals and should not need to be told, the way he had had to tell players in Japan. I also introduced the new element of my own slipping performances. He agreed. 'I invited my friends over to see you play,' he said. 'And I think they were surprised because I had told them so much about you. They have not seen the best of Tony Adams and neither have I.'

I told him that against Blackburn I had been unable to run and jump properly because I did not trust the ankle, that I felt it would give way. I could keep on playing, I told him, but I wasn't doing myself justice. 'I have had high standards here at Highbury and if I can't maintain them, then I think I would be better off at another club where it is less demanding.' He did not agree with that idea. 'Tony, you have too much pride,' he said. 'You will not be able to do that.'

He was right. I could not just go through the motions with football. It wasn't in my nature. In which case, I said, I would rather go through to the summer, then pack up the game. If you are a bricklayer and you have your right arm cut off, then you can't do your job. Perhaps someone or something was trying to tell me to find alternative things to do with my life. As open-mindedly as I was trying to lead my new life, I was quite depressed about that thought. Retirement was a huge one. Arsène said we would talk again, once he had thought things through.

Two days later, on the Saturday before a Monday night game at Wimbledon, Arsène phoned. He had decided, he said, that I should have three weeks of not playing but of getting myself fit again, if that was going to be possible. I knew it was make-or-break time but I actually felt relieved that I would not have to keep playing, when I was getting so little pleasure out of it and not performing to the best of my ability.

It enabled me to have a good Christmas, which included the players' party at the Café de Paris in the West End of London. That was a really good night and brought the boys much closer together. The Frenchmen were all amused by Ray Parlour's dancing, Marc Overmars liked the place so much that he wanted to get a subscription and everyone let their hair down. After all the stick we had been giving each other in the previous month, it was a night when we started to get to like each other and I would come to look back on it as significant in the team's development.

In these days after the Bosman ruling, and with players from abroad costing less than their English counterparts, it is a delicate balancing act for any manager seeking to blend the best with value for money, the overseas with the domestic player. I think Arsène got it about right with a 50-50 English and foreign mixture in the squad and I would hate to see that disturbed too much, as it has been at some other big clubs.

Fans do still want to see local boys, I think, and I want to see a new Tony Adams come through. And when it comes to adapting, in some ways it can actually be more difficult for the English rather than the foreign player, with we homeboys having to accept what they can bring to our game and trying to integrate them into the set-up. At Arsenal it took a while, I have to admit, but when it came together on and off the field, as with that get-together at the Café de Paris, it was beautiful.

I also took the children away for five days up to Norfolk over the New Year, which did me good, and went to consult Gillian Morgan, a physiotherapist at Bisham Abbey who works with some of the England team and advised me on my posture. She told me that my right buttock needed strengthening to improve my jumping ability and gave me some exercises to do. Arsène flew in Philippe, his masseur and osteopath, from France and he manipulated my whole body, which was unbelievably beneficial.

On top of all this, I went to see Eileen Drewery, the faith healer that Glenn Hoddle has used so often with England. I was open-minded about it, believing in taking help wherever I could get it, and was willing for it to work. I agreed with Eileen that the body heals when it is meant to. If I wanted it to get better, she added, that would aid the recovery process. Then Arsène suggested that I go to the South of France for some work with a specialist conditioning coach he knew. Little did I know what I was in for.

Before flying out to the Côte d'Azur, I took in our FA Cup third round tie against Port Vale at Highbury, which we were lucky to survive into a replay with a goalless draw. Vale played some good football and we were a collection of individuals rather than a team. I was nearly out of the competition before I had kicked a ball in it.

When I flew into Nice Airport on the first Sunday in January, Tiburce Darrou was waiting for me. He was a tanned and stocky grey-haired character, a trainer who had worked with many tennis players, including Jimmy Connors and Yannick Noah, and had been an assistant coach with Paris St Germain. He was tough, abrupt and right for me at that time.

After a medical examination that night, I was put through my paces on the Monday morning, running, jumping and cycling, the Alps in the distance forming the backdrop for my 10 km circuit around Antibes. And so it went on for a week, the warm weather seeming to make all the hard work more bearable. I had massage and hydrotherapy at the health centre where I was staying between Nice and Antibes, and swam in a salt water pool. Every day I would have lunch on the beach at Juan Les Pins – pasta with fish or chicken – and walk in the blue Mediterranean. The cold water acted like an ice pack on the ankle and enabled me to do more work in the afternoons, which included training one day with the Olympique Antibes basketball team.

Tiburce also had me hopping up the 30 or so stone steps from the beach on my right leg – and no danger of me now falling down them like in that nightclub five years earlier. 'What is the matter, go back home. Your ankle is fine,' Tiburce told me. I was still a bit concerned what would happen when I kicked a ball, but I sensed he was right. It felt good on the last morning, the Friday, when I went through a session of ball work with him at Antibes football ground and there was no inflammation afterwards.

It was more, though, what happened on the Thursday night which helped convince me that I should abandon all thoughts of retirement and get back to doing my job. With Tiburce I went into a restaurant in Antibes and there, sitting in a corner with a group of friends, was Marco Van Basten, my tormentor in 1988. At first we just nodded recognition, but then at the end of our meal I went over to say hello and to ask him how he was. It clearly still hurt him that serious injury had forced him out of the game at the age of 28. 'I wish I was still playing,' he said wistfully. Now you can get carried away with the idea of signs – and Ray Parlour is very funny when he cites that scene in *Life of Brian* where the disciples pick up Brian's sandal and say, 'a shoe, it is a sign' – but I genuinely believed this to be a moment from which I was supposed to learn and take encouragement.

The time had come when my ankle was ready to heal. It still creaked and it cracked, and still does today, because it was worn and had had a lot of football on it, but now the rest, the manipulation, the posture work and all the physical exercise had combined to make it stronger, at a time when it was meant to be. I felt Tiburce was trying to break my ankle that week – but really I was trying to do it myself, to determine whether my career could go on or not. After my week in the South of France, I had a new enthusiasm for the season. I was going to be on players' cases when I got back. I was going to see if we could turn this season around.

One reserve game convinced me that the ankle would hold up, against Chelsea at Enfield. Football felt like fun again. Chelsea had a little guy in midfield who looked about 14 and I said to him: 'Weren't you round my house talking to my daughter last night?' The poor kid looked really embarrassed. David Rocastle was in the Chelsea team and I just said to him, 'Rocky, we are getting too old for this.'

Just to be sure, Arsène held me back until the end of January and I missed the FA Cup replay at Port Vale. That night I was at home, just pottering about, trying to avoid the game because I am a bad watcher and get really emotional. In the end, I found myself tuning in to Capital Gold to get the final score only to find the game still going on, at 1–1 in extra time. I wandered about the house, making a cup of tea, reading a paper, but I was drawn back to my kitchen for the penalty shoot-out. It was excruciating, much more difficult than playing. 'Why are they letting him take one?' I was asking myself. 'Who's going to ruin their career here?' I wondered. Part of me wanted to get out of the Cup, another wanted us to have a run. In the end, I sensed that David Seaman would prevail and as we went through 4–3 on penalties, I felt sorry for Allen Tankard who missed one for Port Vale after having such a good game. It was the night Ian Wright sustained the pulled hamstring that then kept him out for virtually the rest of the season despite his own visit to the South of France.

I actually came back against Middlesbrough in the next round ten days later and it is strange how key moments in my career have coincided with visits there, such as my return after admitting my alcoholism, and the time when I got angry with Bruce Rioch when he suggested to Dennis Bergkamp that he might be rested in midweek. Perhaps that was in the back of my mind as I climbed on to the coach at the hotel to go to the game and felt a need to say something to Dennis. Spontaneously it came out.

'You've been over here two and a half years, Dennis,' I said, half in sarcasm, half in motivation. 'Isn't it about time you won something? It would be a shame not to with your ability.' Then I walked on quickly to the back of the bus.

It needed saying, I thought. The worst thing in football is the unfulfilled talent, people like George Best, though he did win a title and a European Cup, and Paul Gascoigne. Dennis had the talent to destroy teams. I didn't want him to go home just a rich man. I wanted him to get rattled and start retaliating with match-winning performances again. It looked as if I made him think.

I had had a conversation with Arsène when I got back from France in which he told me that sometimes I needed to put people in their place, to remind them that I was captain. I knew I had to back it up with talent and performances, though, and now I felt able to do that. I would later do the same with Patrick Vieira when, before a game at Crystal Palace, some of the older players were complaining about him not training as hard as he should be. I left it a day or two then said that we had worked very hard when we were his age to learn the game, won six trophies, and had earned the right now to pace ourselves with so many games to play, but that he had not yet. I think he took my point.

Anyway, starting at Middlesbrough, I wanted to show everyone that I was back and in that game we started to pass the ball well, to get a rhythm going. Without Wrighty, we now had to get goals from elsewhere. Marc Overmars and

Ray Parlour responded early on as we overwhelmed Boro' and there was no way back for them after that. In the end it was perfect, Paul Merson getting a goal back for them on a big day for him, but we won comfortably.

That goal came when Alex Manninger, who was beginning a run of 13 games in the team with Dave Seaman having broken a finger, came charging out of his area past me. It became a regular conversation point with me and Alex. 'Right, you are not going to come running out today, are you?' I would say and he would smile and shake his head. I enjoyed helping him, telling him when to leave his line and furthering his education process and he responded like a good professional. I made a point of not leading the team out until Alex was ready. 'You're the man,' I would tell him.

The following midweek I was playing in a Coca-Cola Cup semi-final against Chelsea. In France three weeks earlier, Tiburce had found a bar with Sky TV for me so that I could see the quarter-final against West Ham, watching the lads battle in the mud and the rain while I was enjoying a balmy evening drinking cappuccino and mineral water.

Now many turning points have been cited in Arsenal's season – such as the team meeting at Sopwell House, the Blackburn defeat – and I do think my return was also a significant factor as the team got back their captain, one who was fit and right and one they could respect again and would listen to, but that 2–1 win at West Ham was certainly a watershed. Patrick and Manu were providing the protection we needed in midfield and everyone was working hard. Later Pat Rice told me that they also pushed Marc Overmars on to counter everything going through John Moncur so that we had bodies forward. Thus we evolved from the 4–4–2 that was not functioning at its best, with Arsène's idea that we press high in the field not really being implemented, to a 4–3–3 where the opposition had to worry about the number of attackers we had.

We really should have beaten Chelsea by several goals in that first leg but had to settle for 2–1 and it was always going to be a battle at Stamford Bridge three weeks later after that. I felt I had a good game, scrapping and tackling in a way I was unable to do before Christmas, but we lost 3–1 and went out of the competition. Looking back, obviously it was meant to be as our League campaign was developing along with an FA Cup run.

Between the Chelsea games I had returned to League action against Southampton, scoring a goal from a corner. 'Ah, very good,' Arsène said afterwards, which ranked as high praise. I really felt I was back after that, that it was lock-up-your-daughters time, but it also worked out well that I had a two-game suspension coming up. After playing in the League game against Chelsea, won by two Stephen Hughes goals, I missed two matches against Crystal Palace, the first in the League in which Gilles Grimandi grabbed the goal in a 1–0 win. We seemed at that time to be locked in competition with the two clubs and after three games against Chelsea came three against Palace.

At home to them in the FA Cup fifth round, we should have had a penalty, but so should they, and it was remarkable that the game stayed goalless. Considering we had several first-teamers absent, I thought we did well, and I believed a stronger Arsenal would complete the job in the replay. So it was. Nicolas Anelka ran through and chipped us ahead, then Dean Gordon brought down Dennis and was sent off. Dennis's free kick was deflected home and it was game over. They did get a goal, with Bruce Dyer beating me to a header from a corner, but that was meant as a lesson, I'm sure. I apologised afterwards to Pat Rice, who had warned me about Dyer's ability in the air before the game, and I said that it wouldn't happen again that season. It didn't.

With Martin Keown coming back into the side in place of Steve Bould, I had to go back to the left side of the defence and for a while I was disoriented. Arsène commented that I looked better on the right, which I took personally and as a comment that I couldn't play on the left. But I thought, 'Hold on, I have won all my trophies on the left,' so it was just a question of getting used to the position again. Perhaps Arsène had been motivating me to do so but I didn't really need any. I went back to basics in training and practised receiving and giving the ball in the left-sided areas. I soon remembered and realised again that I could come inside and play with my right foot like Alan Hansen, who also used to play on the left.

The Palace win gave us another quarter-final against West Ham, with whom we would also go on to have three battles in quick succession. We drew 0–0 at Upton Park in the League before the Cup game at Highbury, in which they played with only Samassi Abou up front. They took the lead, though, when Ian Pearce's shot went through my legs and past an unsighted Alex Manninger, and though we equalised with Dennis Bergkamp's penalty, it was the type of game we could have lost on the counter-attack as we struggled to break them down. Everyone thought it was all over now, that it was West Ham's year; they did have a very good home record, after all. We were just relieved to be still in the competition and I had a hunch that we could still do it at Upton Park.

First we had the simple matter of two League games away from home, at Wimbledon and Manchester United.

The first one, a 1–0 win thanks to Christopher Wreh's great shot, took us to within nine points of United with three games in hand and all was set fair for an epic struggle on the second Saturday morning in March.

I felt really confident that day. There was no fear in me, just a calmness, and I knew we had the capability to win. In February, as part of the England squad for the match against Chile, I noticed how tired the United players looked and really began to think they might have shot their bolt in the Premiership by then after their pace-setting of the autumn. Other things were also in our favour; they had been concen-trating on a Champions League quarter-final against Monaco and they were also without Ryan Giggs, who was very important to them. They were the ones with the anxieties, the insecurities.

I knew immediately that I was on the top of my game when a ball came up to Teddy Sheringham and I nipped in ahead of him to win it. Then I was on the ball and they closed me down but it was no problem. I just knocked it away. At the other end we had plenty of opportunities and though it took a late goal from Marc Overmars to separate the teams, I always had faith that we would win the game. The result may have said 1–0 to the Arsenal again, but this was not a result we ground out. We were well in control. I said to Arsène in the dressing room after the game that the last time we won at Old Trafford, we went on to win the League. Now its destiny was in our hands, probably much to the annoyance of Alex Ferguson, as we were only six points behind United now, with our three games in hand.

Before any of that, though, there was the replay at West Ham to fulfil and it was to confirm the old Arsenal at their best. Things did not look too good when Dennis Bergkamp was sent off for an elbow to the face of Steve Lomas and at that point, even that early in the game, I was thinking about penalties. But we grabbed a lead soon after through Nicolas Anelka and the rearguard action that followed was really enjoyable – sometimes being down to 10 against 11 can inspire you – and I was disappointed when we conceded an equaliser to John Hartson. Now it was a question of holding on for penalties, though I had fanciful visions of surging forward and scoring a winner. My destiny that night, and that season, was to be something different, though.

After our usual nine-a-side game in training the day before – one touch, but two if you passed it forward, shot or crossed – the five penalty-takers had some practice. I wasn't one of them but just knocked one in for a bit of fun. Now here we were, in an FA Cup quarter-final and the two teams involved in a penalty shoot-out. Now here I was, the first five penalties not having settled it, finding that I had to shoulder the responsibility for taking one. I didn't much like the idea but felt I should take courage with others unwilling to risk it.

I just wanted to get it over with as quickly as possible. I put the ball on the spot and ran up hastily. I didn't know where I was going to put the ball, but then I thought that the goalkeeper wouldn't either. As I began my run-up I wondered what I had done. All the fans were braying 'ee-aw' at me, at the ground where I first recall the chant, and I thought that this could be the biggest mistake of my life. Before I knew it, I had stroked the ball and it had dribbled home. It was a completely pathetic penalty, I admit, and I had this illogical idea of following it in to knock home any rebound. As I ran back to the centre circle I exhaled deeply and smiled the smile of a relieved man.

Then, all of a sudden, Abou had hit a post with his shot

and we were through. Alex Manninger had been the real hero with two saves and I was delighted for him because he was a good young pro with a good attitude. Before Christmas, I thought David Seaman had been unusually wobbly just a couple of times and Alex coming in and doing so well for this period acted as motivation to him, I'm sure. I think Dave's pride was stung.

But Arsène made it clear that David would be recalled when fit and he returned for the next game against Sheffield Wednesday. There was a nice moment in the dressing room before the game when Alex went to David's peg, hung up his clothes, turned and smiled and said, 'What's the problem?' David smiled, too, and just gestured to him to move his stuff. That was another 1–0, and yet another followed at Bolton three days later. Now we were closing fast on United as we turned our attention to an FA Cup semi-final against Wolverhampton Wanderers.

There is a tradition at Arsenal that you do not train the day before a semi but Arsène was ignoring it, to the annoyance of some of us. As soon as we got out on the field, though, a thunderstorm broke and it was all back inside. Arsène may be right to ignore superstition in favour of doing the right thing, but this was meant to be. We were aware that the 1979 Arsenal team had also beaten Wolves in the semi-final – and at Villa Park, which I always consider a proper semi-final venue – but I just couldn't let myself think about that.

The game itself saw us again into our good rhythm of passing and moving and after Chris Wreh gave us an early lead, it was again as good as over. For the fifth game in a row we had gone a goal up and we hadn't let the game slip away. To be honest, it was men against boys, as it had been at Middlesbrough in the fourth round. You always have a little fear in Cup games, but I always believe that if the favourites have courage, are near full-strength and show strength of mind, they will always win. It is the same in the Final, in which we would now play Newcastle United.

By a quirk of the fixtures, they came to Highbury the following Saturday and were no match for us, Nicolas Anelka scoring twice and Patrick Vieira once with a brilliant long-range shot. Newcastle were never really in it, with Alan Shearer hardly getting a look-in, and we shouldn't really have let in a late goal to Warren Barton. In a way I was glad we did, though. It was the first goal we had conceded in ten games and talk of records was becoming a burden. We could also wind up David Seaman, saying that Alex had kept all those clean sheets and now he had spoiled it.

Our next game on Easter Monday took us to Blackburn and, except as psychology, I couldn't see why Alex Ferguson was telling everyone how good they were after United's own game there the previous week when they had scrambled a win. Blackburn were without Chris Sutton and they were losing to everyone at that time. Even so, it was impressive the way we went three up in ten minutes with Dennis, back after suspension, and Ray Parlour, twice, scoring and Nicolas Anelka making it 4–0 by half-time. I was just annoyed with Remi Garde for letting his man go to give a goal away in the second half.

Wimbledon came to Highbury on a good run five days later, but they had no chance as we gave a powerful attacking performance. I got things going with a header from a corner – and the following midweek would have one disallowed against Portugal on my 50th England appearance, when there was less physical contact as I went up for the ball – and the 5–0 win was notable also for Manu

Petit getting his first goal for the club. It was notable, too, for us now going to the top of the table for the first time since October – a point ahead of United and with two games still in hand.

The next Saturday at Barnsley was, I thought, one of my best games of the season. It was much more of a scrap, with them fighting for their lives, and the first twenty minutes were intensely hard work. Then Dennis curled home a great goal and the pressure eased. Marc Overmars's second made it comfortable in the end, if not the beginning. Now the title was in sight. Two wins in the next week would give us the crown. One game at a time, though, had to be the realistic, if clichéd, aim.

I was actually very nervous before the game against Derby in midweek. I had echoes of '89 and Dean Saunders, us nearly blowing it when we lost at home to them. It was tough stuff, mainly because they were angry after losing at home to Leicester 4–0 the previous Sunday, which had prompted their manager Jim Smith to threaten to sell them all. We can compete, though, and did. Manu's goal settled it – after waiting all that time, two had come along at once for him.

That to me was a really big win, the one that probably decided it, in fact. There was just no way we were not going to beat Everton the following Sunday to clinch the title, even without Dennis Bergkamp, who had pulled a hamstring against Derby. As Nigel Winterburn said to me, if we couldn't beat such a lowly team, then we didn't deserve to win it. The boss was getting a bit worried, I think, because he saw we had two away games to finish with, against Liverpool and Aston Villa. 'You're still getting to understand Arsenal,' I said to him later. 'We don't get in these positions to let it slip.'

Slaven Bilic's early own goal – though I would have headed it home if he hadn't – calmed everyone down and thereafter we were able to play a bit of football. I knew there was no way we were going to lose the game after that and the only unpleasant moment I had was when Mikael Madar came on and spat at me for some reason. I turned to Duncan Ferguson and said, 'What's his problem?', to which Duncan replied, 'Oh, just kill him.'

When we got to 3–0 up, with Marc Overmars having scored twice, and with the game almost over, I decided to have a bit of fun. I passed the ball into midfield to Steve Bould, who had come on as a substitute – actually, I would have liked his calm assurance alongside me from the off, but that's another matter – and kept running forward. 'Put me in, put me in!' I shouted to him and he looked up and chipped a great ball through. As it was coming, I thought, 'Concentrate. Just push it forward with the first touch.' I knew that would set me up. And although I pushed it on to my weaker left foot, the touch with my stomach was good enough. I swung at it and the next thing I knew the net was bulging. 'Just like Roberto Carlos,' someone said later but I said, 'No, just like Tony Adams.' Besides, he doesn't score from there. The corner flag maybe … As the ball hit the net I just thought, 'Wow'. It was a beautiful moment and as I closed my eyes to savour it, I simply felt a great calm and peace.

Soon I was walking past a giant can of Carling Black Label, the drink that had got me started on that last seven-week series of benders after Euro '96, and lifting the Premiership trophy. It seemed symbolic and ironic. In April I had been criticised by some Arsenal fans on the Internet for not staying to applaud them long and loud at the end of every game. I replied that sometimes I did – at Barnsley they were magnificent – and at other times I didn't need to stay out there fuelling my ego; I had done my job well and that should be enough. Now I was happy to celebrate with them, to walk round the pitch and slowly drink in the day, rather than the alcohol of '89 and '91.

Back in the dressing room, I went round and spoke to people individually, to the boss to say that I told him we would do it, to Nicolas Anelka to say well done, to Gilles Grimandi to point out how crucial his winning goal against Palace had been, to Martin Keown to tell him with a smile that I would win more medals for him. Liam Brady came in to remind Bouldy that he had the copyright on those chipped passes. At one point, Stephen Hughes sprayed beer over me and some went on my lips. It made me angry and I told him so – after which the poor kid spent the whole time apologising to me. I calmed down and told him not to worry. I just went and sat in Pat Rice's office and had a cup of tea and a Mars bar.

From there I went home because my dog needed walking. It was a beautiful evening there on Putney Heath as I gazed across at the church at the end of my road and it was all so peaceful. I still wanted to be with the boys, though, and joined them later at the wine bar in Dover Street in Mayfair that we had also used in 1991. All the Arsenal staff were there, office people and players, and I just took it all in, enjoying the music, talking to people, having a good meal until about 3 am. Then I went home and got on with the rest of my life. Which included an FA Cup Final.

I can honestly say that I didn't give the Double one thought in the build-up. 'What has 1971 got to do with playing a Cup Final in 1998?' I thought. It is just so different when you are on the inside of things. For me, it was a job to be prepared for and done; for everyone else around the club it was an event, an occasion. I heard all about the parties in Islington still going on after we had won the title but I had work.

We allowed ourselves only two distractions, one a Cup Final record, the other the fittings for our suits, the Hugo Boss all-black outfit which I thought made us look super cool, very 'now'. David Dein said that the idea to do a version of 'Hot Stuff' out of *The Full Monty* came to him in his sleep. At first I wasn't keen but the team wanted to do it, the younger ones especially for the experience, which in my view can be very tedious, standing around for two hours. In the end it was fun, though. I was actually willing to do the Full Monty for the video unlike the other boys but then I have nothing to be ashamed about. We did not get involved in any money-making exercises, except for donations from the media to the Arsenal Trust which helps fund children's hospitals in North London. It is good these days that most Premiership players are well enough paid not to need to supplement their incomes.

On the Friday we suffered a setback when Dennis Bergkamp was ruled out of the Cup Final, the hamstring he had pulled against Derby having failed to heal. He was shooting for goal from a free-kick in training when it happened – just as I was telling him to chip it so I could get on the end of it. It was sad for him, as he had also missed the Everton game, but I couldn't let it get to the team, who seemed worried initially. Of course, we had lost a great player but we had to carry on. 'Oh no, we've lost the messiah,' I joked as Arsène, Pat Rice and Gary Lewin attended to Dennis on the touchline. 'The boss is crying. We're all doomed.' It achieved the effect of lightening the mood.

We did a little work on set pieces then, with Pat Rice and me organizing. It was something Arsène let us get on with. Early on, he had wanted Patrick Vieira, for example, to patrol the near post when we were defending corners, but I pointed out that it had always worked well when Steve Bould was there and Arsène accepted this. It was one way in which he was sensible enough to leave well alone.

We had two League games before the Final and lost both. I was rested for the 4–0 defeat at Liverpool but returned for the game against Aston Villa, about which I was more tense than for Everton or Newcastle. I just do not like games with nothing at stake; I can tell because I channel-hop agitatedly in hotel rooms the night before with the television remote.

On the Friday night before the Final, Arsène sat us down in a team meeting at the hotel in Chelsea we use. 'I have been observing everyone since we won the title,' he said, 'and we have changed. We got here because we were a team and we looked to our own performance. Lately we have been looking at each other's performances.' It was calm and determined and designed to shock. I personally didn't feel in any need of it but he may well have refocused some people's attention.

After that, I went for my regular reflexology from our masseur, then to my room to watch *Frasier*, the neurotic sitcom psychiatrist, with whom I have to say I identify. I felt no need to channel-hop. After his regular session of eating for England, my room-mate Ray Parlour was already sleeping – and snoring – for England, catching up on rest after being at home all week with two young children who wake him up constantly. It may have had something to do with him being Man of the Match the next day.

I also slept well but woke at 7.30 am with those usual negative voices that take some time to disappear – Will I be tired? Have I slept enough? I had breakfast with my friend and confidant Steve Jacobs – toast with strawberry jam, but don't tell Arsène – and talked it all through until the doubts passed. Then it was a fifteen-minute walk around Chelsea Harbour and fifteen minutes of stretching. We always eat four hours before a game, but lunch at 11 am felt strange. All the usual pasta, chicken and vegetables were on offer but I just felt like poached eggs on toast, with yoghurt and apple pie to follow. We weren't used to 3 o'clock kick-offs on a Saturday.

The team talk was at 12.55 pm and lasted just five minutes while Arsène named the team. No one was really surprised or too disappointed; we had seen the way it was shaping up in training during the week. Chris Wreh, rather than a fit-again Ian Wright, was always going to be Dennis's replacement. At 1.05 pm we left. Not once had we discussed Newcastle. We were confident enough that if we played well, we wouldn't need to worry about them.

I made it my business on the coach and at Wembley to make sure that everyone was taking it all in and enjoying it. I told them that I was pre-occupied the last time in '93 and hadn't really savoured it. I told David Platt that if it was meant to be, after doing our best that is, then we would win. I told Martin Keown to calm down and not to worry about the 90-degree heat because he was fitter than anybody in the Newcastle team. In my team talk, I told them to seize the day and not let anything pass them by.

'Come on, boys,' I said as a last remark before going on the pitch. 'Let's make some memories.'

When the game kicked off, at first we could get no rhythm and I was disappointed we were not pulling them about. Afterwards, my Dad said I should have been a traffic policeman, so much was I getting everyone to manoeuvre.

'Martin, Nigel, come here, go there,' I was saying. Patrick and Manu were getting frustrated, I sensed, because they wanted to do something special. 'Just do a job today. Keep it simple,' I said. It was a time for being patient.

Then Manu found Marc Overmars with a through ball and he scored a goal similar to the one which had turned the title race in our favour at Old Trafford. After that I felt it was game over, to be honest; even this early midway through the first half; even when they hit the bar and then the post, Martin Keown treading on the ball and Alan Shearer seizing on it. Alan's tackle on me, for which he was booked, was water off this duck's back. I saw him coming and rode the challenge.

When Nicolas Anelka made it 2–0, I found myself looking up to the Royal Box at the trophy as I had done in 1988 that time we lost the League Cup Final. 'Stop it,' I told myself. Then, in all honesty, I found myself wishing Newcastle would score to make the last ten minutes more exciting. I love all the do-or-die stuff.

At the final whistle, I went to each of the Newcastle players to shake their hand. It is important, I believe, as captain, to spend time with the losers. Apart from the fantastic Geordie fans who were so good to us, I felt most sorry for Robert Lee. I lived next door to Robert's mum and dad in Essex and they also bought my house. I can remember being drunk in the gutter with him once on an Under-21 tour. Then Arsène was embracing me and telling me that we had performed an amazing achievement.

'Now Arsène,' I said. 'You have seen the best of Tony Adams.'

It was a lovely moment with a coach I had come to like, respect and admire more and more. I need to work with people like that, but I never thought it would be someone who had never played the game to the highest level. It shows how you should always be open-minded about people.

As I walked up the steps to get the Cup and my eighth major medal, David Seaman told me to slow down. He likes to be in the pictures next to me. I should also wait, he said, so that all the others could get on to the row and be in shot. There we are, so experienced at winning trophies that we are even organizing the photos, all getting bunched up before we lift the Cup. I gave it a good high lift this time.

Back in the dressing room, I asked the dressing room attendant if he had anything cold to drink. 'Beer?' he asked. I just smiled. It was the same bloke who had provided me with that can of Carling after the defeat by Germany at Euro '96 some 21 months earlier. 'Sorry, I forgot,' he said almost immediately and brought me a bottle of iced water.

Waiting for me back at Sopwell were Mum and Dad, for whom I had hired a limo for the day. They had been looking after Oliver and Amber at the game; Clare was very sorry but she had a netball tournament in Norfolk that day. That helped to keep my feet on the ground. I stayed to enjoy the company and the bonhomie till about 12 then drove home, returning to Highbury at 9 am for the traditional procession through Islington. This one was unbelievable, better than '89 even. This time I had no need of the tinnies being thrown up to us.

When I got home in the afternoon I felt strange, flat and empty feelings. It had been the same after winning the Premiership. The amount of emotional energy I had invested in the achievement had drained me. It was done, we had won, but it was over and I was sad. Probably a bit jealous, too, of all the boys getting drunk, and I had echoes of all my previous trophy wins. Those feelings passed, though. And this time the feeling of achievement that replaced the quick buzz was deeper and more lasting.

The Double. It is almost a mythical achievement and for me as time has gone on I have come to realise just how momentous it was. A chill has gone down my spine from time to time, in fact. And I think it is going to get better as time passes. We have done more than shut that '71 lot up, as I jokingly told Pat Rice. We have taken our place in English football history, I have become the first Arsenal captain to lift three League trophies, and we have joined the Highbury legends.

SEVEN

Top Guns

Results make football teams, people make football clubs. Over my long career with Arsenal, I have encountered a wide range of personalities and players, all with different characteristics, assets and defects. It is fair to say that life at Highbury has never been dull, even if we have had to endure the 'boring Arsenal' tag at times.

When it comes to coaches and managers, the first big influence on me as a full-time professional was Don Howe. When I joined the club full-time at the age of 16, Terry Neill was the manager, the PR man who was good with the press, but to me, a young player desperate to learn the game, Don was the straight man of the double act, the one grafting away. The senior players seemed to like Terry, a Northern Irishman who talked a good game, and they told stories of the golfing, of him organizing the whip-rounds. At that time, I wasn't interested in the business of management – the contracts and the press, that sort of thing – or the socialising. The only time I really spoke to him was when I signed my contract.

Don did what I liked best. He would be out on the training pitch with his bobble hat on, getting muddy with us, running the knackers off me. 'You, make a five-yard run. You, this is how you give an angle. You, this is how you come off a defender,' he would shout. I was pleased when he got the job himself after Terry.

A lot of people see Don as a sort of cheerful, friendly old figure, but I feared him a lot, and certainly respected him. He could be ruthless in his own way. Once, when I was still only 16, I was injured for a game one Saturday but thought I would be all right to go out in the evening. He phoned my home and Mum and Dad told him where I was. I had to go in for treatment on the Sunday morning and Don was waiting to give me both barrels. To try and gain some sympathy, I told him I was ill as well. It only made things worse. 'You're nothing but a little boy who thinks he's back at school,' he shouted. 'In nightclubs. Not good enough. What's going on with you?' I nearly cried but it was part of the toughening-up process. Not everyone with talent can endure being chewed off like that and they drift out of the game. Mind you, fifteen years later I might be able to answer back better.

Then again, Don understood what you were going through as a player. When Terry dropped me after my debut, it was Don who came to me before the West Ham game in which I wanted to play so much and explained the reasons why, urging me to be patient. He was also the motivator, the organizer and I remember him, for example, shaping us up to beat Liverpool one season.

I was personally very sad when Don went. I think he found it difficult to deal with such maverick characters as Steve Williams and Charlie Nicholas and he was being labelled as a coach rather than being seen as a manager, who could buy and sell and deal with players. When he was Terry Neill's assistant at the time of the League Cup defeat at Oxford, followed closely by the game at Manchester United, he gave the older players a bollocking, saying 'Look at Tony Adams. Why can't you all show his attitude?' Then, in his final season as manager, there came a 6–1 defeat at Everton, after which Paul Davis bravely got up in the dressing room to say: 'You're all prima donnas, you lot.' I think in many ways Don felt the same. More and more, money was starting to come into football and he could never understand why it motivated players so much when the game, and trying to win things, should simply do that. I think he liked my single-minded attitude, and I gave him no trouble when it came to signing a contract – the last he negotiated as Arsenal manager.

That day he left was so strange. There was I delighted with my performance in the 3–0 win over Coventry, in the players' bath next to a guy looking miserable, his thoughts elsewhere. I don't think he was enjoying it any more, all the cares of management were probably not for him. I didn't understand all the press speculation about Terry Venables coming in to replace him and the politics of it all. All I knew was that Don Howe knew football and had my total respect. It was probably good for him to go to Wimbledon a little while later, to be loosened up by lads who enjoyed a laugh, who may not have had great talent but who were willing to work hard. It was no doubt a lot more satisfying winning the FA Cup with that team in 1988 than dealing with some of the problem players he had at Arsenal.

For a few months, we had Steve Burtenshaw in charge and he was hilarious. 'Kick, bollock and bite,' was always his pre-match catchphrase. On the last day of the season in 1986, we were mid-table and playing Oxford United, who needed to win to stay up. 'Now,' said Steve, 'I probably won't be in this job next season so all I've got to say to you is do your best for yourself – kick, bollock and bite and all that – but if Robert Maxwell comes in here and puts a load of brown envelopes on the table, we are throwing this game.' It was all tongue in cheek but we did lose, 3–0.

When George Graham became manager that summer, I could not have realised it would be the major footballing relationship of my career. At first, I was still upset that Don had gone and I had had no stability to my early career. I was still only 19 and this was my fourth manager. Is this what professional football was going to be like?

People who had known George said he changed, the moment he got the Arsenal job. For example, now that he was in charge of one of the top sides in the country, he changed all his drinking pals, they said. It was the same at the club. He was going to sort out or get rid of the prima donnas, one by one, you could see it. Once in training, Gus Caesar kicked Charlie Nicholas up in the air and when Charlie complained, George just ignored him.

The motivated ones like me enjoyed all this. I felt like I was on trial again, like I had been with Terry Burton, the youth team manager Tommy Coleman, and Don Howe. But it was a trial I knew I was going to pass. The older pros never had a chance. George used to call them the 'pension players' and he packed them off to go and pick up their last couple of years of pension somewhere else.

For a long while George was very reserved, very closed with the boys and kept his distance. After a couple of pre-season tours and after winning a couple of trophies, he loosened up a bit but you never really involved him in any of the laddish things that went on. Once in Norway, I went up to him, put my arm round him and asked him how he was, just so I could put a lemon on his shoulder without him noticing. It was just a silly joke and gave the lads a good laugh, but George was not happy about it. He was even less happy when Niall Quinn once put a condom there.

There was this image of George as a disciplinarian but he was very pragmatic about things. The reality was that if you were working hard in training and giving it your utmost in games, then he turned a blind eye to some things. If you were out of favour, you could expect him to come down hard on you. When the Pizza Hut incident happened with Ray Parlour, for example, he went berserk with Ray, who wondered, not surprisingly, why I was not also getting a bollocking. 'He's doing it for me, week in, week out,' George said. 'When you are as well, I'll back you to the limit.'

In public George would say that everything was dealt with in-house. 'Yes, I'll be fining the player,' he would tell the press and could be seen to be a hard manager. But it would take a very strong manager not to have one rule for one and one for another. The business of running a team depends on treating individuals differently, after all. There were, though, certain things that you just couldn't get away with because Arsenal did have a rule book, and George did things by the book.

It was issued to you at the beginning of every season and contained information like the manager's home telephone number and all the do's and don'ts, such as don't go into licensed premises 48 hours before a match – which I confess to doing at 18 years of age – and don't go into the ticket office on the day of a game. And although Arsenal paid my wages while I was in prison, they also fined me two weeks' worth. That was the set fee for drink-driving designated in the rule book, which also contained fines that could be docked from your wages for bookings and dissent. David Seaman and I once got fined £100 each for not turning up for training the day after an England international. Well, I hadn't got home after a session until 8.45 am, had I? Paul Merson, by now in recovery, had gone in and shown us up. What a creep.

George always loved the image of the Arsenal, the tie and the club blazer, the bust of Herbert Chapman in the marble hall. That was where he and I differed. When I used to have to polish the statue in my days as an apprentice, I never could see what Herbert Chapman had to do with me getting in the first team. We were always told as kids: 'Remember who you are, what you are and who you represent,' and David Rocastle and I used to spout it out as a joke. The first time I came across the 'Good old Arsenal' thing, the idea of it being some sort of professional Corinthian Casual sort of club with high moral standards, was when a couple of other Gunners started singing it to wind up some of the Liverpool lads on an England trip, Stuart Pearce joining in for effect.

Where George and I did coincide was in our fiercely determined attitude towards the job. It was probably why he made me captain. He could see in me a person who could carry out what he was trying to achieve. 'Desire plus talent equals success,' he used to repeat and I would agree with him. A lot of my relationship with him was unspoken, though; we walked the walk rather than talked the talk. Mostly I knew instinctively what he wanted. He would show us so clearly on the training ground what it was, so it was just a question of me reinforcing it.

There were a mixture of feelings around him. The dominant one was fear, because of the power you knew he had. He was stronger than us off the pitch. I could probably have eaten him alive if he had been a centre-forward, but the body language off the pitch, what with that Scottish mask of his, definitely said: 'I'm the boss. Be careful.' We poked fun, as far as we could, at that stiffness about him.

But there was also an admiration for him at what he was doing for us in winning trophies.

On the coach to away games he would sit at the front, with the card school taking place in the seats just behind him. We'd tease him a bit – though stopped short of calling him by his nickname among the players, 'Gadaffi' – and wind him up by doing the things he didn't like. 'Stop swearing, Wrighty! Language, Bouldy!' he would shout. Sometimes someone would put a blue movie on the video and at the first sign of a woman's breast, he'd be outraged.

'What is this?' he would complain loudly. 'Get this off.'

'But boss, we're grown men. We can watch this,' someone would reply, but he would then put on whatever film he wanted to watch, and he loved his films. Anything without nudity in it. We didn't really mind, it was all good banter, and we were successful. These were the happy times.

At least until what I called the Tuesday club – the drinking sessions I organised – had been in session for a while. These took place in weeks when there was no midweek game and after a physical day on the Tuesday of running up and down the terraces, we were free until Thursday and could go out on the piss. It developed a camaraderie and was good for us.

Then, all the grievances about contracts and tactics would come out as the beer went down. It was like talking about the headmaster behind his back. 'We're fed up with George. Go and tell him,' the lads would say. I never did. I didn't really have the capability at that time. I didn't see him as approachable and I didn't have it in me to confront him. He was the boss and we were achieving. I probably didn't agree with them most of the time, anyway. They said the 'Son of George' stuff tongue in cheek, but they probably meant it. 'Every time you talk to him you're signing a new contract, and we haven't had a new one for four years,' they would moan.

Actually, I probably should have been more assertive when it came to the subject of contracts after we won the '91 title. If I had held out for more then, maybe the other lads' wages would have gone up and the resentments they felt towards George in later years, the feeling that he wasn't doing enough on our behalf with the board, might have been averted. Instead, he was able to say, 'Look, Tony Adams is only on this amount,' to other players and insist to the outside world that our wages policy was as good as anybody's, because Tony Adams wouldn't stay if it wasn't. He definitely had the upper hand in that department.

You would never socialise with George. It just wasn't done. On something like a pre or post-season trip, on the night before he was allowing us to go out he would personally check out the nightclubs in whichever city we were in, then give me a list of two or three for the lads, keeping the best one back for himself. Occasionally, by accident, we would run into him in a club we weren't supposed to be in. He was always dressed in a very dapper way, even when in casual clothes, and usually reeked of Paco Rabane aftershave, as Martin Hayes always pointed out to us.

George was an astonishing worker on the training field, and would very rarely take a day off. Those times when he wasn't there, we'd treat as a day off. He liked to do all the coaching himself and was highly motivated. The work was never frivolous. About once a season he would let you have a five-a-side kickabout, but he had to be in a very good mood. Then he had to win. But he'd gone really as a player, and he would lose patience. 'Right, that's enough,' he'd say if he was losing and walk off to do something else. He reckoned he was a great header of the ball, and in fact old footage of some of his goals bore him out. He used to show Alan Smith how to do it. He would walk across a room moving his head from side to side. 'Your flick, your flick, your flick,' he would say. Then he would walk back the other way, head going back and forward like a chicken, neck muscles straining, and repeat: 'Your power, your power, your power.' Yes, it was quite comical.

He was a very canny motivator. He used the media, the way Alex Ferguson has with Manchester United. 'Look at them,' he used to say. 'They hate us. They hate the way we play, but it's successful, isn't it?' I remember once that Johnny Giles had written a column about me, saying that I couldn't play. 'Look at that, Tony. Look what's he's saying about you,' George said. 'He hated me back in 1971 because we beat Leeds and he's taking it out on you, saying you can't play. You know what we're trying to achieve here, don't you? Don't let him get to you.' By the end, so impressionable was I, that I would be agreeing with George and wanting to get out there and prove Johnny Giles wrong. Somehow, I would end up hating him as if I had played in '71 as well, when I had never even met the bloke.

George's team talks were always very passionate, precise and economical. If it was a home game, we would meet at South Herts Golf Club and four hours before kick-off be presented with his dossier on the opposition that he had the chief scout Steve Rowley compile. On the day before, you had worked on how you yourselves were going to play, on all your set pieces, and now you found out how the other team set themselves out. You knew the strengths and weaknesses of your immediate opponent, what formation they would adopt, what set plays they would use. Then George would go through it all.

It would go something like this: 'Now, their keeper. Been a good keeper but getting on a bit now. Doesn't fancy crosses these days and he's a bit overweight so get shots in on him. First corner, Tony, put him in the back of the net. The right-back can't tackle, so take him on. That central defender, Wrighty pull him wide on the left wing, he goes walkabout. The other one's too slow so run at him, make him turn, get some balls over the top of him. Left-back, he's gone. Midfield, close them down, they don't like it if you're at them all the time. They'll pack it in.' And on it went in that deep Scottish brogue that Kevin Campbell was always the best at imitating. 'Tony, your man does a bit with his left foot so push him to his right and win your headers against him. If you don't, you're in trouble. Martin Keown: You're marking this bloke today. Stick to him like glue. If you don't, you're out. Wrighty: I want 10 runs from you in the first half.' And if Ian didn't make 10 runs in the first 45 minutes, there would be an argument in the dressing room at half-time. It got personal once or twice. If Wrighty went off to the toilet, George would shout after him: 'That's it. Go and sulk like a baby.'

We would leave the golf club about two hours before kick-off and George's next input would be in the dressing room ten minutes before the start. Nigel Winterburn was always in the toilet at this point and George would usually shout to find out if he could hear him. Once he had got the distant 'yes' from Nigel, George was off again. 'Lee Dixon, get your tackles in ...' right the way through the team, leaving you in no doubt about your job for the day. Maybe we became robots in some areas of the game, but everyone knew where they stood and a lot of players like that. 'We have standards at this club,' George would say and he made sure you knew what they were.

He was rarely elated at the end of the game if we had won. Sometimes, you would know from that smirk of his that he was pleased enough with you. Usually, he would knock you down after the match and build you up for the next one during the next few days. His first assistant, Theo Foley, was a cheerful Irishman who would always build you up, but later George's next assistant Stewart Houston was another knock-downer. A pat on the back can work better than a kick up the backside. Sometimes George would go over the top in his criticism. I remember Paul Merson once taking the wind out of his sails, though. He was really ripping into Merse at half-time of a game and Merse, still in his drinking days then, simply said: 'Well, I told you I wasn't fit.' George just fell silent while everyone else sniggered.

The worst time with me was at half-time during a pre-season friendly against Celtic, when George accused me of not trying. I just went quiet, then went out in the second half and kicked everything in a green and white shirt. You knew that George was really upset with a performance when he was quiet.

I've thought about whether I liked George and decided that the word 'like' is too simple. If you took the football out of the scenario, I think we'd get on famously well because we have a lot in common. We are both driven. That was why in the end I was so sad at the time of the European Super Cup against Milan in early 1995 when I felt he had let his intensity for the game slip and showed little enthusiasm for the contest. Also, I think that beneath the smart image, the tough guy, lies a more vulnerable and sensitive man than people imagine.

Could he have done anything to help me address my drinking? Who knows. Perhaps there were times when he could have been tougher with me, rather than indulging me and enabling me to keep drinking. Perhaps he could have been concerned for my welfare rather than that of the team at times. But I was an alcoholic denying I had a problem, so it would have been hard for him not to deny it too. I do know he could never have stopped me. And he was a realist. He needed me performing and didn't want to do anything to upset that. If I had not been performing, then he would have come down on me.

The 'bungs' episode I could never understand because of our different attitude to money. After he had lost the Arsenal job and was banned from the game for a year, in the period before he took the job at Leeds, he phoned me once and asked me to get my Dad to give him a call to arrange to come round to his house in Hampstead for a chat. That was the way we did things; I always used to take my Dad to contract talks.

It was a lovely afternoon and George showed us around his garden, which he was very proud of, and offered my Dad a drink. He had been busy, he said, writing letters. He received so much mail. He told Dad that I had been brilliant for him. I think George still felt angry and bitter about the way things had turned out at Arsenal, where he thought he should have been a hero rather than a figure who left in disgrace. He wanted me to explain to the players why he didn't do as well financially for them as he might have, that his hands were tied. 'The club was bigger than all of us,' he said and told me to get as much as I could in my next deal. There was still a formality between us, and I think his pride was covering up his true feelings.

That night I felt sadness around him, rather than the resentment that some of the players may have nursed. What we achieved was amazing and I will be able to look back on so much success in my career because of George Graham.

Maybe I was good for him. He was good for me, too.

I couldn't say the same of Bruce Rioch, because I was hardly there for him. It was such a shame that a painful time in my life coincided with his time at Arsenal, because I liked the guy and appreciated the things he was trying to do. That night on the pre-season tour of Sweden, I was staggered that he wanted me to sit up with him and have a beer and talk about me, about the game. I think it was about 5 am before I went to bed. He said he wanted me to 'express myself' and I don't think he was too impressed by the way George had the team playing in the last couple of seasons. Bruce wanted a more exciting and open game, involving more dropping-off and counter-attacking.

For me it was an interesting period, what with new ideas I was also getting from Terry Venables at international level. Under George I had always done what I was instructed to do; it worked, after all. Sometimes, though, I would wonder whether the press had a point about ball-playing centre-halves. They always seemed to love players like Mark Wright. 'Forget Mark Wright,' George would say. 'He's never won anything. He's a weak link. As soon as he brings the ball out and loses it, bang, we go into the space he's left. You know your job Tony, and you do it well.' He was right, but just sometimes I'd go away and I'd be kicking the ball into touch, keeping clean sheets, and wondering if there was more to enjoying the game than this.

Under Bruce, and later Arsène Wenger, I was encouraged to start playing and I think people were a bit surprised. They might even have realised that I wasn't a donkey after all. And I felt like saying, 'Well, of course I'm not. I've been telling you that for fifteen years, but no-one would listen. I've been under orders. And I was winning things. But I can play. It actually takes a good player to perform in a restricted way for the good of the team, you know.' After George, Bruce was also very different in the way he would open up to you. I remember him one day coming into training talking about having had a really good pillow fight with his young son. He loved his family and his home life and I respected that. But footballers being footballers, they took the mickey out of him behind his back. George never left himself vulnerable to anything personal like that.

I think one of the mistakes Bruce made was in the way he dealt with certain players, notably Ian Wright. Now, I think even George found Wrighty a difficult character to deal with sometimes, but he realized he was the best when it came to being an out-and-out finisher and he knew how to get the best out of him. He would yell at him in training and games. 'Wrighty, make some runs. You're not doing it!' And Ian would get fired up and shout back. 'You Scottish bastard! Yes I am.' And then he would make some runs. And then he would score a goal. So George would let him have his head.

Bruce started laying the law down, telling Ian that he shouldn't be doing promotional stuff, that he should start wearing a collar and tie, that sort of thing. Ian resented it. He also didn't like being told, as Bruce did one day at training, how John McGinlay had done things at Bolton when Ian knew he had twice as much talent. It worked for Bruce at places like Middlesbrough and Bolton where he turned ordinary players into good ones, but he had trouble when it came to international superstars. He couldn't bully players at Arsenal. He was another of these old-fashioned football men who demanded discipline and found anything outside of the game distracting. It made sense that his father had been a sergeant major.

You could also see that he had once had trouble keeping

his temper in check. He would get very angry with some of the younger players who didn't have his motivation and couldn't do things properly; he would go in very hard on them in the tackle during training. He used to tell the boys that he had had to do a lot of work on himself. 'I lost it once,' he admitted. 'And I have to watch myself.' As someone who was full of anger himself, I could understand. Bruce was a very good player, a World Cup player with Scotland, and it can get frustrating trying to teach people with lesser ability.

It was also a frustration for him that he was never in total control of the club the way he had been at Middlesbrough and Bolton. After George, the board decided they were going to do all the transfer deals and just asked Bruce for names of players he wanted. At first, he gave them sensible ones, like Tim Sherwood at Blackburn, but when they were unable to get them and would not let him go for players himself, the joke around the club was that he was starting to take the mickey by giving them names like Pele and Maradona. Certainly Alan Shearer was one name he advanced at a time when the signing would have been impossible.

In such an atmosphere, Bruce was clearly not going to thrive and with a striker who didn't like him as well as a captain who was never there, his days were numbered. He had looked like an Arsenal man, with his upright image, but now I think the old guard had had their say and the vice-chairman David Dein took more control, saying that the club had to modernise. In came Arsène Wenger with his ideas from abroad about fitness and tactics. Bruce had been the bridge between George and him because Arsène certainly was different from anything the boys had experienced before.

Whereas with George I simply lived on my wits and instincts, I found myself with Arsène taking much more notice of his methods. I suppose it had something to do with the age I got to as a player and also with a new awareness I had acquired in my life. I have to say I like Arsène a great deal, I think he is a really nice guy.

He has a lot of qualities. He is a thinker, a listener and he cares a great deal about the welfare of players, as was seen when he sent me to the South of France for a week's rehabilitation when he could have been pressing me to play at what was an important time for the team. He is certainly an educated man, well qualified, and I think he knows professional footballers inside out. He can tell just by how a player runs whether he is fully fit or not. In fact, I don't think he actually needs a fitness coach on the staff. He knows himself how to get players into the best working order. Training is short and sharp, conducted with a stopwatch.

He likes to keep his methods mostly to himself, but I don't think I am revealing too much when I say that training can often last only 45 minutes. We will have stretching and a warm-up, then play a 10-minutes each way small-sided game and finish with a run round the pitch. The first time he introduced us to his stretching routines was at Blackburn when he called us all down into the hotel ballroom and put us through the routine for half an hour. There was some joking amongst the boys, who were all pretending to be still sleepy and putting on the tiredness, because we probably feared change. But just because it was different didn't make it wrong. It helped that we went on to win the game that day and now it is second nature to us.

He does set out a diet for the players, but it is not regimented. After all the chicken and pasta at lunchtime, the English players like a bit of spotted dick or bread-and-butter pudding and custard, for example. The French and Dutch players do poke fun at us. Arsène also issues us with vitamin pills and supplements. Before a game, I still like a Mars bar and a cup of tea and he will say: 'No Tony, no sugar. You have to eat more carrots, more raw vegetables.'

We also have regular massages and once a month Arsène will fly in from France a guy he trusts called Philippe, who is a mixture of osteopath and masseur, who realigns players' bodies. I now feel fitter than I ever have and can touch my toes with no trouble, and can bring my leg up behind my head. I know Steve Bould also says he feels fitter and more flexible than ever and the older players can now see the value of it all. If it extends your career, that means your earning power goes on, after all.

I would say that Arsène is a very good judge of character but not necessarily a Tony Adams-type motivator, certainly no shouter and bawler. He is a professional and finds it hard to understand that players themselves may not always be, that they may need firing up. He likes players to take responsibility for their own game and that has been a culture shock for some of the older players who grew up under George and were used to being told what to do, rather than think for themselves. Sometimes English players like to know where they stand. They have certainly developed a respect for him, though, mainly because he didn't come in and try to turn everything round overnight. He left the good things well alone.

Arsène is exceptionally thorough and focused on football. It is his life. Often, on his day off he will fly to France to watch a match. If not, he will stay at home and watch a video. He is very studious. After his initial nickname of 'Clouseau', the players then called him

'Windows' because of those boffin's glasses. I think he can forget that players may not be as dedicated to the game as him. Certainly, I think he gets annoyed by all the talk about money in the game and is concerned by players' wage demands.

I think he has also had to learn about the passion of the English, not that he doesn't have a passion for the game but that the crowd like to see people living the game. It seems strange, the English teaching the French about passion. At Highbury, for example, they have enjoyed Patrick Vieira getting in tackles and will cheer loudly when he does. It was not so long ago that it was standard fare, and they would only really get excited when it was sustained. Now the crowd has accepted that patience is required when it comes to the European game, but at home in some games you need to match fire with fire and have it in your belly.

Sometimes Arsène does not appear a great communicator when it comes to team talks. They are certainly minimalist in both instruction and motivation, as is his coaching. He likes to make observations, rather than give orders. But then it was a skill to recognise that all that the back four had learned under George Graham could not be improved upon. He expects players to know their job without having constantly to tell them. He likes to let players go, likes them to have the freedom to perform.

Arsène's method is different to George's, but then both ways have worked and brought success. For me, both were perfect at the time of my life I found myself in when they were in charge. People always think that change is going to be for the worse, but it has been shown to me that this is not the case. And I have seen great change.

Playmates

WHEN I was 16, Don Howe took me with the first team to a pre-season friendly at Wolverhampton Wanderers. I had been told I was doing well and I was delighted. I revelled in just being on the coach and having a three-course meal, enjoying all the luxuries I now take for granted. I even thought I might be on the substitutes' bench, such was my confidence and ambition. I was somewhat disappointed, therefore, when Don told me to spend my afternoon watching everything David O'Leary did.

What an eye-opening experience it was, though. Don told me to take note of how David prepared for the game, how he ran and how he played, even how he stretched – and he was performing stretching exercises long before they became fashionable. People said that David lasted as long as he did – a record 724 appearances for the club – because he didn't make tackles. I saw that day that he didn't have to, because he was such a clever defender. I began to think. Yes, the guy's had a long career. He's looked after himself. There must be something to it. And I began to learn.

Then, a short time after, I was sitting at Highbury watching a first-team game in which Willie Young was playing alongside David. When Arsenal won a corner, a woman next to me up in the stand started the chant of 'Willie, Will-ie, Will-ie,' and everyone joined in as he ran forward. Now Willie wasn't a great player, although he may have been a good header of the ball, but it was a lesson to me that being a wholehearted player would get the crowd on your side. You had David with a bit of class and Willie who would run through brick walls. It occurred to me that I could be a mixture of that. They were probably the first two colleagues to make an impression on me. In two decades with the club since signing as a schoolboy, there have been many more.

My first partner in defence in the youth team was Martin Keown. He once came and stayed over at my house in Essex and when we went out to a club, he provided some good entertainment by dancing on his own, this boy from Oxford going through whatever repertoire that was out on the floor at Ilford Palais. Martin has had to endure a lot and has come through with great character. At that age, everybody poked fun at him. Once, he fell asleep under a sun lamp and came into training with an orange face. He also had to have matching T-shirt and socks, it was his trademark.

Also, someone once put a hot teaspoon on the back of his neck and he turned round and thumped the guy. Actually, he usually had a fight in training once a week, because he was so intense about his job. One day, he asked Don if he could kick Charlie Nicholas in training because Charlie was nutmegging him all the time. Martin was never part of the gang, but it paid off for him because he was very dedicated and he made it whereas some of the gang didn't.

My first real pal in the first team was Kenny Sansom. As a player I admired him because he was quick, enthusiastic and talented, but it was as a drinking partner that I really enjoyed his company. He was so outgoing and funny and was always telling jokes at the bar and doing impressions. At that time, he was exactly what I wanted to be. All his jokes were centred on pubs, such as: 'An elephant walks into a pub and asks for a pint of lager and a packet of crisps. The barman says, "That'll be three pounds and fifty pence please" and tells him that they don't get many elephants in here. So the elephant says, "Well, I'm not surprised at these prices."' I once saw him do his Lt Columbo impression in front of Bobby Robson on an England plane: 'Mr Robson, my wife thinks you're terrific,' he said as everyone laughed.

I became David O'Leary's partner in defence when I first made the first team and I soon noticed how he could get by in every department of the game. He could jump with the best tall strikers and cope with the quickest, smallest ones. Sometimes it annoyed me how laid-back he was when I was so wound-up. Stewart Robson always said that it must be hard work for David to walk his dogs and used to joke with him that he ought to get the butler to do it. David always needed someone around to motivate him and I think he was lucky that he had characters like me and George Graham, something David came to acknowledge himself. George always used to say that David was fortunate to get his medals when he was playing in a back three ten years before everyone else.

There were times when David and George didn't get on because David was a composed and constructive sort of player and George liked tacklers and defenders who would go through people. David was a 'nicker' of the ball, who would guide forwards wide rather than close them down. But he adapted because he was a good and clever pro. I came to like him a lot and we became room-mates, one of several I would have including Niall Quinn, Gus Caesar, Martin Hayes, Paul Merson and Ray Parlour. While David was grateful in the end that he had this precocious kid pushing him all over the place, for me he became a father figure at times, later trying to point me in the right direction on occasions when my drinking got out of hand.

At first I was annoyed that George replaced him with

Steve Bould, especially when Bouldy gave away a goal in that first match of his at Wimbledon. It had been the same when Lee Dixon came, because I had always loved Viv Anderson at right-back for his enthusiasm and how he made goals for me. But with Nigel Winterburn also having arrived, George clearly knew what he was doing. We were to develop into a unique back four that would last more than ten years. You wonder if it will ever happen again.

Lee's main asset has always been his mobility. He came to a big club and seized his chance, getting forward, crossing the ball well and scoring some great goals out of the blue. He was never going to help me get goals from set plays by heading the ball as Viv had done, but as a quick covering player he helped me at the other end. Later, he developed into a very knowledgeable player who could read the game well, knowing the angles and where to be. I know all this stuff about 'If Lee Dixon can play for England, so can I' hurt him, just as the donkey stuff hurt me. We are human beings, after all. During one of my absences through injury, I was once in the directors' box at Aston Villa watching the game when Lee sliced a ball into touch by mistake and somebody there shouted it out. I just turned round and said, 'Excuse me, but he's a friend of mine.' It shut them up. It is also rubbish. You don't play for so long at the top level without having some talent. It's no fluke.

In analysing Lee, you are really speaking about Nigel as well. You could almost hold up a mirror across the field. They were probably the first of the wing-backs that are now so common in the English game except that as well as being good bombing forward, they were better defensively than most wing-backs are these days. Nigel, having been brought up at Wimbledon, probably likes a tackle a bit more than Lee, who's more of a nicker, though he can also get stuck in. Nigel was probably unfortunate to be playing the game at the same time as Stuart Pearce, which limited his international appearances. What is amazing about the pair is the consistency of performance they have shown. There have never really been any lasting troughs with them. They have been good pros; fit, agile, flexible and reliable.

Then you come to Bouldy, who seems to have more hair now than ten years ago. He was just what George needed – and Steve, in agreement with George, thought Mark Wright was too flash a defender. 'You can take risks in midfield and attack,' Steve has always said, 'but not at the back. You'll get found out over the course of a season and give away goals.' Steve has always had more about him than an out-and-out stopper, though, which strangely enough Graham Taylor never recognised when you might have thought he would be Graham's sort of player. Terry Venables did, and he liked defenders who could use the ball. I also don't just want stoppers playing for my country; you can get those over on Hackney Marshes. Defending is an art. They must be able to run, tackle and head the ball as well as having positional sense. It's not just turn up and kick everything in sight. Steve has been saddled unfairly with that description.

Steve doesn't take chances, mind, and in some ways I have striven to be like him. If I was looking for a centre-half, he is what I would go for: calm, strong, determined, never loses a header. Rock solid. Get the ball and give it. End of story. Now sometimes I might find that boring, because I feel I have got talent bursting out of me, but it's a talent in itself just to do the simple thing well. In our '91 title-winning team, I thought he was the best in the country at the time. Now, I think Arsène Wenger has been good for

Bouldy. He has extended his career by fitness stretching, all the new exercises probably getting him an extra year or two at the highest level.

Of course, you can take four good defenders but they don't just become a good unit by accident. The durability has been down to the characters themselves but also down to hard work. And it can be repetitious and tedious. Then it works. In training with George, we would constantly work on forwards against defence. At first it was one on one, with the ball thrown to the attacker and the defender working him. Then two v two, to learn how to work as a pair. Then a back four moving together – as comically the *Fever Pitch* and *The Full Monty* films made great play of – getting organized, dropping off to cover the run. 'No, no, no, stop. Like this,' George would interrupt. He would stand with his arms outstretched. 'My shoulders are the centre-backs and the palms of my hands the full backs,' he would say. And he would move his arms to show how the movement of all four components should be linked.

Contrary to perception, we never set out to step up and catch people offside. If a forward is intelligent enough – like Gary Lineker, Ian Wright or Dennis Bergkamp – to bend his runs and pull off a defender, you can't do that. If there is no pressure on the ball in midfield, you have to drop and you can't play offside. But if there is pressure on the ball, then you can squeeze up. And we did hold a line. It was simple and we did it every day. If you can get a midfield four working on the same lines to cover the back four, like AC Milan did in their heyday, then you are in business. Then, if you've got a front two also doing it, as a centre-half you can play until you are 35. Good players working hard was the maxim, the same ethic as Manchester United have these days and we try to retain. Some people thought that the defence might not be so tight with the arrival of the new rules that made attackers who were level with the last defender onside instead of offside, and ruling out the tackle from behind. 'It's not quite so enjoyable now, is it, Tone?' Steve Bould said to me, tongue in cheek, lamenting that he could no longer take the forward as well as the ball, but in all seriousness I thought we adapted well, as good players do. It was the same when the back pass rule was changed; we changed as well. Looking back and watching tapes of old games, you wonder how you ever conceded a goal. You could do your fancy turn to shrug off the attacker, then knock it back to the keeper. Simple. No such luxury now.

It was a compliment to Arsenal, really, that it was our defence that was being questioned and nobody else's. It was because we were seen, I'm sure, as the best. I do think we have to be careful about taking tackling out of the game, mind. I remember as a kid being on the beach in Spain and going in strongly when I was playing with the local kids and they hated it. The absence of contact makes the game dull for me, it just makes it like basketball. I'm sure the crowds want to see contact as well. Our game in England is strong and passionate and that is why it is watched all over the world more than any other.

Such was the system in place at Arsenal that players could come in and do the job almost seamlessly. We won two Cups with Andy Linighan in the back four, for example. He worked on it too, he knew the drill, just as Martin Keown did. It was also physically very taxing, which was why George collected centre-backs, it appeared, for fun. You never knew when another would be needed due to injury or suspension. And of course sometimes George liked to play a three. Mostly he would say that if you've got two good 'uns you don't need three, but in away games where you were going to get bombarded, at Watford or Wimbledon, or when you had wide areas to defend, like at Old Trafford, then it made sense. We also used it against Liverpool, when they played the split centre-forward system of Rush with Dalglish deeper. Rush was actually quoted once as saying he didn't know where to make his runs against Arsenal. Was Dalglish talented or what? I can still see a curler into the top left corner past Pat Jennings at Highbury. Apart from individual moments of skill, we could be caught out now and then, though, as Graham Taylor showed with Aston Villa and Howard Wilkinson with Leeds, by two big wide men either side of a central striker pulling the three around.

Sometimes in those situations, we would be saved by our goalkeeper and I have never seen one better than David Seaman. Before him, I am afraid I saw Pat Jennings past his sell-by date and as a confident kid, I used to moan at him. David O'Leary always insisted that Pat was the best, but I am afraid I never saw it. John Lukic in 1989 was magnificent, coming for every high ball, which as a defender is what you want from your goalkeeper. At that he was almost in the class of Bruce Grobbelaar, whom Alan Hansen must have loved because he never had to head a ball.

I don't think Dave realised how tough an environment it was going to be when he first came to Arsenal, and having scored against him when he was with Queens Park Rangers, I didn't realise he was as good as he was. He can actually play, as well; he can juggle a ball better than me. He was also fortunate to have Bob Wilson as his coach, which was another strength of George's – getting good people around him. George tried to integrate Dave into our training, working with the back four and having him kick the ball up to Alan Smith in certain areas, but after ten minutes or so, George always got the message from them that Dave and Bob felt that they should be off somewhere else working on all the specialist things that goalkeepers work on.

But Dave respected what George was trying to achieve and liked the demarcation of the goalkeeper being expected to police a certain area of the field and the defenders knowing which areas were theirs. We tried not to let teams penetrate deep into our box on top of him and David's part of the deal was that he came for the ball. He didn't come enough for George sometimes but he came plenty. He always did his research as well, and a lot of angles and positions that other goalkeepers adopt these days are down to him. He has also worked on techniques of saving where you don't have to dive. It's the same with a defender; you don't always have to run around like an idiot to do the job properly. Who was the best, Peter Shilton or David Seaman? It is an impossible comparison because of the way the game has changed. Both were the best of their eras.

It is the same with midfield players. I know Arsenal fans have pined for a Liam Brady for a long time but the game is much quicker now. Could 'Chippy' still have been as creative at the highest pace in the systems we had to play to win league titles? I know Arsenal won the FA Cup with him and he was an exceptional passer at that time, but we were in the business of winning Championships in a more demanding time, for which you needed strength and pace and work and determination, as well as talent, all rolled into one.

It may surprise the Highbury faithful, but I actually think Michael Thomas was better than Liam Brady. He was an incredible athlete and would run up and down the pitch for you all day long. And he was strong. He could do press-ups with George Graham sitting on his back. He had the right attitude for the team. Once, when Norman Whiteside did something nasty to David Rocastle, Mickey came from midfield, Viv Anderson from right-back to converge on Whiteside and sort him out. You wanted Mickey on your side in those days.

David Rocastle, now there was another. Actually, if you are going to compare anyone with Liam, it is Rocky. He could dribble past four players and put the ball into the roof of the net with a mixture of strength and skill. He also got back and helped out Lee Dixon as well. Not only could David dribble and pass, he would tackle and work as well, even though he was blind as a bat and had to wear contact lenses. Unfortunately for David, he was never quite the same after a bad knee injury. As a defender, half of your work is done in your head but with a player like him, it was explosive pace and he never quite recaptured it. You can do a trick all day long, but if your full back can get back to cover it, you don't have much of a chance.

When I started, we had Graham Rix, who was an excellent passer as well but who would soon find the likes of Michael Thomas snapping at his heels. Vladimir Petrovic was another talented guy. The first choices in the centre, though, were usually Paul Davis, much more of a worker to go with his talent than people gave him credit for, and Steve Williams. Steve, who was a classy and dynamic player, introduced me to the money side of the game and I think he ended up quite a wealthy man. He could also be quite spiteful on the field and irreverent off it. He always used to wind me up by saying that Mark Wright, with whom he had played at Southampton, was better than me. He also told David O'Leary that it wasn't right that a centre-half kept playing a full season with no injuries or suspensions. Rumour has it that at Southampton he once goaded Alan Ball by asking him what he had ever won.

Under George, the midfield had to be solid and I know the fans were never really impressed by John Jensen or even Stefan Schwarz, though they knew what was expected of them. I always liked as protection Mickey Thomas and Paul Davis as a pair, the one physically, the other verbally and we needed people to go hunting as pairs in there.

Then the French duo of Patrick Vieira and Emmanuel Petit developed quickly after linking up and came to provide the same shield for the back four, one going forward and one sitting back, Patrick playing the short balls and Manu the longer ones. They became a good blend. Mickey and Patrick were similar, dynamic box-to-box players with an ability to score goals but Patrick's defensive contribution gives him an extra dimension, especially at set plays where his height is invaluable.

For all the criticism of our central midfield, I think we have always had areas of the park that were exceptional; wide on the left, for example. I am afraid Perry Groves doesn't quite fit in the highest company here, but he did provide one of my funniest moments at Highbury, when he was once being carried off and fell off the stretcher behind the goal at the North Bank End. We could hardly play for laughing. Perry was renowned for making amazing recoveries from injuries; no chance during the week, then fit on a Saturday.

Brian Marwood made a huge impact first, then Anders Limpar, who was really hot in '91. Brian was more the solid pro, Anders was all quickness of feet with no backlift, who had trouble sustaining his talent. Into the left-wing tradition came Marc Overmars, who really got it back after a flat middle period during the 1997/98 season and blossomed in the spring. He has been a real flyer and really was a key figure in the third title, not only with his ability to get by defenders and get crosses in but also for his goal-scoring knack, as he contributed fourteen goals during the season.

We were lucky in the past that we also had Paul Merson, who could play either wide on the left or up front, where he preferred, just off a target man but because of the players we had, and because of his own versatility, he was switched quite a lot. Paul was what you might call a luxury player, only because of the skills he had as a passer and finisher but he was always willing to sweat, though by his own admission it got tough when his own addictions to gambling, drink and drugs were in full flow. I was lucky, too, that he was in recovery when I decided to quit drinking as he was a great help and encouragement to me. Before he made his move to Middlesbrough, we helped each other out when we were rooming together.

Merse was one of the clever and exceptional players that people overlooked when they tagged us boring. The fans always saw Charlie Nicholas as exceptional in my early days at the club, but I am afraid I didn't at that time. Sure, he could do things with the ball but talent without application was not my idea of a professional footballer and he was never going to be a part of what George was trying to do. I couldn't look Charlie in the eye sometimes, so little respect did I have for him in those days. There would be stories of him out on the town every night and pieces of paper with phone numbers on used to fall out of his pockets when he got changed for training. I never wanted all that. I never played football to get the birds, even though they stood around the touchline at school. I was too busy in my world, trying to get on. He used to poke fun at my dedication and once he pulled all the buttons off my shirt, which really annoyed me. Now I understand more and taking into consideration my drinking days, I am in no position to judge him. I feel less harsh towards him and I think he himself regrets quite of bit of the excesses of his time in London.

My first mate was Niall Quinn as we came through the youth team together. We had a lot of laughs trawling round the North London social clubs, up and down the Holloway Road, and I was very disappointed when George replaced him with Alan Smith. It shows sometimes that players are not the best judges of other players and that your heart can rule your head because 'Smeggy' could do all that Niall could do and more. He held the ball up, made runs, got into the channels and scored goals, twice winning the English Golden Boot. He was a great header of the ball, well taught by George who had been better in the air than me, my Dad used to say. Alan would certainly be in my top five of headers, along with David Platt, another who is aggressive in the air and times his jumps well.

Alan was always such a nice guy as well, no airs and graces to him. He was 50 years old when he was 25, I think. He always hated being called 'nice'. He wanted to get booked to show that he could be a bit of a hard nut, but that only ever happened once, in the 1993 FA Cup Final replay. 'I can be tough you know,' he would say to me. 'Anyway, what's wrong with being nice? You're too mean, you are.'

The striker who has had the most impact at Highbury in my time, though, is undoubtedly Ian Wright, breaker of Cliff Bastin's goalscoring record of 178 for the club. He is quite simply the best finisher I have ever seen. He will never be a Dennis Bergkamp in terms of football intelligence, nor an Alan Shearer in the art of being a defending centre-forward, but his passion and love for the game, allied to his lightning pace and reactions, has made him a phenomenal striker. I never let him score against me when he was at Crystal Palace, mind. He joked that he was holding back because he knew he would be joining us.

The one problem with Ian, from a team point of view, is that he became such a focal point for attacks. When we had Niall Quinn in the side, the temptation was to knock the ball long to him all the time. With Ian you could hardly help yourself sending the ball over the top for him to run on to. It can make you lazy, so that you were looking for the 1–0 all the time and if it didn't come off, you didn't have other options. In an exceptional side like that of '91, I don't think it would matter, but when you are not all-round so talented, you lose part of your game and other players do not contribute as much. I know my own return of goals went down, because quite often Ian was popping up in positions at set pieces that I might have taken. I confess to wondering if we would ever win another title with Ian in the team.

There are several reasons why Ian did not play for England more often than he did. Two were Gary Lineker and Alan Shearer, both exceptional and with a need to be the central striker, with a deeper man playing off them. In international football, the one-on-one marking is a lot tighter and you have to play with your head rather than your heart more often. Also, the ball over the top is never going to be so successful because most international teams have very clever sweepers who pick it off. Still, Ian probably should have played more often than he did.

As a character, he could be more shy than people believed him to be, what with the image he projected on television, but there is no doubt that he was very bubbly and kept everyone entertained, even if it was hard work being around him 24 hours a day. He is a loveable, flamboyant, charismatic and honest guy and I just hope he never loses any of that. The problem is that people always want a part of him and he doesn't know how to say no. He will not refuse an autograph even if he is out for a quiet meal with his family – and I think at times that is being unfair on your family who need and deserve your full attention. It all takes its toll on him.

'People love flash people,' he once said to me. 'Yes, Ian,' I said, 'but be careful what it does to you. All this need to be constantly energetic may be at your expense.' I told him not to lose himself, because I lost me, but I don't think he will. He is at that time of life when he is taking stock and moving on, most evident in his transfer to West Ham, and I think he will make the right decisions. Of course, he has had his disciplinary problems and I have to be honest and say we were annoyed when they hurt the team sometimes, with him being suspended, but as the tattoo he has on his arm says: let he who is without sin cast the first stone.

It is strange how images can deceive. You would think in many ways that Ian and Dennis Bergkamp would be opposite people and in terms of noise and silence, they probably are. But Dennis's Iceman look also conceals a passion for the game. He really cares about winning, it is just that he shows it a different way. In that respect he is like Arsène Wenger, cool and sophisticated, unassuming even.

Anyone who outfoxes me at Wembley, as he did in 1993, must be quite some player. It was a hell of a goal, that chipped volley. Working with him every day, though, helped me to see that he was only human and enabled me to get revenge in Euro '96. He does have very quick feet and great intelligence and vision and you can miss what he does when he doesn't have the ball as he takes up some clever positions. I can give him no higher praise than to say that when he came to the club, his reputation having preceded him, I was determined to get the better of him in training after he had embarrassed me before – which was probably behind me being unable to look him in the eye, in fact, at first.

Dennis's contribution to the third title of my career at Highbury earns him a place in the Arsenal XI I would pick from my time with the club. It is always difficult comparing players over different eras and I have to say it has been a complete headache trying to get a balanced team. In many ways, the defence picks itself, but further forward I have had to make some difficult decisions, not least to leave out Ian Wright, the club's record goalscorer, from the starting line-up in the interests of the team. Still, it is a great problem for any manager to have. The one deficiency of this team is that it may lack some pace, but I do feel that if the movement is good you can cover for that. If we can't, then it is made for Wrighty to come off the bench. Of course, the formation is 4–4–2 and it lines up:

Seaman

Dixon   Adams   Bould   Winterburn

Rocastle   Vieira   Davis   Merson

Smith   Bergkamp

Substitutes: Wright, Thomas, Parlour, O'Leary, Overmars.

Manager: Graham, G.

EIGHT

England...

I looked out of the window of my hotel room. Snow was falling over Madrid. It never snows in Spain. Well, that's it then. The game'll be off. I won't get picked again. I'm only in this time anyway because he's got injuries. Mum and Dad and my sisters are flying out as well. Oh, well. Nice while it lasted.

That was the agitated state I was in on the morning of 18 February 1987. The day before, Bobby Robson had taken me to one side, said some nice things about me – that I had made a great start to my career and had a great future in the game – and told me I was going to play for England against Spain in Real Madrid's Bernabeu Stadium. Now the papers were saying I was to be the youngest central defender, at 20 years and 4 months, to make his debut since Bobby Moore. Except I wasn't because this snow was settling in the fields down below my window here just outside the city.

I knew I was close to the full squad because I had captained the Under 21s, having been through all the levels from Under-16 up, but I can't remember how or where I was when I first heard I was in the squad a week earlier. In those days I was resistant to the good feelings, wouldn't remember them. I would have been more likely to have been able to recall where I was, had I been left out, because I would probably have cursed and told myself I was better than the players they had picked. The part of Tony Adams that likes to be criticised so he can prove people wrong was dominant then. This was long before the part of Tony Adams who quietly enjoys his achievements and can recall them held sway.

I was more concerned about the plane journey than anything else, because of a fear of flying and not being around all the familiar Arsenal faces. A hundred things were going through a young, nervous, insecure mind. I was still trying to prove myself at club level, let alone internationally. How were these players I try to kick every week going to take to me? I had to play against Glenn Hoddle in training. He might show me up. Luckily Viv Anderson and Kenny Sansom were in the squad and Kenny took me under his wing. Or maybe he thought I was a soft touch – but was wrong. He had me in the card school on the plane with Peter Shilton and I won a few quid. It was the same going to training the day before the game.

And the same going to the ground for the game. Because it had stopped snowing and the match was on. Kenny was still being good to me, trying to take my mind off the game, but he was not happy that I was taking money off him. I was still feeling a bit overwhelmed in such company. Unlike at Arsenal, where I felt safe to express myself on and off the field, I was quiet and reserved. But it was still a funny thing about me. I may have got in only because Terry Fenwick and Mark Wright were injured, and I may have been feeling very apprehensive, but there was still a determination in me to do well and prove myself to everybody. Because deep down, I knew I could.

I was exceptionally fortunate to make my debut alongside Terry Butcher, and Bobby Robson had told me to watch everything he did and learn from him. Butch was a guy I could really relate to because he was so aggressive and cared so much about his club, country and profession. Meeting him, seeing him in training, being alongside him was to help me so much in my future England career. People said he was a bit slow but I thought he was technically excellent; good header, good left foot. I would pick him in my team ahead of someone with more talent simply because of his attitude. My one criticism was that he didn't use the ball enough, but then at that time we were stuck in quite rigid roles and didn't venture anything that we weren't asked to do.

Really I was too inexperienced to be playing but what an experience it was. I saw for the first time how the game could be slow in two thirds of the field, then all of a sudden quick in the final third. I was up against little Emilio Butragueno, the 'vulture' as he was known in Spain, and he was making runs all over the place. It was a real eye-opener. Of course he scored, and of course I blamed myself. I took responsibility, in fact, and felt quite down. As a young defender making your debut, the pressure is on you twice as much as if you are an attacker, with all due respect to Michael Owen, who became the youngest England international this century when he played – and excellently – against Chile as an 18-year-old. If a defender concedes a goal, it feels to him like the end of the world. If an attacker misses a chance, well, it doesn't seem quite so serious.

Looking back, I actually performed reasonably well. I was enthusiastic and worked very hard. I feel I grew up as a player very quickly as a result of the experience. It was, though, an early insight into how you can perform well or badly and both can go unnoticed if there is a different agenda for the media. Or at least you could in those days before there was so much space in newspapers, or air time on television and radio, devoted to sport in general and football in particular.

We won 4–2 and Gary Lineker scored all four, with Glenn Hoddle making all four. With the runs Links could make, that sort of score was always a possibility. Of course he was the main story, especially as he was at that time a Barcelona player coming into the home of Real Madrid and seeing off the country now providing him with his living. He had the bit between his teeth because at the time Johan Cruyff was playing him wide on the right for Barcelona and he had a point to prove to him. The sub-plot for the media, as it often seemed to be at that time, was: why doesn't Hoddle play like that all the time? Soon would come the other question with him: why isn't he in the team all the time? I was down the pecking order in terms of stories – though I'm sure it would have been different if I had made any more real howlers.

On the coach back to the airport, Kenny told me I was playing cards again. He and Shilts were my type of characters but gambling wasn't really my drug. I just wanted to give them the money to shut them up. But of course, being the person I was at that time, I didn't say anything. When I got home, after an Arsenal game on the Saturday, I got stuck into my – then – second drug to celebrate my England debut. A mate of mine who was a publican let me have a 166-pint barrel and I threw a party at Mum and Dad's house. They had stayed out in Spain for a few days' holiday and I found myself hurriedly clearing up on Sunday, the party having spilled over from Saturday night, before they came home. I think it helped that I signed my first England shirt and gave it to Mum and Dad.

Bobby Robson seemed to think I had done reasonably

well and I got another couple of caps in that first season, in Turkey and at home to Brazil. It was too soon for me to face the most charismatic and successful nation in world football, though. I didn't really savour the occasion and can't even remember which Brazilian I swopped shirts with. I had just won the Littlewoods Cup with Arsenal and wanted to be on the beach, drinking. There was also a match in Scotland, where I was a substitute, to fulfil at the end of that season. All I remember about it – apart from Mark Wright taking my place and performing very well, as he was prone to do away from Wembley, where I think he found the burden of expectation very high – is the training, during which I nutmegged Glenn. It was something I would bore my team-mates rigid about when I reported back for pre-season training.

By 1987/88, I was now Bobby Robson's first choice and played in 11 of the 12 matches that season. To be honest, I think there was a shortage of good centre-halves during the late 80s, with Bobby trying out a lot besides myself, including Gary Mabbutt, Gary Pallister and Dave Watson to go alongside Butch, and sometimes to replace him if he was injured. By far the most important game that season was the one against Yugoslavia in Belgrade, which we had to win to qualify for the European Championship finals in West Germany.

I spent most of the days leading up to the game in hot baths trying to ease a thigh strain, which also had the beneficial effect of taking my mind off the game because I was fearful about performing well. The game itself was on Armistice Day, 11 November, and Butch the great patriot was reminding us of our duty even in the tunnel as we waited to walk out on to the field. He was banging the wall with his fist but he was never out of control, just highly motivated and vocal – and very frightening to the opposition who looked across apprehensively at this aggressive, impressive figure. It must have helped because we were four up in an amazing first half hour when everything we did came off. I even scored my first international goal, meeting John Barnes's inswinging corner from the right around the near post powerfully to head home. My second was to come in a 2–2 draw against Holland in a friendly a few months later.

On the back of that 4–1 win in Yugoslavia, we went to West Germany with the nation's hopes high, but then again, when have they not been when the national team has travelled abroad for the finals of a major championship? It was with some justification, too, because it was probably just about the best team that could have been picked at that time. Following three defeats by the Republic of Ireland, Holland and the Soviet Union, we were home with our tails between our legs, however.

The problem, in my opinion, was that we were very much stuck in rigid formations at that time. Yes we had quality players, players you pine for these days in Bryan Robson, Hoddle – who was not a happy man at the championships with the way he was out then in, as he often seemed to be with England – Peter Beardsley, Lineker and John Barnes, but in formation we were flat and square with little movement except up and down the pitch. Trevor Steven would work the right flank, Barnes the left. Beardsley, when Bobby Robson had almost stumbled on him as the partner for Lineker at the World Cup in 1986 after trying target men, was the only exception as forerunner of the split centre-forward.

We missed the injured Terry Butcher badly. The team needed his stature and I needed his reassurance alongside.

Mark Wright, my partner, probably felt the same. Mark and I were similar types at the time, both young, and would have benefited from a stronger character than I was internationally in those days. It didn't help either that Gary Lineker was so listless and lacking sharpness at the tournament, something which would be explained when he was diagnosed with hepatitis soon after.

Also, we were out of European club football at the time as a result of the ban following the Heysel disaster and had little experience either of emulating or coping with continental opposition. All of a sudden players were making runs right, left and centre and you wondered how to defend them. Our midfield players were not used to making such runs themselves, or coached how to.

It was not until we got back into Europe, not until we had an influx of foreign players and coaches into the Premiership, not until Terry Venables melded it all together for England, that we really began to develop tactically. I think we also had foreign players on pedestals in those days and saw them as supermen because we weren't seeing them every week. Now we are up against them in training, seeing them much more on television, and realising that they make mistakes and are human too.

Not that there was too much tactical about the first match, against the Irish. Their players knew our players, we knew them. They had a rigid formation, we had a rigid formation. It was an English cup tie, like the Liverpool v Wimbledon FA Cup Final of that year, in which the underdogs had their day, and the party atmosphere in Stuttgart fostered by the Irish supporters certainly helped them. After Ray Houghton headed an early goal, we hit the post through Gary Lineker and Pat Bonner saved everything else thrown at him. For the Irish, it was their one big game while we were thinking about playing a campaign of five. Some hope. Thus was shown to me the importance of not losing the opening match of a tournament. Just a draw keeps you in with a chance. After a defeat you can feel you are almost out of the competition. And a few days later we were.

Everybody looks back on the game against Holland as the night Marco Van Basten tormented me. It was certainly his match, as he scored all their goals in the 3–1 win, but I feel that too much of the blame attached itself to me. I confess to feeling with Van Basten the way I had with Ian Rush in the early days; somewhat out of my depth. I was astonished that he was the same height as me, 6ft 3in, and also at the athleticism he possessed. He was also stronger than me. At 12 stones, I was still growing. I was determined to give it my best shot but at a tender age I was up against the best I would ever face.

Perhaps I could have got closer to Van Basten for the first goal as he turned me comprehensively, but it had been Gary Stevens who gave the ball away. For the second, Ruud Gullit – a strong, massive figure who covered an amazing amount of ground in those days and was outstanding in the air – flicked the ball on and Van Basten escaped Bryan Robson, who was marking him. Then the third goal went in on the right flank and I was on the left. In theory, we were marking zonally as a defence, not man for man, except at set pieces. We were, as a team, destroyed by the best striker in Europe, who would go on to score one of the great goals of all time, an amazing volley in the final against the Soviet Union as the Dutch deservedly took the title. But because I found myself up against him in areas of open play, I was the one in particular who was blamed. I have to admit that I was at fault; it's just that I wasn't the only one and I wasn't that bad.

Even with all that, it could have been different. After Bryan Robson equalised, Glenn Hoddle hit the post. If that had gone in, and I had then headed a few away, I would suddenly have been the bee's knees. Instead I am a pilloried scapegoat. At 21 years of age. I could only agree with the criticism in the media that I was too young. If there had been a better crop of England defenders around at that time, maybe I would have taken longer to make my mark. But most of the other things said about me were over the top and probably due to more senior players being considered above some of the flak flying. It then seemed to count for nothing that against the Soviet Union I scored the best goal of my four for England, heading home from 12 yards Glenn's free kick.

The next day we made the mistake of arriving back at Luton airport just as a charter of fans had got back. I was a particular target for the abuse as I hurriedly tried to get the money into the machine for car park payment and had to make a dash for it to my Fiat Uno, the car I had won for being Young Player of the Year the season before. These were the days before the FA laid on cars and drivers for you. Luckily the Fiat was a nippy mover so I was able to make a clean getaway. Back at my local pub a few hours later, I sought solace in familiar company and booze, embellishing stories of Euro '88 – how I had confronted the fans who jeered me, rather than ran from them, and denigrating England team-mates and management behind their backs and without being rational or constructive in my criticisms. All because I knew no better how to cope with it all.

In a perverse way, it was all an invaluable experience. I came back fuelled with a determination to prove people wrong about me again, to show that I was better than they were saying. I learned much about the ways of the media, about handling top strikers, and the peculiar pressures of tournament play. It is probably something in my character that I take more from failure than success. I still didn't feel able to assert myself properly with England, and I was inhibited among so-called superstars. I would be glad to get back to Arsenal where I was comfortable and appreciated and could be myself, shouting out orders. The next season Arsenal won the Championship.

In the autumn after the debacle of Euro '88, I was retained for matches against Denmark, Sweden and Saudi Arabia. But even though I scored the goal in the 1–1 draw in Riyadh, Bobby Robson was critical of my performance, so I knew which way the wind was blowing. I had been having trouble with my distribution at this time but Tony Cottee actually said to me afterwards that he thought I had passed the ball well. Perhaps the way I was then, I took it too personally but I remember thinking that George would never have said the things Bobby did.

Anyway, the next match was the following February in Athens against Greece and I had a slight muscle pull so did not make the trip. As I watched on television, and saw my replacement Des Walker playing well, I knew that my international place was slipping away from me.

At the time, the media seemed to have hit on a formula for a central defensive partnership; one speedster, one stopper. Terry Butcher was coming back and was the ideal stopper, Des Walker fitted the other bill and did very well in the role. I was very resentful and jealous, though. I didn't think Des was the best on the ball, and that was probably proved when he went to Sampdoria after the 1990 World Cup, even though they played him out of position. I think I was the more constructive player and, as my career has shown, could play either on the right or left of a defence as required. I have worked very hard in extra training on my left foot.

I continued to feel that I was the man for the job but that if that was the way that Bobby Robson and the media were thinking, then I was probably better off out of the scene. At that time, the newspapers had considerably more clout with the manager than they do now. There was nowhere near the amount of live television coverage of the game as there is these days and managers had to go by what they read or heard rather than what they saw.

A lot of enthusiasm for international football went from me at that time and I simply wanted to play well and win things for Arsenal. I did make a squad of 26 for Italia '90 but it brought only more disappointment. Upon releasing me – along with David Rocastle and Alan Smith – Bobby Robson told me to keep myself fit, and that I was on standby. I then went on my week-long bender to Rhodes and came back to watch the tournament mostly in a club near my home, then in Rainham.

Actually I quite enjoyed it. I would drink the afternoons away, ordering pizza, watching the games until I got bored and went to serve behind the bar. I would always have a bet on a game – like Niall Quinn to score the first goal for the Irish. I was delighted when David O'Leary scored the winning penalty for them against Romania. I cheered England on but in all honesty I was indifferent to their fortunes. I was jealous that Mark Wright was playing so well and scored against Egypt, that they ended up playing with three central defenders as I always told everybody they should. It was an exciting atmosphere when they played West Germany in the semi-final and I would have given my all if I had been there but the way I was then, the booze spoilt it for me in the end.

That World Cup signified the end of an era for England, with Bobby Robson moving on to PSV Eindhoven and Terry Butcher's international career ending, but Des Walker and Mark Wright became the men in possession under Bobby's successor Graham Taylor. Our Euro '92 qualifying group, though, contained the Republic of Ireland and this was a job for a good old-fashioned English stopper. After two years in the wilderness, this was a job for Tony Adams. It was the match that Graham controversially dropped Paul Gascoigne and I thought he was right to do so. He spoke famously about Paul's 'refuelling habits' but I was in my own world at the time and did not know then what he was talking about. I believed more that it was not Gazza's type of match, he was not mentally prepared for it and physically he wasn't in good condition. Instead, Gordon Cowans played and did well. David Platt scored and we should have won but a 1–1 draw was no bad result at Lansdowne Road at that time.

At that point my prison sentence intervened and I must admit I thought quite often in Chelmsford about whether Graham would recall me for the return match at Wembley. Once he saw that I was fit again on my release in February, he put me in and just a month after coming out of prison, I was playing for England again. Unfortunately I did not play as well as I can, and had a mixture of feelings about being up against my old friend Niall Quinn, who eluded me to give the Irish their goal in the 1–1 draw.

But again that was it for a while. I probably wasn't quite fully fit for that match but I had done reasonably well and was fit the following season in the last stages of qualifying for the European Championship finals and for Sweden itself. Again I was on standby for a major championship, however, and I was even fitted for the team suits. Instead,

Graham took Martin Keown, Des Walker, Keith Curle and Mark Wright. When Mark was injured just before the finals, Graham was phoning me daily saying that he was trying to get UEFA to agree to me being flown out as a late replacement but nothing came of it.

Instead I went on holiday with Jane to Cyprus, where I had also been with Arsenal on an end-of-season tour, a month or so before our wedding. It was a nightmare. Jane had migraine most of the time and poor little baby Oliver screamed with colic, so I spent a lot of time pushing him in his pushchair, mostly in and out of bars.

Perhaps I should have held a resentment against Graham that he left me out for all of that 1991/92 season but I never did really. He had, after all, brought me back after I had come out of prison even though he had to endure some criticism for picking a jailbird for England.

Then, after Euro '92 went all wrong and he took a lot of flak for pulling off Gary Lineker, he was brave enough to come to me and say in a conversation at a hotel in Luton where England used to assemble: 'I'm going with you, son. You can be my No. 1 now.' I had been knocked down several times playing for England and each time, after a rest and period away from it, I always wanted to come back. Now I had to prove myself all over again, but I was up for the challenge. It was good just to have been encouraged, to feel that I was the man, because by now I was feeling good enough.

The qualifying group for the 1994 World Cup finals got off to a good start when we took the lead against Norway at Wembley with a goal by David Platt but a long-range shot by Kjetil Rekdal meant we took only a point. Three comfortable wins followed, 4–0 at home to Turkey, 6–0 at home to San Marino and 2–0 in Turkey, before another home draw that would also eventually prove costly, this time against Holland.

Again we began well, taking a two-goal lead by half time through a beautiful free kick by John Barnes after only two minutes and Platty again – his sixth goal in three international games – but the Dutch bounced back. Dennis Bergkamp, who had the Indian sign on me at that time, got a brilliant goal back with a chipped volley and Des Walker got outpaced by Marc Overmars and conceded a penalty that Peter Van Vossen converted for a 2–2 draw.

It left us with a tricky task, needing good results from demanding away matches against Poland in Katowice and Norway in Oslo in the space of four days at the end of the 1992/93 season. What a trip it was to prove.

The omens were not that good in the tunnel before the game in Poland where I thought Carlton Palmer was going over the top in his attempts to help motivate the team. Whereas Terry Butcher had concentrated on us, keeping his distance from the Yugoslavs but instilling fear in them in 1987, now Carlton was going up to the Poles and shouting insults in their faces. This time, the opposition was motivated instead and we endured a torrid first half, falling a goal behind. Later, Graham would describe Carlton as being one of several 'headless chickens' in the team and there were some poor performances, but fortunately we were rescued by Ian Wright's late equaliser after he came on as a substitute.

During the journey to Oslo, I got talking to Trevor Brooking who told me not to worry, that he had been in a worse situation than this in 1981 during qualification for the Spain World Cup when England had lost a match in Switzerland and went on to win in Hungary a few days later. The important thing was not to lose the first one, he added, and we had achieved that. If only such positive thinking had been apparent in the camp before the game.

Once in Norway, Graham called a team meeting at which he went through the team, asking us to mark our performance out of 10. Wrighty gave himself 10. 'Well, I scored the goal so I ought to get top marks,' he said and everyone laughed. Poor Des Walker owned up to having a bad game and gave himself four. It was excruciating for Des and as his partner, I thought I ought to give myself four too. Afterwards, Graham awarded his own set of marks, which mostly tallied except for Wrighty, who got eight.

I'm not sure what the object of the exercise was but all it succeeded in doing was undermining morale. Putting people through it was just horrible and everyone walked out of the meeting, I believe, with less respect for Graham Taylor. I certainly did. And several must have felt how I did with Bobby Robson after the Saudi Arabia game – if you feel that way, don't pick me then, but don't slaughter me like this, especially with a big game a couple of days away and certainly not in front of the other players. I think it was then that Graham lost the full backing of the England players, something a manager simply cannot afford.

Thus we hardly had much stomach to implement the tactics that Graham had decided on, of three at the back. We were in disarray, anyway, whatever the reasons. Chris Woods's confidence was shot in goal, Paul Ince was good and angry, Carlton Palmer was a recipe for disaster because he was so hyped-up and now we were going to play a system we were not wholly familiar with and with only two days to work on before a massive match.

The day before the game we trained at an air base well away from prying eyes because Graham wanted our tactics kept secret. I had confidence in my own ability and had played in the three before at Arsenal, but I don't think the manager's work on it inspired us. We played a square, rigid three of myself, Des Walker and Gary Pallister and passed the attackers across to be marked as they moved. It was similar to what we had done at Arsenal now and then but less expert. Lee Dixon and Lee Sharpe were the wing-backs; one suited to it, the other not, as an out-and-out winger. Up front, Les Ferdinand and Teddy Sheringham were just deployed standing up there. There was little movement.

The Norwegians, who were themselves playing a rigid 4–4–2 formation which would be found out at the World Cup Finals where the top teams easily pulled them around, made it just like an English game and that night they were better at the English game than we were. In fact, being well-organised and the pitch being small, they reminded me of Arsenal. They also put a man on Gazza, kept him quiet, and it was all over, 2–0.

I was fortunate that after a long, hard season in which we had won two Cups at Arsenal, I could get back home, naturally to get back on the drink. The rest of the squad – in disgrace, as the papers pointed out – had to go on to a tournament in the United States, where they were beaten by the host nation and Germany and drew with Brazil. It was supposed to be a warm-up for the Finals of the following year but there would be none for England unless we could beat Holland in Rotterdam in October.

Whoever worked out this schedule of three away games against our strongest rivals, punctuated only by a home match against Poland, which we won well 3–0 in the September, wanted their head examined. In fact, these things are decided at fixtures meetings after the draws for the qualifying competitions and involve lots of haggling and bartering. You never seem to end up with the games when you want them. I think it was one of Graham Taylor's beefs that the programme was less than ideal.

Unlucky 13 October 1993 was just one of the cruellest nights of my career, though I suspect Graham looks back on it with less fondness that I do. The build-up was unreal and I tried not to let the occasion seem too big, tried to stay positive and focused on the job. It was difficult, though, because there were fans and journalists in our hotel and we were not cut off as we should have been. I was signing autographs just before the game.

On the night, we were going OK, Paul Merson hitting the bar, and suddenly David Platt looked as if he was in on goal with one of what he liked to describe as his Martin Peters runs. Ronald Koeman, though, pulled him back and although we got a free kick on the edge of their penalty area, which came to nothing, Koeman stayed on the field when he should have walked. Later FIFA would discipline the referee as an admission that he got it wrong. But it was too late. It was just so big a decision and, as would be seen, careers hung on that moment.

A few minutes later Koeman curled home a goal at the other end from a free kick and we were struggling. Then I missed a header, Dennis Bergkamp latched on to the ball and he shot past David Seaman. Game over as, soon, was Graham's management of England. It only remained for a bit of salt to be rubbed into the wound when, in a match I missed, we fell behind against San Marino in a matter of seconds before winning 7–1 an ultimately meaningless match.

The nation, naturally enough, was devastated, though I have to say that personally I did not feel as bad as I had after Euro '88. I didn't think I had done anything wrong, hadn't performed badly. There was the odd isolated incident when I could have done better but I felt I was growing as an international player. I was starting to feel comfortable at that level, beginning to enjoy the big games and, with Arsenal going into Europe in the Cup Winners' Cup the next season, gaining more valuable experience. Also, this time I wasn't the one getting it in the neck. Graham was the one with his in the noose, as one paper so tastefully mocked up.

Often when a new England manager takes over, you wonder if you will be his cup of tea, whether you have been too closely associated with failure and whether he has his own players in mind. Though he was still open-minded on many things at first, I think Terry Venables had earmarked me for his team. I knew from some of the early things he was saying that I had a good chance at least; he wished he had had me at Tottenham, for example. At Spurs, he had also gone out of his way to work out how to stop me from set plays. I knew also that he was a good friend of George Graham's and that George would have told him how highly he valued me. I think he just wanted it all confirmed on the training pitch and we were immediately on the same wavelength. And it was fun.

I played in all Terry's early games, including the two end-of-season matches against Greece and Norway at Wembley where Steve Bould got the two caps that became so precious to him. The Two Dobermans, David O'Leary used to call us. After the first game, I remember Terry telling me to get the boys to bed soon as he headed for his room at 11 pm. What a thing to say to an active alcoholic. There were a few of us still going strong at 6 am.

We had to go through a whole load of friendlies at Wembley in the build-up to Euro '96, technical exercises really, but there was a lot of strategy in what Terry was trying to achieve. First he looked at all the older, tried and trusted players to see if they could still do it, then he brought in the younger ones. Paul Parker, for example, gave way to Gary Neville; Terry liked that quick defender who could play centrally and also move outside comfortably to full-back. He tried to get away from old-fashioned positional terms, though, and just wanted flexible defenders, midfield players and attackers. He never made a great many changes from match to match, though, always just two or three, unless injury forced more on him.

Then he would experiment with formations, a back four and a back three. Within that three he would sometimes have one dropping off or one who played just in front of the other two so that the withdrawn striker that most international opposition played with could be countered. If you felt uncomfortable stepping up from the back line, he said to me, get back level with the other two when the ball goes wide. Everyone had 'starting positions' for when we gained possession as well as lost it.

We would play a 'Christmas Tree' of 4–3–2–1, with two mobile, interchanging attacking players just behind Alan Shearer as the spearhead. Or sometimes just one withdrawn – Teddy Sheringham proving the best – as the team's pivot. It was all designed to accommodate skilful, versatile players who could pass and move and pull the opposition out of their shape to create space. It was also all geared towards Euro '96 when we could encounter a variety of opposition and needed a variety of options to beat them. In addition, it was exactly what we had been crying out for after all the time we had been tactically behind the better nations – not technically, because I always maintain that we have as much talent in England as anywhere.

I quickly became very comfortable on the training

ground with Terry. In fact the only other person I had been so comfortable with was George Graham. I hadn't felt so in tune, I have to admit, with either Bobby Robson or Graham Taylor. In pure footballing terms, therefore, I thought I was the right man for the job when Terry made me captain for the first time – meaning that I had captained every team I had ever played for – against Romania in October 1994 in the absence of the injured David Platt.

It was now nearly five years since I had been imprisoned but it still seemed I had some time to serve, though. I turned on a Sky television discussion programme which was wondering how such a man could be leading his country. A couple of the papers, bless them, were also outraged by the prospect of an ex-con as captain. Paying your dues, forgiveness and rehabilitation did not seem to mean much to some people. Anyway, it was an honour I felt I deserved and one I certainly enjoyed, even if Terry did give us a coating for a sloppy first half hour when we went a goal down before drawing 1–1.

David was back as captain for my next game, against the Republic of Ireland in Dublin when some England fans forced the game to be abandoned by hurling missiles on to the pitch and at Irish fans. I have to say I was still in my own self-centred world in those days. I hadn't noticed it going off because I was concentrating on the game but at the referee's signal I got off the pitch quickly, unscathed, and was more concerned about whether we would start the game again. Jack Charlton was running about the dressing room area saying how sad and disgraceful it all was, but all that occurred to me was that we had been playing badly and that it would be a relief for it to be called off as we were a goal down.

I inherited the England captaincy again in the September

of 1995, when injury again plagued David Platt, and then kept it when he failed to regain his place in the team, through games against Colombia, Switzerland, Norway and Portugal. Then at what was that dark time in my life in early '96, I had to have the knee operation and just making the Finals, let alone being captain, began to look bleak. The pre-tournament trip to China and Hong Kong would determine my fitness.

It was hard enough just being there amid all the confusion I was in. My marriage – though I was not seeing it clearly at the time – was in the early stages of breaking up, and I was beginning to understand, instinctively if not intellectually, that when I drank I did not know what would happen to me so that it would be better if I stayed off it altogether. It was Jane's birthday while I was out there and I went out into the shops in Beijing to buy her some things, anything, I thought she would like; wind chimes, books on Chinese philosophy and religion, just to try and impress her.

Luckily football was a welcome distraction – my old, reliable first drug of choice – and I came through the match against China intact. I was the business again, and back in business. I could put aside all the pain I was in with the death throes of alcoholism about to engulf me, as well as the worry about my wife, and concentrate on Euro '96, for which I would again be England's captain.

Which was how I came to be in this meeting with Terry Venables at the England base at Burnham Beeches shortly after we returned from Hong Kong. All hell had broken loose in the papers because two television screens had been broken on the Cathay Pacific flight back. Terry had to know what happened. Coming on top of the night when some of the players had gone out to the China Jump club and been pictured having a beery night out, our image had taken a bit of a knock. From my point of view, it was all pretty ironic, really. I hadn't been to the China Jump club, with its 'dentist's chair' where they pour booze down your throat, but was in somewhere similar called Joe Bananas the year before on the Arsenal tour with Ray Parlour that night when he got into trouble with the taxi driver. As a result of that, and what was going on with me, I stayed well away.

The same was true on the flight home. About 20 of us were seated in the upstairs section of the jumbo jet and I was up front having a conversation with people for a change – Gareth Southgate, I remember – when I would normally have been at the back myself getting drunk, singing some songs and possibly doing some damage. Footballers need a release like any other people in life. Some can handle it, some can't. Some were drinking and playing cards and it did get a bit noisy. In fact, Terry's chief scout Ted Buxton came up at one point and asked everyone to keep the noise down. But there was no confrontation with the Cathay staff. In fact, an off-duty co-pilot came out and had a drink with the players at one point.

There was a story that a couple of the boys lifted a sleeping Dennis Wise into an overhead locker and shut him in, so that when he woke up, not surprisingly panicking, he banged on the locker until it opened and he fell out. All I can say is, I don't know. I did walk back down the plane at one point but everyone was dozing or passed out by that time. I didn't see anything, certainly not any broken TV screens but then you know how it is at the end of a long-haul flight where there are newspapers, blankets and plastic beakers strewn all over the place.

I didn't really care, anyway, who did what. I told the

team meeting that the most important thing was Euro '96 and we should stick together for the next few weeks, put aside all differences and rivalries, and be united in the cause, whatever may or may not have happened. If somebody wants to own up now, they can. Nobody did. 'OK,' I said. 'It is too much for somebody to own up to publicly, too much for one person to handle. We are all going to be responsible and worry about things after the tournament. If someone wants to tell Terry privately, then so be it.'

I don't think anyone did but then perhaps people had forgotten in the course of the drinking what did happen. I know during my own drinking that I could convince myself at times that I hadn't done certain things. Anyway, the squad agreed that we should be in this together, as with everything else, so David Platt and I then went to see Terry to tell him. 'Right,' he said. 'Then we will take collective responsibility.' It was issued to the press in a statement, became our buzz-phrase and actually brought the squad together.

It was soon after this that Terry took me to one side and told me that I was to be captain through the tournament. He had already told David Platt, who was bitterly disappointed, I know. I thanked Terry but told him, 'You know what you will get from me, whether I am captain or not.' One of Terry's problems, I think, was that he was unsure whether he would be picking David.

The Manchester United boys, especially Gary and Phil Neville, were impressed with the camaraderie, which Alex Ferguson had also used with his 'them v us' portrayal of the press. There were papers lying around the hotel during the tournament but few chose to read them. Don Howe said that those who did want to read them should do so in the afternoon rather than being negative for the whole day. It all combined to stoke a team spirit, in a way that artificially trying to create it doesn't, and it became a very happy camp, very focused on the task. We watched a lot of films, both feature and football. I drank a lot of tea, became tea boy for the team in fact, and spent my time on the phone to estate agents and solicitors trying to buy Jane a house now that it seemed we were splitting up. It felt good here inside the squad. By just letting events unfold and using adversity to our advantage, we grew stronger.

After everything, it was a relief actually to get the first game against Switzerland under way. The hype and the build-up had been amazing with all the 'Football's Coming Home' feel-good stuff and we had to get our heads into football and get used to the atmosphere. We didn't play well despite getting off to a good start with Alan Shearer's goal, but there were a lot of factors in that; the heat, the nerves, picking up the pace of the game. Personally my main worry was getting booked for a little mistimed tackle. One more and I would miss the Final – that's how I was thinking. We got out of it with a 1–1 draw, which was the important thing. Not to lose is the aim of the opening match.

For me, the Scotland game was the big turning point. It was reminiscent of Euro '88 and the Republic of Ireland, thinking about which sent the odd shiver down me. If we won, I couldn't see us losing to Holland or failing to reach the next stage. Gazza was really up for it that day, as Gary Lineker had been that day of my debut in Spain, wanting to impress the nation where he earned his living at that time with Rangers. His goal, the lob over Colin Hendry then volley past Andy Goram, was outstanding, and later he would have the brandy and cigars out at Burnham Beeches as befitting his self-image there as lord of the manor.

Before then, there was still plenty of work to be done and

I was sickened to concede a penalty in bringing down Kevin Gallacher. When David Seaman saved Gary McAllister's kick, though, I rushed to plant a kiss on the cheek of my Arsenal team-mate. And when Alan Shearer headed home Gary Neville's cross, we knew we were as good as in the quarter-finals. There was no way we were going to lose to the Dutch in our third group match.

That feeling was confirmed the day before the game in a 90-minute team meeting. We already had so much confidence after beating the Scots and now we went through exactly how the Dutch played, the strengths and weaknesses of each one of them, how they worked for each other and created space. Terry had done a lot of work on them because there were elements of their game – like the back three of a central defender and two full backs, into which a holding midfield player stepped if they were defending – that he wanted to incorporate into ours. Every player left that meeting convinced he was better than his counterpart and that the Dutch were simply there for the taking.

So it proved as we annihilated them with one of the best England performances I have been party to. Dennis Bergkamp no longer had the psychological edge over me while at the other end the Dutch could not handle our 'SAS' of Shearer and Sheringham, who each scored twice in the 4–1 win. One of our great nights. In the dressing room afterwards, I thanked the boys. 'This is my revenge for '88 and I've waited eight years for that,' I said. 'The only shame is that Van Basten wasn't playing. He bottled it.'

Celebration turned to perspiration for our quarter-final against Spain, who were a good side and getting better. It was one of the most tense and intense afternoons of my career as both sides kept the game tight and a chess-like battle of wills was played out. In some ways we were fortunate. They had a goal disallowed for a marginal offside decision and I managed to get a last-ditch tackle in on one of the Spaniards as he burst through. I was chuffed with myself. It was a great challenge, I thought.

Before every England game I had played since Hungary in the April, I had had a pain-killing injection in my right knee. Now, as we were about to start extra time against Spain, today's was wearing off. 'Stick us another one in, Doc,' I said to the England medic Dr Crane and, covering it up with his medical bag so that no-one watching on TV would be alarmed, he pushed the syringe in again. I had no care about the long-term damage then. This was an instant decision in a big match.

Extra time was again just so tense as neither team wanted to concede the 'golden goal' that would end the game. Once we got through that goalless, I felt we would go through. We had David Seaman for the penalty shoot-out. Enough said. It was also Stuart Pearce's moment. When he scored his penalty, to banish the ghosts of 1990 when he missed against Germany in the World Cup semi-final, it was for him as it had been for me against the Dutch.

And so on to West Germany and the end of the nation's dream we had come so close to fulfilling. We were the better side. They were not as good as they were cracked up to be. Andy Möller was their only exceptional player, I thought. I was not to know it at the time but it was to be also the beginning of the end of a personal nightmare. And, of course, the end of Terry Venables's tenure and beginning of Glenn Hoddle's reign, which would see me awarded my 50th cap and us go through a tough qualifying competition and on to the World Cup finals of 1998 in France.

NINE

... And
Englishmen

Not many players appear alongside someone who goes on to be England coach, then play under him. In fact, of more than 1,000 players who have worn the Three Lions on their chest, there are only three: me, Stuart Pearce and Gary Pallister. I actually pre-date both of those two, by making my debut alongside Glenn Hoddle in that match in Spain in 1987.

It is partly due, of course, to the fact that Glenn was the youngest England coach of all, at 38, when he was appointed in the spring of 1996. Most playing colleagues of previous England managers would have been far too old to have been considered by them. But it all shows how long I have been on the England scene as well and just how many managers and players I have seen come and go; come full circle, in fact.

In some ways, Glenn and I had some similar experiences under my first England manager Bobby Robson, during whose tenure I learnt all the vagaries of international football. It is not as simple as you might think; you're good enough, you play for England. Sometimes it does actually work out that way, but there can be so many variables out of your control. So much depends, for example, on what injuries there are at any given time – injuries being the reason why I got my debut in the first place. It depends, too, on who is available in your position. A player not considered good enough in one era might be just what is required at another time. You hear people saying, 'Oh, he should have played 100 times for England' – certainly of Glenn, who won 53 caps – but you have to take into account who else was around in his position at the time. Then there are the side issues, such as whether you have the press on your side and they further your cause.

The biggest single factor, though, is whether the manager likes the look of you and whether you fit the ideas he has in mind for how he wants the team to play, as well as what his needs are at any given time. As a midfield player, Glenn went in and out of fashion, with prevailing thought saying something like 'last year we needed passers but this year we need workers' and because he was viewed as someone who would not work hard for a team. As a defender, I was seen mostly as a stopper who could not distribute the ball well, wrongly in my opinion, and I think many people eventually had to acknowledge that.

I know also that I have been chosen for England at times when I have not been playing particularly well for Arsenal. Then again, I have been left out when I believe I have been steaming at club level. It was why I endured wilderness years, one under Bobby, in 1988/89 when I thought I was doing well, then in 1990/91 under Graham Taylor when I was a significant figure in an Arsenal team that could lay claim to being the best in the club's history. In both years Arsenal won the Championship. In other seasons when the team was below par, I won recalls. Hard to explain.

I have to be honest and say that I felt Bobby Robson was a bit bumbling at times. When I first turned up for training, he called me Paul Adams because, I was told, he once had an apprentice by that name at Ipswich, where he was manager previously. It was not unusual. When he first called up Luther Blissett, he had to go over to Kenny Sansom and ask him what the new lad's name was. He couldn't quite get it into his head properly, though, and from then on started calling him 'Bloother'. Bobby had this habit, and I don't know if it was an asset or a defect, of switching off. The lads used to say sometimes that the light was on but there was no-one at home.

He had got some success at Ipswich playing in a certain 4–4–2 formation and had his favourite players, like Kevin Beattie and Terry Butcher, and was always trying to find players like them in spirit and style. That said, I think he was not a bad judge of a player and he was right to love the Chris Waddles and the Peter Beardsleys. You wonder, though, if Bobby made the best of some of the talent that was around, because we were stuck in rigid systems for a long while and didn't do as well as we might have in tournaments.

Bobby was fortunate in my opinion to have Don Howe as his right-hand man in that era of managerial partnerships, front man and power behind the throne, like Brian Clough and Peter Taylor. One of my most embarrassing moments with England came in Germany just before we played the Soviet Union at the European Championship finals of 1988 and a few of us were in a lift when Peter Reid started cursing very loudly about Bobby not picking him even now, when we were out of the tournament and all the other midfield players had screwed up. Behind him, unknown to Reidy, was standing Don Howe.

Don was an exceptional coach at Arsenal and then with England too. Although his playing era had been the 50s, he never lost his enthusiasm and love for the game and kept learning, stayed modern, all through the various changes of style over the years. He proved with Wimbledon in the 1988 FA Cup Final when they beat Liverpool what he could do with a team, how to organise them. And if Don says he likes a player, then that's good enough for me. I don't know of another man with that experience and knowledge – people say Roy Hodgson, but I have not had the pleasure of working with him – and what worries me is that men with his feeling for the game are growing older without any really outstanding English coaches emerging to replace them. It is shown in the fact that Dave Sexton, my first manager at Under-21 level and who taught me how a man could be quiet and get people's attention, remained at work with the Under-21s, like Don, well into his sixties.

Bobby Robson was good at dealing with the FA officials at Lancaster Gate and the media, who were always knocking him but loved him anyway because he was so accommodating to them and gave them good quotable material. The description of him always seemed to be 'avuncular' but Gazza thought he was his granddad. They still speak fondly of him at the FA, I know, and in fact it was hard not to like Bobby, no matter what I thought his short-comings as a manager might have been. And of course he gave me my chance.

Graham Taylor, who took over from Bobby after the 1990 World Cup finals, gave me another chance after I had been to prison. Many things have been written and said about Graham down the years but I can only go by what I experienced. I thought he was a very intelligent man and I liked him personally. He thought about things deeply and tried to make things interesting and lively.

Whenever we met up as a squad there was always champagne on the table and Graham would give an introductory speech at this little reception – he was fond of talking, was Graham – usually to announce that we were definitely going to win the match. One day, just before an important game, we got on to the coach to go to training but instead Graham took us to Windsor for a walk round and a cup of tea in a hotel. It helped relax us. I think they also had to go to a post office to get a passport photo for someone.

I probably had more sympathy for his methods of direct football, though with England it was never as pronounced as it had been when he was bringing Watford up through the divisions to runners-up in the old First. He had better players, after all, who needed to pass the ball. Still, he wanted the ball put into the opposition corners from the kick-off, wanted it played forward early, and his aim was a high-tempo game. It was nothing new to me. I had been introduced to Charles Hughes, one of Graham's influences as the FA's director of coaching, early in my development and also because we played a direct way at Arsenal, though with modifications, George Graham always insisting on some finesse in the attacking third of the pitch.

I did have respect for Graham's methods, which included extra iron as part of a diet designed to help maintain a quicker paced game, and the motivational side of his nature, which saw him recruit a sports psychologist. But I did have reservations. I think the way of playing was short-sighted because if you did reach the finals of a major tournament, you would not be able to sustain the effort right through if you had ambitions of winning the trophy. It was all right for the Republic of Ireland and Norway but they were always shattered if they made the second phase, which represented the summit of their ambitions, bearing in mind that finals tournaments always take place in heat.

Graham had a fixed way in his head and was too stereotyped, in my opinion. In the end he also became obsessed with the media, which may have been understandable to some extent after the way they portrayed him grotesquely as a turnip after the Euro '92 defeat by Sweden, but it became distracting. In the run-up to the World Cup qualifying game against Holland, he was far too concerned about keeping the papers happy when he should not have bothered.

As for the notorious Channel 4 Cutting Edge documentary that followed him around, I wanted nothing to do with it. In team meetings I would always make sure I was out of the camera shot. I didn't want cameras up my nose. I was playing for England and concentrating on that. I have never seen the programme, which everyone tells me ridicules Graham, and I don't think I ever want to.

He also made himself look foolish, I think, because he didn't surround himself with the best people. His assistant Lawrie McMenemy liked me a lot, thought I was a real man, I think, but I can't say I ever had that much to do with him. He was another media man in my eyes. As for Phil Neal, you almost felt he was making you stand to attention when Graham was approaching. 'Come on lads, the boss is coming,' he would say. You can't have respect for someone like that.

What can I say about Steve Harrison, Graham's warm-up man? Actually, that's exactly what he was. Or perhaps entertainments officer might be a better description. The warming-up was supposed to be physical preparation before the actual training session but it was as if he was a comedian warming up an audience. He was probably the funniest, or daftest, bloke I have come across in football and there was never a dull moment. I'm told his dad was a comic who played the Northern circuit and that makes sense. Steve could have been a professional himself. In fact we all went to a show one night and he was better than the comedian.

One morning we got on the coach and he was sat on the roof of it throwing stones down at us. Then at Bisham Abbey we were running round the pitch and he was leading us. As we went round a corner he kept straight on and ran into the bushes, leaving us wondering what was going on. Then he would do his Norman Wisdom walk. At a team dinner one night, he suddenly burst into the room wearing a dirty mac and when he opened it, he was naked except for a rubber chicken tied round his waist. I have never seen Gazza so quiet. He was completely upstaged by this bloke.

Footballers can be very judgmental, which was another problem for Graham. There is the old thing about 'show us your medals' when it comes to taking charge of players. The fact that he came from Aston Villa and they had won nothing under him, even if they had done reasonably well to be league runners-up, counted against him with some players. There was also the question of him not having enough international experience, of not having played for England or coached abroad.

I think that at times he should have had the courage of his own convictions more. He did that time in Dublin when he dropped Gazza, and he did when he brought in Paul Merson for the Holland game in Rotterdam. I also felt that he wanted to drop Gary Lineker at times but was too worried what the press and public would say. That time he took him off in Sweden in 1992 was, in my opinion, the right decision at the wrong time. Had Graham followed his heart more, he might have got us to the World Cup finals in 1994 and everything would have been different then.

But I was grateful to him for recalling me and he made an impact on me with some of the things he did, made me feel more confident as an international player. That said, in the end I was not that upset to see him go because, quite simply, he didn't achieve anything and that is the first requirement of being the national team manager.

I never saw the same deficiencies in Terry Venables, when he took over from Graham in January 1994. Terry had won a Spanish League title with Barcelona and the FA Cup with Tottenham and everyone knew him already. There was a bond with him because he was an Essex boy like me – though I did feel I also had some rapport with Graham, who was from the North – and immediately I felt at home on the training ground with him as I had not before with an England coach.

He won my admiration also for bringing Don Howe back on to the staff and with Bryan Robson in the fold as a coach as well, I could not think of three better people to be in charge of the England team. It is crucial to have figures who are respected by international players. There you had a team manager, a coach and a players' player. You could say things to Bryan that he would understand, having recently played for the team and with the shrewd footballing brain he had, and things that would not go any further; your reservations about tactics or certain other players, for example. Don was just obsessed with the game. At this time he had studied the Dutch closely and analysed the Brazilians. In meetings, Don would enthusiastically be getting carried away and saying how we should play like them and Terry would say, 'Hold on a moment, what can we take from them to suit us?'

Terry was a laugher and a joker but he knew when to be serious, when to calm things down. I remember one night during Euro '96 when he was giving a live television interview and Steve McManaman and Robbie Fowler ran across the background making faces. He took it in his stride, just laughing and shrugging on camera, saying he thought it was past their bedtime. Then when they did it again another night, he simply said to them the next morning that once was funny, twice was not. They got the message very simply without the need for any disciplinary stuff. I thought that was good man-management.

He liked to work at things gradually, and did not expect players to absorb a lot of information in too short a space of time so that it got forgotten. He was a five-minute man who didn't like too many meetings or too much talk. A lot of people said that his business dealings got in the way of his real work but I know nothing about that. He may have been a ducker and diver, a loveable rogue or whatever, but to me he was a football man who knew his job in depth. I could work with anyone like that because it also described me.

With Terry, everyone felt they could speak up in team meetings, that he appreciated the honesty and that grudges would not be held. With other managers, you were often worried that your place was in jeopardy. Above all, he made the best of the talent available. He would go into great detail on the training ground. And training sessions were his equivalent of meetings; he was happy to spend time there.

Take the times when he played the 'Christmas tree', the 4–3–2–1 formation that he thought was effective against certain opposition. He would tell everyone where they needed to be when the ball was in certain areas of the pitch and we liked that knowledge. Movement was what he liked. 'If he goes there, you come in here. The problem is with the Christmas tree is that there is no width when we're attacking so when we break out with the ball, so-and-so, you get wide,' he would say, for example. One of its main functions was to get skilful attacking players like Steve McManaman on the ball in areas where they could hurt the opposition – Steve with his dribbling skills – and it worked.

At the back, Terry put more time and effort than anyone into actually carrying out ideas rather than just paying lip service to them. Like three at the back. He would tell you where you should be in a given situation and he liked me, as spare man, to step ahead of the two markers to track a deep-lying attacker or forward midfield player so that we didn't lose the all-important numbers game in midfield. When I expressed a concern that I was leaving the middle exposed at the back, he simply explained to me how I should drop into the back line when the opposition sent the ball wide.

It all made sense to me and as an experienced player I was consulted a lot, which I enjoyed. Terry even took me out to a West End restaurant early in his management to talk football with me, about players and the forthcoming Euro '96, about starting positions and movement, and fascinating it was too. Except that of two bottles of white wine that Terry ordered, I drank a bottle and a half and it started me on a two-day bender.

The role of spare man in a back three was later seen differently by Glenn Hoddle and caused some discussion between the two of us. Where Terry wanted me to move forward, Glenn wanted me to drop off. I think he was particularly worried that we could be caught out by the ball over the top after the goal that Gianfranco Zola scored for Italy which beat us at Wembley during the 1998 World Cup qualifying campaign. Glenn and I didn't always agree, as would be seen on the road to France '98.

As a player there is no doubt that Glenn had a great talent. If we had been able to integrate him at Arsenal, it would have to have been as a withdrawn striker playing just off a target man. He probably would not have been able to fit in the midfield system we had, where work-rate and protection of the back four was everything. At international level, though, with games not as physical or frequent as in the league, you need that type of player more, someone who can unlock the opposition.

For England, at the time when he was at his peak and with the players we had then, I would like to have seen him playing just behind the front two in a more mobile and fluent team. I thought we were very naive in the late 80s and I'm sure Glenn did as well. No national team manager really got the best out of him. In another time, another place, I'm sure someone would have, someone such as Terry Venables, and Glenn could have operated in several roles. At club level Glenn was appreciated at Tottenham but not far beyond. I have to say he always made my life uncomfortable for Arsenal by opening me up with those little balls into the paths of Steve Archibald and Garth Crooks, passes that defenders can't quite get to. He probably had his best season in this country, before going on to win a French title with Monaco, in that flowing David Pleat team of 1986/87 when we beat them in the League Cup semi-final.

When Glenn became coach, everyone thought that this would mean that Matthew Le Tissier would become his man, as a gifted player who had not always been appreciated. Both, after all, have been national debates as well as players in their time. My own opinion of Le Tissier is that he could have been one of the great players if he had shown more ambition by going to a bigger club than Southampton – yes, such as Arsenal – where he would have been expected to add hard work to his ability, which he had in abundance. Unfortunately he became a media figure to me. In 10 years playing against him, I don't think he ever gave me a problem and by not contributing on the defensive side he often looked like a liability to his team.

Anyway, it was David Beckham, another Essex boy, with whom Glenn most empathised. He always said that David had the rare ability to see the furthest pass first and I think he was probably talking about himself. Beckham also has a lot of grit and determination that Alex Ferguson has brought out. It would have been interesting to see what the Manchester United manager could have made out of Glenn.

Actually, I would have liked the chance as well. What I would most have enjoyed is being in the fantasy football position of player-manager of my own England XI, involving the players I have appeared with.

It was something I talked over with Terry Venables after Euro '96 when I called in at the club in Kensington he used to own, Scribes West, for a chinwag. It was August and I had just quit drinking – I even managed to get up on the karaoke and sing 'Wild Thing' without a drink. 'Come on,' he said to me. 'You've won two league titles playing 4–4–2 and now you've played in my systems. How would you go about setting up your own team?'

My preferred formation would actually be three at the back in Terry's concept of it, rather than the three stopper-type centre-backs, but it is something for which you need a bigger pitch than Arsenal have at Highbury to maximise its potential.

Starting with the goalkeeper, it comes down to a choice between Peter Shilton and David Seaman. I played in front of Shilts in his later days, when he was a legend, and I was a bit in awe of him, even though I gravitated towards him as he was one of the lads who liked a bet and enjoyed a drink. He was a lovely man. In my early years with England, I think I wanted to become like him, in fact.

Shilts was a reaction goalkeeper, a brilliant shot-stopper and I think he went on so long at international level, which he preferred to club football, because he did not have so many crosses to deal with. He was always very agile and alive and also very talkative, a man who was always organising his defence. A defender likes that, even if someone like Peter Schmeichel might get on your nerves now and then, because you know you have a commanding figure behind you. That also communicates itself to the opposition.

I have to say, though, that I think David Seaman surpassed Peter. Dave just has a presence and aura about him that inspires confidence and can deflate the opposition, who wonder how they will ever get the ball past him. Often he has not had to make the spectacular save because his positioning and angles are so great. Some may look at some of his saves down the years and think, 'Well, what's so special about that?' but look at how some goalkeepers save exactly the same shot. I have been with him watching television pictures of a keeper flying about his goal and Dave has just said: 'One for the cameras, that.' He has been simply the best I have ever played with and he gets my nod.

In defence, I would like to play with Terry's idea of a three that he adapted from the Ajax system. It involves having a dominating central defender – me, of course – who can play the ball out, flanked by two who can be central defenders, with their marking ability, as well as full-backs; rare players, I know, but then that is what international football is all about. When the team is defending, a holding midfield player drops back to become an auxiliary defender so that the other two can become more traditional full-backs and deal with the danger from wide. I suppose the best examples of that type of player are the Dutchman Frank Rijkaard and the Frenchman Marcel Desailly.

My choice on the right would be Viv Anderson, who could play as either a full back or central defender and thus is perfectly qualified. He was also quick and could head a ball, which are major requirements, and was a great influence in the dressing room. On the left I would have Kenny Sansom, not because he was my pal but because he was mobile and flexible, could explode forward but was tough in the tackle. Now I know people will point out that so far I have chosen only Arsenal players but aside from being flippant and saying that it's my team anyway, I will just ask which club has consistently had the best defensive record over the last decade and a half? Viv and Kenny were part of the team that laid the foundations for the celebrated back four that helped Arsenal win three titles.

The great thing about a back three like that is that it gives you so many options further forward; the aim of the game, after all, is to score goals. It is why Terry Butcher doesn't quite make it into my side, though I loved him as a partner in a back four and for the way he helped develop my international career. I don't think either that we have had a really quick, intelligent defender over the last decade, like the Italian Franco Baresi, who would demand selection. Paul Parker and Des Walker have been sharp – though I think the obsession with pace was because we were rigid in formations and needed to counter movement with speed, rather than tactical thought – while Mark Wright was clever, and Martin Keown a good man-marker, but we have not had a real all-round defender.

It is a better system, too, in my opinion to have two players who were full-backs by upbringing rather than more orthodox central defenders because then you don't need wing-backs as such, players who are neither great defenders nor attackers but who fill in as both, and you can employ instead more specialist attacking players. If you are not careful, with the 3–5–2 formation, you can get as rigid as the old days, albeit in a different way, and lose sight of the flexibility and mobility that Terry Venables rightly believed was necessary for the modern game.

But before we get carried away, we need our holding player to help out at the back and Paul Ince fits my bill. He is very strong, a good leader, and I want people in my side like that when a battle comes along. He can also pass the ball and get forward, make things happen around the opposition's penalty box. Not that with my team, we would probably need it. Having said all I did about Glenn, I would want him to line up on the right of my team, in a David Beckham sort of role, because I think he could hurt teams from there with his crossing ability and long passing. Also I think in this system he would still get plenty of opportunity to express himself. I also want to use a Paul Gascoigne at his peak in that role behind the strikers.

Gazza. I've grown up with him, used to drink with him. I've loved him to bits. We have had similar lengths of careers both with our clubs and country and there have been some similarities in our lives, though they have taken different paths. I remember once after an England B game against Italy at Millwall we went to a nightclub in Dartford along with Dennis Wise and the two of them were tastefully pictured in the *Sun* with a finger each up one of my nostrils, my nickname then being Big Nose.

Even with the issue of his weight, I have understood

what Gazza has gone through, though I have been luckier with my own metabolism. During my drinking, I went up to 14st 4lb and went down to 13st in prison before settling at my optimum weight of 13st 9lb. We did lose contact for a while because it got confusing when he went to Tottenham and we thought we had to hate each other, but we always got together for a drink with England. When I stopped drinking, I think perhaps he started to look at me as if I was on a different planet. He couldn't make out what I was about.

I used to deny that Paul was a major talent when it came to club games against Spurs, because that was the only way I could deal with the situation. We reckoned we could put a stopper on him and nullify him, like we did with Stewart Robson on Glenn Hoddle. I have to say, though, in that semi-final of 1991 he did for us pretty comprehensively with that free kick, then by setting up the third goal. But then he always could get up for one-off Cup games. What about a whole league season? You could never guarantee the number of games he would play, what with injuries. And take the Cup Final of '91 for Spurs against Nottingham Forest. Having done that to us, he went out next time and smashed his leg up with a reckless challenge. The fact is that he has never been able to do his job consistently and that type of player will always find it difficult to. Maradona at Napoli was probably an exception but how many games did Paul play at Lazio? In fact, it was 43 in three seasons.

The difference at international level is that you need greatness over a few games rather than consistency over a season and with Gazza you always have that potential. You want players who can open teams up, which is why you pay £7.5 million for Dennis Bergkamp. Gazza is exciting in that respect, he can open locked doors. The strength he had when he was on those diagonal runs that we tried to get him to do was second to none. When he drew defenders to him, two or three at a time, he was creating space for another player and could then release them into the space with a little pass.

When you get him focused on his football and just give him the ball, he can be exceptional. You take all the peripheral things out – the media, the public expectation, the managers even – and just let him go and play and he would do it all day. You just couldn't stop him. As Don Howe used to say about him, he doesn't like the discipline of running on the training ground, but give him a ball and he'll go on until it gets dark. The problem is that professional football is so much more than just that, though.

Another problem is that Paul comes as a package, with all the attendant baggage. For a start, he is a bag of nerves. Now, everyone is up and down before a game and everyone has their own mannerisms, like Perry Groves driving me mad shaking his leg incessantly in the dressing room. I was always alive in my stomach before England games – and used to take medicine to settle it in the days before I calmed down – while every inch of Gazza's twitching body was alive. He just cannot wait to get that ball. He used to love me shouting because he could get involved and join in. It was a release for him and I could get him going.

For a league season, I would rather have a consistent performer like Alan Smith with me in my team. Now whether Alan could have scored that goal against Scotland, chipping the ball over Colin Hendry's head then volleying home, is quite a different matter. Smeggy could not win games single-handedly – though you could argue that he did against Parma – but probably contributed to the overall picture more often.

I think Paul Gascoigne is at his best when he simply gets his escapism in fishing and nothing else. Sometimes you just have to say, when he is being a nuisance around the team hotel, 'Look Gazza, just naff off and go fishing.' I saw David Seaman confront him before Euro '96, telling him to sort himself out, that he was letting the boys down. After his fishing, you can let him come back and do his training with the ball, do some shooting, and hopefully you have a good chance of getting him to play for you. When you get him bubbling, telling jokes and having a laugh – and he is a joke machine – then he forgets about his other problems in life and you have him on your side. I don't think you can cage a tiger like him. Some people can stay in a hotel without needing release for six days. I didn't used to be able to and nor can Gazza.

Before Euro '96, when Paul Merson was still gambling, he and I used to share a room together on England trips and Gazza would always be in there, with Merse setting up deals for him. I was a bit jealous of that. I wanted to be considered a loveable rogue, too. Then during the tournament, he would swan about Burnham Beeches with his brandy and cigar and playing snooker as if we were all guests at his country house weekend. I do think managers have turned a blind eye to some of his antics down the years as long he performed on the pitch, but I'm not sure that they have all done him a favour. Terry always got the best out of him because he knew him inside out and didn't try and control him. It is difficult. You have to let Paul fly but he runs the risk of crash-landing.

I just hope he finds the right path for him in life. I do feel for him, with all the attention trained on him. I know he would be happier in his working men's club in Newcastle with his mates, having the odd kickabout. I just hope it all sorts itself out for him and that he gets to a stage in life where he wants to change. Underneath it all, he has a great heart – on the pitch too, which is why, despite all the minuses, I would still pick him. He is a team man, unlike many of the most talented players who simply see a game as a stage for their ability, and realises that football is not like golf or tennis where you play for yourself.

Working just behind him on the left there would only be one choice in my England team. Like Shilts, I always admired Bryan Robson for his ability to work hard and play hard. I used to hope that other players would be saying that about me as well. About a month before Euro '88 he organised a night out for the players but I declined, being young, naive and thinking I ought to be in real training. Robbo was still stronger than me the next day. He was an extraordinary professional.

And talented, too. He just had a terrific football brain, knew the game inside out and had an amazing sense of what was happening in the game. He had a great engine for getting up and down the pitch, could head a ball, was tough, strong and could be ruthless in the tackle. Above all, though, he had fantastic awareness. When Terry Butcher went up for the ball, Robbo seemed to anticipate where the header was going and get there first. He knew how and when to arrive in the right places at the right times; it is a footballing intelligence that I believe I also possess. David Platt has it too. Many players don't, though, and for me it is this real awareness that separates the average from the best. They know when to close down and when to commit themselves or to stay on their feet. Beyond the best are the unique, like Maradona, a player who could command the whole pitch, pulling people around, opening up space.

Another element of Bryan's game was that he was a good talker, not just to his team but to the referee as well. He would sit in that midfield, having a dialogue with the ref so that when there were important decisions to be made, he might be on your side. Robbo was everything that I wanted to be in the late 80s; England captain, successful, strong, not scared of anybody or of having a ruck, fond of a drink. They used to give him man of the match automatically at Wembley. That was the presence of the guy.

Wide on the left but not tied to the touchline would have to be John Barnes. 'Digger' could pass, he could move, he could dribble, had great balance, could cross a ball. What more could you want? I know that he was seen by fans as someone who never performed for England the way he did for Liverpool. There were reasons for that. Too often he was stuck out on the left and had to stay there. At Liverpool under Kenny Dalglish, he was given licence to come inside, allowed to roam and fly. That's why Liverpool were the great side they were in the late 80s. I know that type of movement was exactly what Terry Venables would have wanted and it's what I would like in my team.

Probably the most contentious selection for England has always been in attack and many have been called. Only two can be chosen, however, which means, in my way of playing, an out-and-out striker and one playing off him to link midfield and attack. In that category, I have played in teams with two outstanding practitioners of the art. Peter Beardsley and Teddy Sheringham are similar players in many ways, unselfish and with an eye for a killer pass, able to pull off markers cleverly and get into areas to hurt teams. Both possess individual assets too. Peter, for example, was quicker and nippier than Ted, who was better in the air and more likely to score goals. I think it is Ted's strength that would just give him the edge for me.

For the last place there are again two leading candidates and as goalscorers Gary Lineker and Alan Shearer have both dominated their eras. You would have to say there is one fundamental difference, however; Alan is the one likely to work harder for the team. I think Colin Hendry once said that he is all-round average and he does contribute in every area. He is an intelligent player, along the lines of Lineker, and also has that talent of awareness in when to move and where to run. He is a great header of the ball but I would fancy my chances against him – as I do against everyone, mind. Neither is he especially quick but like Alan Smith, he holds the ball up well and brings other people into play. He is also very determined around the box and very aggressive, not that his rough and tumble has ever really bothered me because it is part of the game. He is, simply, an all-round centre-forward and a good leader, too. Not many people know it, either, but behind the public straight-laced figure is a real prankster who likes to cut people's ties or hides their socks; the Wimbledon Crazy Gang sort of stuff.

I have to say my attitude to Gary Lineker has changed. In my early days with England, I don't think he respected me or thought I could play. I disliked this arrogant, golden boy image he had. When he was playing for Tottenham, I also hated the fact that he often did well against me, like scoring in that '91 semi-final. I was young and I would try to kick him up in the air on the pitch, and bad-mouth him in private as my way of dealing with this thorn in my side in the North London rivalry. 'We'll have him,' Steve Bould used to say. What can he do anyway? That was my rationalisation. He can't go past five people. He can't head the ball. He made his name on the back of Peter Beardsley's efforts for England and Alan Smith's for Leicester. 'Did he send you a thank you card at the end of the season, Smeggy?' I used to ask.

What could he do? Well, he could make the most penetrating runs I ever saw – helped by Don Howe, who used to say, 'One run for the defender and one for yourself' – and if you delivered the ball properly he was almost certain to get you a goal. He worked on his timing and although Ian Wright was, in my opinion, probably a better finisher, there was a cleverness, a cuteness, to Lineker's runs that I don't think anyone else has demonstrated for England.

I think off the pitch he has also loosened up now that he doesn't have to be seen as this goody two-shoes any more. Ian Wright's wife threw a surprise party at Terry Neill's Sports Bar at Holborn Viaduct in London to celebrate Ian's record number of goals for Arsenal and I got talking to Gary there. It was amazing how well we got on now that all the stuff of the past had been shed. So there you have it; you can't play Shearer and Lineker together because they would take each other's space and be rendered ineffective together. I plump for Gary.

And there you have my England team, too:

Seaman

Anderson   Adams   Sansom

Hoddle   Ince   Robson   Barnes

Gascoigne   Sheringham

Lineker

I think they could play together and I would certainly enjoy finding out. I can almost hear Terry Venables licking his lips now.

TEN

Cheers and Booze

'Tony, I cannot believe it,' Arsène Wenger said to me one day as we sat drinking coffee at Sopwell House, Arsenal coach and captain just talking things over. 'I cannot believe how you achieved everything you have with the way you abused your body and your mind. You have played to only 70 per cent of your capacity.' Neither can I believe it really, but that is alcoholism. Some people have this idea that alcoholics are just down-and-outs on the street but very often they are people who achieve highly and cling on to doing their job very well because they know they will go under if they let that slip.

I have looked back to see where I crossed that invisible line between what some people call social drinking and the sort of alcoholic drinking of those seven weeks after Euro '96 but I can't recognise it. It just crept up on me. Some people say they are born alcoholics. I believe I drank myself into alcoholism. It wasn't that I needed to drink to celebrate victories or to console myself after defeats. I just needed to drink. There is an old saying in football: 'Win or lose, on the booze,' and that was me.

I don't look back and blame anyone or anything for it, not my Mum or my Dad, not George Graham, not football. In fact, that was when I accepted that I was an alcoholic –

when I ran out of people to blame and took responsibility for myself. It took a lot to get to that point, though, when booze stopped working as relief from the pain I felt in life; like football had stopped working from about 1994 onwards.

That was mostly a private pain that few people got to see. Of course there were the very public escapades that drink had caused – the prison sentence, the 29 stitches in my forehead, the Pizza Hut incident. But behind those were many more private episodes that have never been revealed, because active alcoholism is a shameful business and only in recovery have I been able to deal with that shame and own up to all the things that did go on.

The longer I do not drink, the more insight I have into both my past and my present. The seeds of my illness – and alcoholism, make no mistake, is an illness and a progressive one that gets worse unless arrested – were there from very early on. They say it is a disease of the personality and I can see the unease I had from quite young.

As a kid, for example, I remember looking out of the window at four o'clock on cold, wet days when it was just getting dark, unable to get out for a fix of my first drug football. I felt empty and lonely. Even then I was thinking about what I could do to fill this void. I was searching for something. The feelings led to panic attacks when I was only 11 or 12 years old, when I experienced a sensation of my heart racing with fear – about what, I couldn't really tell you. About nothing in particular and everything in general. I would jump out of bed with hot sweats, thinking that I was going to die.

Then there was the shyness. I remember a girl who lived a few doors away when I was 14 coming up to me and insisting that she was going out with me now. I complied, of course, and we walked round the block. It was real Nick Hornby stuff, though, from his novel *High Fidelity* rather than *Fever Pitch*. After we had kissed, she dumped me. I was left wondering what I had done wrong. I felt rejected and ashamed, unwilling to talk about the feeling with anybody. I didn't feel attractive to girls. I had greasy hair, after all. I was going to concentrate on football. I was good at that and didn't get any of this feeling of inadequacy with that.

School was an ordeal for me. Because I lived in Rainham and went to school in Dagenham, I had a different set of mates and was playing two different roles even then. I felt uncomfortable and feeble there. I was not good academically and would panic during lessons if I was asked to read anything out. They called me 'the wheelie kid' because I couldn't pronounce the word 'really' properly. I was ridiculed and felt useless.

Football rescued me from all that. It was why I liked being out in the open air, away from the confines of classrooms. Also I had my mates in football who looked up to me. I was a star in that crowd. Exciting things were happening for me at Arsenal and it meant that I could look towards things there. It also, I'm sure, stunted my emotional growth but that is with hindsight. Then, my instincts carried me along.

In my last year at school I didn't take the mock examinations at Christmas because I was ill and the prospect of the real things terrified me. I was dreading the oral exam in English especially and had been for five years. Signing for Arsenal and going on an England trip got me out of it and as a result I got my first experience of escaping from fear. My Mum and Dad would just tell me to do my best with the exams and of course they were being encouraging and helpful, but the fear of facing up to them was just too much for me.

Alcohol did not enter my life for a long time. I didn't even like the taste of it early on. I can see the start of an obsessive personality, though, in the way I would consume a whole gateau or cheesecake before bed every night and burned it off at training the next morning. When it came to drinking, as a 17-year-old I would mostly stick to bitter shandy. In another year or so it became lager with a top of lemonade. Then it was on to cheap watery lager.

I wanted to become a proper drinker because all the people I liked, the ones I wanted to be like, enjoyed a drink. They were confident and funny and outgoing, all the things I wanted to be. I had to work at liking alcohol. It was the effect, not the taste, I was after. I tried Special Brew but got frightened off it because I woke up in a wet bed in a hotel room after six cans one night. I didn't want to be that bad. So I once asked one of the senior Arsenal players then, Graham Rix, if Guinness worked to get you drunk. When he said it did, I gave that a try. And so I drank myself into liking Guinness. I so much wanted to be a good drinker.

At first it was just Saturday nights after games. Everyone did it and I saw nothing wrong with it. I deserved some release after working hard all week. I probably didn't start till about 9.30 pm but it would go on until 3 am in a nightclub. I was comfortable doing it, always ready for the next pint half way through the existing one. I didn't want to chat up the birds and I didn't want my mates to. 'Leave them alone, lads. Let's have a good night on our own,' I would say to them. I drank as much as I could get down my neck, probably about 10 pints. I was a shy, awkward character who needed a drink so he didn't have to worry about it.

Though I mostly wanted to avoid confrontation – and I never thought I was an aggressive person when drunk, even if others may have disagreed – booze could bring out a destructive side to me. One night around this time after a party, for example, I recall staggering down the High Street in Old Brentwood and breaking off every car aerial along the way just for the hell of it. I suppose I could say it was just the over-exuberance of youth and that a lot of people do such things at some time. Perhaps, but I also know these days that, when sober, I would not do such a thing and nor do a lot of young people.

In my routine at this time, I would get home and go to bed without having any sort of blackout, so I considered that everything must be all right. Alcohol was there on the rare occasions I did find female company, always in nightclubs. As a young man of 18 and 19, and with all the peer pressure a young footballer gets in the dressing room, I wanted to find a girlfriend but was frightened and needed drink for Dutch courage. The booze enabled me eventually to have sex; or maybe it was another excuse to get drunk. Of course I lied about it to the boys, told them I had plenty of girlfriends. Come to think about it, the dressing room was about the only place I ever talked to people then. It was banter, actually. Drinking and 'birding' made me a man. But I was a man subconsciously unwilling to face up to all the feelings he was experiencing and didn't know how to deal with.

Mostly, though, football was still enough for me and isolated instances warned me about the dangers of drinking. There had been the time Don Howe rang up on the Saturday night, to be told I was at a nightclub when I was supposed to be resting an injury. I was furious with my Mum for telling him. He was furious with me and it shook me for a while. Then there was the first time I missed training on a Monday. Or coming in to training still stinking of booze and someone remarking on it. Not being able to do my job did alarm me. Without that, I was worried that there was not much to me.

Not even those concerns – and this is the power of alcohol over an alcoholic and his or her powerlessness over it – would get in the way for too long, though. Saturday spilled into Sunday, a day which came to play a big part in my drinking. It was partly out of boredom, partly out of loneliness. The rest of the week I was occupied with the game and Saturday was the peak of the week. Sunday was anti-climax, Sunday was empty. In those days when I was single, I would get up at about 10 or 11 am, just about manage a shower, though I never shaved on my day off, and be down the pub for midday. Then the usual story; back home at two or three for a sleep. The routine of many. I knew nothing else. I was not an educated young man, had a limited attention span and had no other interests. No problem still, it seemed.

When live Sunday football was introduced, it gave me an excuse to stay down the pub all day. In the 1989/90 season, for example, on the day of the FA Cup semi-finals between Liverpool and Crystal Palace, Manchester United and Oldham, I was out drinking from midday right through both games. I started off at Cardinal's in Romford and managed to pay attention to an exciting first game, which Palace won 4–3 after extra-time. In those days, pubs closed in mid-afternoon and I had to go over to my mate's pub in Billericay to see the second match. But the drink took over, the game began to bore me and eventually I was too drunk to see it. When later Arsenal had to play on a Sunday, my drinking was really spoiled. That became a pain in the neck.

It also later became difficult if we were playing a Tuesday game because I would not be fully recovered.

If we weren't playing, I would now, in my early twenties, be out drinking all day on a Sunday. The idea of a sleep had gone. If I felt tired I would just have a few more pints until I chased the feeling away – something I did with so many feelings. Blackouts were now creeping in as my Sunday routine developed and I would lose my memory of large parts of the day. At least they meant I never suffered from the room spinning as so many drunks do. Also, I rarely had hangovers. Later, during bad days I would come to think that if maybe I had, they might give me an ability to stop drinking. Too often I was just able to get up and do it all over again.

Piecing the bits together I recall from several years of it, I can say that the day would start at midday with the first pint of Guinness. It was a bit difficult to get down but I worked on it over the years. I persevered. Then once I had hit two or three, I was off and running. Four, five and six came easy. At three o'clock, I would order up four pints in case Bill was going to close the Chequers for the afternoon kip he liked. Being the sly sort that alcoholics become, I would try to get him on the vodka and orange he also liked and usually he would agree, after a couple, to keep the place going for a select few of us. 'It's just for you, Tone,' my mates would say. 'He likes you in his boozer.' It wasn't just because I was a famous footballer, though. Bill once told me I was the best Guinness drinker in his pub. Yes. What an accolade, I thought; what an achievement. I had won medals and England caps all over the place but this made me really proud.

I had indeed mastered Guinness and I could drink it like other people drank lager. On good – or bad – days I could drink four pints in an hour. A session would probably be about 20 pints. In the evenings I could do a couple of bottles of wine on top. My mates would say that it was because I was an athlete that my capacity was so high, that I had a fast system and that my body could deal with it. I thought wetting the bed, which was becoming more frequent for me, was also my body's way of dealing with it. In fact, I welcomed it because I thought it was not rotting my stomach and that I was getting rid of it ready for Monday training. Some clear thinking, that.

The most embarrassing example of the bed-wetting came during the European Championship finals of 1988 in West Germany. After we had lost the second game to Holland, Bobby Robson told us all to stay focused on the next game against the Soviet Union but as team captain, Bryan Robson thought we would be better served by a night on the beer drowning our sorrows. As an alcoholic in development, it suited me.

When I woke up the next morning, my bed was soaked and a chambermaid was standing in the room holding her nose and saying 'pee pee'. It was even more embarrassing when word got round the camp and I came down to breakfast to hear the lads laughing and repeating 'pee pee' at me. I tried to laugh it off, but underneath I was ashamed, unable to talk about this hurt with anybody. Enduring the mickey-taking, as well as the media, hardly come into your head as things you will have to deal with when you dream about being a professional footballer.

Anyway, on Sundays I would either move on from my starting point of The Chequers, or if Bill did close in late afternoon, I would find other little pubs and clubs I knew around Hornchurch. Perhaps even get a cab up to Niall Quinn's place in Enfield and we would do a few social or

Irish clubs he knew in North London. Then I discovered Ra Ra's, the nightclub in Islington where I met Jane, and I had somewhere cheerful to go on those gloomy Sunday nights. This is rocking, this'll do for me, I remember thinking.

Although Niall and I went on that bender a week before the 1989 title decider at Liverpool, Anfield itself was just too big an event for drink to play a part in the immediate run-up. In those days I could white-knuckle it, as is said of drinkers who clench their fists and grit their teeth as they desperately go without a drink. Football still had me first and booze came second. Mind you, that night I needed it afterwards, as proved by the bender I went on. It had to be competitive football, though, that kept me away from the stuff.

In March of 1990, for example, I was picked for England B to play the Republic of Ireland in Cork. It was a Tuesday game but I wasn't going to let that get in the way of my Sunday routine. My body had not recovered enough by the time of the game and I was given the run-around by Niall Quinn and David Kelly as the Irish won 4–1. Then in May of that year, booze was definitely more important to me that day I was due to be going to Singapore with Arsenal.

Going to jail had little effect on my drinking or my perception of it as any sort of a problem. In fact, though I lost my driving licence, I gained a drinking licence; because I didn't have to worry about the car any more, I could get drunk more often and get people to drive me about. Ray Parlour, who lived near me in Romford, was particularly helpful. Sometimes after training if I couldn't wait until we got back to Essex for a drink, I'd drag him into a pub in nearby St Albans.

Jail must have had some effect on me, though, and I know other people around me thought so. I think I shut down my emotional system in jail as a way of dealing with it and there were a lot of pent-up feelings. I went through a self-loathing period, as I would call it now, though at the time it just seemed like me developing a few party pieces.

Before prison, I had often done some mad things for the entertainment of the lads, like the time on an Arsenal mid-season break to Bermuda – where all the boys wanted to play golf but I just wanted to drink – when I head-butted a concrete pole. After jail, I began to smash glasses over my head, to their amazement. Mostly it was for private consumption but on a trip to Dublin, we were in a basement drinking club in Leeson Street in the early hours amid a party of Oriental tourists. I think I mistakenly picked up one of their drinks and the bloke took exception, shaping up to me in a Bruce Lee pose. I grabbed a pint glass, stared at him and just crashed and smashed it on the top of my head. Bruce Lee and the other tourists left pretty quickly. The boys laughed. I was seeking approval, showing how tough I was.

I also picked fights with people, such as David Hillier. Shortly after I came out of Chelmsford, I went to Paul Davis's golf day – where I played only a few holes, fuelled by a morning drink and the Scotch in my bag – and that night we were going on a mid-season break to the Meon Valley Country Club near Southampton. There I just turned nasty and went for David, punching and bloodying his nose. There was also some horseplay with Michael Thomas, whom I had in a bearhug that he broke easily enough. That should have told me I was suffering from an illness. One, Mickey was a good friend whom I respected. Two, you don't go messing with Michael Thomas. He was a strong boy.

Because Sunday was my drinking day, I would often turn

up drunk when England assembled at Burnham Beeches. I started off driving down there, then got into driving down there drunk. Once, I had to stop on the hard shoulder of the M25 for a pee, to my great embarrassment. After that, I took to taking a taxi down there so I could drink from noon to 7 pm without worrying.

On arrival at Burnham, I would be straight into the bar. I had all these feelings around England of inadequacy or being overawed in the early days, but at the same time thinking I was the bee's knees. I remember being in the London nightclub Tramp one night after a game during the Bobby Robson era with Terry Butcher – who asked me after watching me dancing if I really was injured as Bobby had told him – along with Kenny Sansom, and seeing all these people like Bill Wyman in there and thinking I had really arrived. This was the life for me. Actually, sometimes I think I enjoyed being injured because it allowed me to have a drink.

If fit, I wouldn't drink on the Monday or Tuesday before the international, however. I had this suspicion even then of what might happen and I couldn't trust myself. I always recall Paul Parker bringing four cans of lager with him and in a very self-disciplined way drinking them moderately over the next couple of days. I couldn't understand that. Who wants two beers? That would have been torture to me. It had to be all or nothing. At Arsenal, Brian Marwood would have just the one glass of wine on a Friday night to relax and I used to think, 'How can I have a problem? I don't drink on a Friday night. I will not drink on a Friday night.' I would conveniently forget about Thursdays, Saturday nights and Sundays, though. And in those free weeks of the Tuesday club, the lads didn't know that I had a Monday club all of my own.

On long get-togethers with England, from a Thursday through to the following Wednesday, before important internationals, Bobby Robson would take us to a local pub to relax, which naturally I enjoyed. Graham Taylor also took us to a restaurant one night and after checking out that it was OK to drink, I did – plenty. I got very lippy by the end of the evening and was giving all the Liverpool lads an earful about 1989. So obnoxious was I being, apparently, that David Seaman and Mark Wright had to pin me down on the back seat, David putting his hand over my mouth to shut me up.

The incident I recall most vividly during Graham's time in charge was in the October of 1992 before a big World Cup qualifying match against Norway at Wembley. After one of the nights out, Paul Merson and I were in the mood for some fun and we crept in to David Seaman's room to fill up his toilet with toilet paper. We thought we were being secretive but he was standing in the doorway of his bathroom watching us do it. Prank over, I stayed on to talk to David while Merse went back to the room we were sharing. The next thing I knew, I was waking up – bed wet – in the room, which no longer had a door to it. I was told later that I had crashed through the door in my drunkenness, or perhaps broken it down, and had asked the night porter, who had been alerted by the noise, if he could sort things out.

Obviously he had not been able to because Graham Taylor was soon marching into our room demanding to know what had happened. He was visibly stunned. I was just out of the shower. 'Who's done this?' he asked, secretly hoping that it was Paul, I suspect, as I was at that time a more valuable player to him. I had been in blackout but Paul had told me that he hadn't done it, so I concluded therefore it must have been me. After I had owned up, Graham said, 'Well, I can't help you on this one. If this gets in the papers, you're out.' He wasn't to know he was dealing with an active alcoholic.

Luckily it stayed out of the papers. The players all kept quiet about it and the staff at Burnham Beeches have learned to be very discreet over the years, which is why England have probably stayed there for so long. The cleaners turned the mattress over and put a rubber sheet on my bed. Later I did receive a bill from the FA for the door, though. It was a lovely oak job and cost me £490.

I was worried about the effect of the incident on my England career but the money never bothered me when it came to drinking. When I once got my credit card company phoning me up to query a nightclub bill for £5,800, I just told them to pay it. In fact I was one of those lucky alcoholics who had enough money so that he was never forced to moderate his drinking. Mostly my mates had a principle of not letting me pay for everything, but sometimes if I needed company and someone didn't have any money, I would just get £300 out of the cash-point and we would embark on a spree. Having money probably meant that I got to my rock bottom a lot quicker than some people do.

If I thought that getting married and having children might calm me down for a while and make me more responsible and adult about things, I was very mistaken. Like attracts like, as Jane's own addictive illness was to prove, and the marriage probably helped me on my way to rock bottom. In the week of the wedding, in July 1992, I was drunk for five days solid. At the ceremony, I was slurring my words as I took my vows. It was a grand, even grandiose, occasion at a country house hotel in Essex for

150 guests and I drank champagne and brandy all day, ending up playing the drums apparently. I arranged it all in a blackout, phoning my Dad a couple of days later to see if I had paid everyone off.

The relationship between Jane and me was to prove a volatile one, not surprisingly given the cocktail of an alcoholic and an addict living together. The signs were there early on. On one of our first dates, we were in the back of a taxi coming back from Chelmsford where we had been to a restaurant called Russell's and we were having an argument. I tried to get out of the minicab while it was coming down the A12 and she punched me, giving me a black eye, trying to bring me to my senses. It probably did shock me for a moment into calming down. On another occasion, we were in Planet Hollywood and someone approached me for an autograph when we were arguing. I told them to piss off and just carried on with the row. Jane proceeded to pour a drink over my head. I knew nothing about any of this until the following morning when she told me. Blackout again.

Around this time in the early 90s I was drinking heavily but because I was still doing my job well for Arsenal I thought everything was fine. At training on mornings after the night before, I would put on an extra layer of kit, sweat it all off and get on with things. In fact, I liked training because it was another form of escapism from myself and my problems. Quite often I suspect I was still over the limit when I turned up for training and I would hope it was just a running day, that George Graham wouldn't get a ball out.

I would also try to keep out of his way in case he could smell the drink on me, and I would chew gum as I sauntered in during the morning. In the team meetings I would sit at the back. If we were doing any ball work, I would often be really agitated and kicking people and swearing and George would tell me not to kick my own players but to save it for the opposition. Then I would get angry with him and have a go back.

There were times when I am sure he noticed but kept his own counsel. Once on a pre-season tour of Sweden I was still pissed from the night before and I was falling about all over the place, to the amusement of the boys, but George never said a word. It might have been the same Scandinavian tour where we were in a pub in Oslo called The Gunners and I was pulling pints for everyone, loving being the centre of attention. George sat in the corner observing it all. I was putting brandy in my Guinness, which was the only way I drank spirits really. I did drink Chivas Regal for a while – in fact I knocked back a whole bottle in one session – because I was once in Marbella with Kenny Sansom and he got chatting to a bar owner who had two Dobermans called Chivas and Regal. That tickled me when Kenny told me and I thought I'd try the drink.

End of season, summer and even pre-season tours were a great release to me; I was a dog off the leash. Because my first drug was withdrawn from me, I needed to indulge fully my other to fill the void. On one post-season club trip to Cyprus I drank for five days solid without eating. At the end, just trying to get a piece of bread into my mouth was a painful and drawn-out process.

Right from the early days, booze figured all the way through the close season and, before I met Jane, I would organise the holidays for me and my mates. I loved all that, the dominant ego controlling everyone, the big talker, making all the arrangements for them that suited me. I can reel them off now – Torremolinos '84, when I went with Martin Hayes; Ibiza '85, dressed up as a woman on stage;

Gran Canaria '86; Majorca '87; America'88, which I hated; Portugal '89; and Rhodes '90. Alcoholic escapades all of them.

That one to Florida was a mistake because there were a couple of mates on the trip whose first priority did not accord with mine. They wanted to do things like go to the Magic Kingdom at Disneyworld. But you couldn't get a beer there and there was no way I was going to queue for the rides without booze in me. I endured walking round for a couple of hours before going back to the hotel and having a proper drink, pondering also on what weird people the Americans were.

The last 'lads' one to Rhodes, after being left out of the World Cup squad, was the worst. I actually hallucinated during that and saw ghosts coming out of the cupboard during the night. There, I was also about to urinate in the foyer of a five-star hotel, had my underpants around my ankles in fact, until my mate grabbed me and pushed me into a toilet. Not that being with Jane changed my behaviour much. In 1993 in Jamaica, I was so drunk at the bar at 6 pm one night that I passed out and the barman slung me over his shoulder, carried me to my room and put me to bed. I woke up at 6 am. It was on that holiday that I first smoked cannabis, one of only a few times in my drinking history as it wasn't my drug of choice, a clear result of having had too much to drink. Sometimes when I was drunk I would also smoke a big cigar just for posed effect.

Back home, in the period before pre-season training, I would be into a routine of pub in the morning – the Albion in Rainham when I was living at home with Mum and Dad – have my lunch in there, then perhaps go on into London for an evening. And get up and do it all again the next day. It was how I met Jane. I was on a crawl around the

Holloway Road area near to Highbury. None of the Arsenal fans who populated the area seemed all that shocked to see me drinking heavily. They never reported me to George or to the papers, anyway. I think they thought I was one of their own and they related to me. Besides which, I could justify it by saying that it didn't interfere with Arsenal anyway.

In the summer just before the 1993/94 season, Arsenal went to South Africa for a series of games but for me it was really an extension of my drinking time. We were not supposed to drink on the flight down but we kept the odd can under the seat. Then I noticed George was drinking champagne, so I got chatting with him, had one myself and from then on, the lads could see we were OK for a drink. Good captaincy, that.

It should have been a real experience, but I was not really in any position to appreciate it at that time. We played Manchester United, winning 2–0, and then beat Orlando Pirates 1–0, after which I was presented to Nelson Mandela. I'm afraid to say it meant little to me then. My knowledge of Nelson Mandela extended to banners demanding his release outside the South African embassy in London when I was on a regular pub crawl around the Embankment area, stopping at every place that sold Budweiser. We were also due to go into the townships to do some coaching but the day before, there was a bombing in which three people died and it was considered too risky.

Now Johannesburg can be a dangerous city and we were assigned a bodyguard who came with us at night when we went out. A few of us jumped from place to place, though, as we trawled through the city and lost him. We came across the Manchester United boys at one point. I offended some white bloke somewhere else and he tried to follow me from bar to bar, threatening to shoot me. I managed to escape from him and ended up on my own at 6 am in a black club smoking a joint that had been offered to me.

None of this type of stuff really bothered me, nor the fact around this time that I kept a crate of cheap champagne in the boot of my car. Then that Christmas of 1993, I began to notice for the first time how the booze was affecting my game. It was against Swindon Town on Boxing Day and I had mistimed my drinking session. I always tried not to have a drink the night before a game but with it being on a Monday, I got dates and times mixed up. I had been drinking until the early hours at home and was still feeling the effects when I took the field. But it was a bit like being back at school; feeling ill but still wanting to play.

If I had been breathalysed I would certainly have failed. Luckily we were scoring goals at the other end – we won 4–0, with Kevin Campbell scoring a hat-trick and Ian Wright a brilliant lob – but George Graham could see I wasn't doing it. It was just too much like hard work. He pulled me off in the second half and afterwards gave me a real dressing-down, calling me a disgrace. I couldn't really argue, just cowered in the corner of the dressing room, and I felt ashamed on the coach coming home. I sensed George knew I had been drinking but results mean everything and that one masked my problem.

It got more worrying a couple of months later when we went up to play Everton at Goodison Park. On the Thursday night before, I was in a club in the West End called Fidenzi's – which opened at 3 am and was used by all the staff of the other nightclubs when they closed – until very late. Then on the Friday night, the sleeping pills I used to take were not working, even though I had upped my dose from two to three tablets around this time. I would not get the rest and recuperation my body needed from such heavy benders as I went on.

Despite Swindon, I still thought that I could hack it, but this time grit and determination were not enough to get me through. I did have a lot of pride – false pride – and desperately wanted to get out there. But when the game kicked off, I was just not in it. Everton were putting balls into the channels and turning me and I couldn't keep up. Lesser players were showing me up. I struggled through 70 minutes before George pulled me off, but this time I had a good excuse. I had told George before the game that I had a stomach upset and that I was vomiting, probably due to something I had eaten. This time, rather than give me an earful, he seemed to admire me for having given it a go. Alcoholics get clever at manipulating circumstances.

Then came the worst of all, that April. We were playing Sheffield United in a Monday night game, travelling up and back on the day so I didn't need to let it interfere with my Sunday routine and I got to bed at around two or three in the morning. Ray Parlour was staying with me, though he wasn't going to be playing at Bramall Lane. When I woke up in the morning, I had the shakes, which were worsened by the knowledge that I had to play in about ten hours' time. I felt really rotten. I knew my body would not recover in time so there was only one thing for it. I only had two pints in The Chequers, just to take the edge off, to settle my stomach. Nobody said anything to me. Typical alcoholic, that, I have come to see. Most people if they are feeling rotten do not think about having a drink – the very thing that has made them feel bad – to make them feel better.

Luckily I had Ray to drive me over to London Colney and the saddest thing about the whole episode was that I was made man of the match in the 1–1 draw. The Sky TV presenter Anna Walker, who is a Sheffield United supporter, made the award of a silver cutlery set afterwards. I knew that I had not been anywhere near my best, however. I sat on my own on the coach journey back feeling rough but putting it down to a cold coming on. I was thinking that the game was getting to be a really hard slog for me and it never used to be. That it shouldn't be. 'You don't smile any more when you play,' my Dad said to me around this time. He was right but I wouldn't acknowledge it and that it hurt. 'Well, work's not supposed to be fun, is it?' I would say defensively.

For a couple of hours on the way back from Sheffield I felt really gloomy but gradually the depression lifted as I started to talk to people about the next game, about our European Cup Winners' Cup run of that season. The worry that the main thing I was clinging on to – my football – the thing that had always been central to my life, was going wrong was lost in a couple of cans of lager. They made me a new man, in the wrong sense of the expression.

Post-match drinking was an easy routine I had slipped into. I used to say to the drinkers in the team at half-time, 'Only 45 more minutes boys and it's job done. Then we'll have a beer.' And it would be straight into the players' lounge. Usually I was pissed after just a couple and would leave with a few cans in my pockets for the journey. At Highbury, I would always get a crate of beer for the opposing captain to take on to the coach and hope that when I went away he would do the same for us. I also liked to smuggle a bottle of wine on board for the meal.

After some of that little lot, I told myself that, yes, of course I could keep doing this. Now I was talking a good game, a hell of a good game. Deep down, I was frightened that I wouldn't be able to play on for much longer and it became Catch 22. I drank because I was frightened and I was frightened because I drank. I couldn't tell which came first.

It was the same when we travelled abroad for European matches. That spring of '94, I was just getting myself together for the Cup Winners' Cup. Having achieved everything else, it was just about the one thing that was still interesting me. The flying to away legs always bothered me but I could never have a drink – the same with England – because we went only the day before and I would not have time to recover so I just had to grin and bear it. The overseas trips were something I never thought about during matches when we were trying to qualify but always did afterwards. When we won the FA Cup in '93, for example, I thought on the Wembley pitch, 'Oh shit. We'll have to fly abroad now.' England summer tours always filled me with dread as well. It was the idea of being powerless and out of control that scared me. I thought that in every other area I was in control. They were the same reasons that the drinking would come to scare me.

Coming back was a different matter altogether, as I knew we could have a drink and the fear got lost amid all the banter and stories. After my first England cap, they presented me with a bottle of champagne on the plane. I was always quickly stuck in. I was probably a bit more sensitive about the mood if we had lost but after 10 or so drinks I stopped worrying. I was also happy if the press were on our plane and we were delayed while waiting for them to send over their reports, because it meant we had more drinking time.

I remember the night we flew back from Copenhagen after beating Parma that May. From Stansted Airport, I went straight to a pub in Billericay where I knew the manager and the staff opened up for us at 4 am. This, though the manager himself didn't get back from Copenhagen until 5 am. When it got light, I went and had some breakfast in a cafe then set off for a bender in the Romford area. I remember also being in The Chequers drinking brandy and Guinness, telling everyone for a laugh that I had told Jane I would be home at three – in the morning.

That May, on FA Cup Final day in fact, I was also out on a bender with Ray Parlour at a friend's stag party in Clacton. As the night wore on, we ended up at the friend's pub in Billericay, where three strippers had been booked. It became, I'm told, a wild night with me ending up doing the Full Monty long before it became popular, and falling over in the process.

It actually seemed to sober me up quite quickly, as sometimes happened to me – I could fall asleep at a table as well and be brand new in ten minutes – because I was soon getting ten people into Hollywood's in Romford, a club where I once insulted Danny Baker and on another occasion started poking fun at John Leslie, wondering where his Blue Peter badge was. Well, at that time I thought it was funny.

Anyway, someone tipped off the *News of the World* about the Billericay shenanigans and it was duly plastered all over the paper. When I got wind that they had the story – which conveniently had quotes and plenty of detail from barmaids and other eyewitnesses – I was with England and had to ring Jane to tell her exactly what had gone on. I was trying to do the decent thing but floundering. It was excruciating. I felt so ashamed that I just had to get drunk again to cover up the way I felt.

The evidence was piling up against me and I look back on those years of 1993 and '94, which also took in other very public embarrassments like the 29 stitches and the Pizza Hut incidents, and can see that the elevator that was my alcoholism was going down relentlessly towards the basement. The Cup Winners' Cup win only strengthened my denial at the time, though, because after all the worries of the spring, I became convinced again that I was still doing my job. So it came to pass that I went on another drinking holiday, again to the United States just before the World Cup finals there, and came back the heaviest I have ever been, a bloated 14st 4lb.

I could be quite demanding, too, I think. When I suffered my injured Achilles that autumn, I remember insisting on some pethadene from the nurses – and I always loved that floating feeling of a pre-med and wished I could have it permanently. Then when I came round from the operation I drank a bottle of Chablis.

That winter, Paul Merson came out publicly about his own addictions but far from seeing it as courageous at the time, as I now would, I saw it as the sign of a weak man. He has never been in my league as a good drinker, I thought. He was always down the end of the bar. I believed that alcoholics were simply bad drinkers – which they are, actually, come to think of it – and it was just that he couldn't hold his booze. I didn't think his condition bore any resemblance to me. I didn't have the same problem as him. I was like that T-shirt: 'I don't have a drink problem. I drink, I fall over. No problem.'

My problem, I thought at the time, was actually other people: my wife, my football manager, anyone else. Anyway, Merse was falling apart. I was still enjoying drinking, I thought, and though it wasn't something I consciously realised, booze was keeping me together, through my injuries, through the departure of George

Graham – after which my drinking just seemed so much more miserable and I spent virtually every afternoon at the pub – and through another European Cup Winners' Cup run.

Besides, I thought, Merse's real problem was gambling. The cocaine I didn't believe. He's an idiot. I can't identify with that. Except that I knew that on the odd occasion when I gambled away a couple of grand, I had to go out and get drunk. It took me a long while to see that different addictions were just different flavours, just variations of the same illness. And there had been times when my standards had slipped. I had smoked dope.

It was the same with Jane. When she was fighting her own battle with drugs I never understood or acknowledged or had any compassion for her pain. I had none for my own drinking so how could I? And at least, I thought, I wasn't a drug addict. Oh yes I was – for the drug of alcohol. As her addiction worsened, we argued constantly, shouting at each other without listening to what the other was saying. There was little trust or proper communication between us. We were both in our own worlds.

How we brought two children into the world or took care of them and her daughter, my step-daughter, Clare, I'm not quite sure. One Sunday when the youngest, Amber, who was born on 26 January 1995, was only nine months old, I fell asleep in the afternoon in charge of them, only to be woken by my mother-in-law Barbara. Clare, then just 10, had rung her to say that the baby had eaten Mummy's lipstick and an upset Barbara had driven all the way over from Muswell Hill. I just wondered what all the fuss was about.

Mostly I couldn't see that my drinking was doing any damage to anyone, except possibly me on those down days when I decided it wasn't fun. I provided well for everyone, didn't I? They have everything they want. But that is the selfishness of the illness. Many people suffer the knock-on effects, especially people close to you; kids more than anybody. I know that good kids can come out of bad homes and vice-versa, but I wasn't taking as much responsibility as I should for their development and well-being, I know. I thought they were happy enough in social clubs and beer gardens with a glass of Coca-Cola and a packet of crisps. Or sitting with me for an afternoon in an Indian restaurant, where I could get a beer.

I think Oliver and Amber were too young to realise what was going on, but Clare was affected at the time. I couldn't understand why sometimes she avoided me or ran away from me. Then Jane told me one day that she was frightened of me. That really hurt, went right through me. And it made me angry. Daddy loves her, can't she understand that? As if that was enough. It didn't stop me drinking; only when I wanted to stop for me rather than other people was that going to happen.

I was a mixture at the time of wanting to please people and letting them down, which is also what booze does to you. I would agree to make charity appearances, for example, or present prizes, then not turn up because I was on a bender. My Dad was often left to pick up the pieces and would appear in my place. I would be really apologetic when I sobered up and run round after people to try and make it up. Towards the end, Dad told me that people down at the pub were calling me a drunk. Underneath me shrugging it off, that really hurt.

Jane was quicker to reach her rock bottom than me in that year of living dangerously in 1996 and quicker to do something about it. I had to endure the bouts of control –

what I now call doing more research into the illness – until I got to that point after Euro '96, the most painful place I had ever been in, when I came to know what alcoholics refer to as the hideous four horsemen – terror, bewilderment, frustration, despair. But I needed all of them; without them, I would probably have kept on the way I was.

No longer was the football enough. No longer could I keep the lid on it and the drinking. Everything else I could order and control, I thought, but not this. I could no longer drink like a normal human being. My body and mind were just not able to continue being a professional, high-achieving athlete and a professional high-class drunk. I just had to throw in the towel and ask for help. And when I did, something astonishing happened.

ELEVEN

My Name is Tony

They gave me what they call a newcomer's pack at my first meeting of Alcoholics Anonymous. It was a collection of little leaflets in a plastic wallet and one asked 'Is AA For You?' There were 12 questions, such as 'Do you tell yourself you can stop drinking any time you want to, even though you keep getting drunk when you don't mean to?' and 'Have you missed days off work because of drinking?' and 'Do you have blackouts?' I answered yes, yes and yes. And I kept answering yes, to the power of 12.

The item that most caught my eye, though, was a poem called 'The Man in the Glass' and I read it eagerly:

When you get what you want in your struggle for self
And the world makes you king for a day,
Just go to a mirror and look at yourself
And see what THAT man has to say.

For it isn't your father or mother or wife
Who judgement upon you must pass;
The fellow whose verdict counts most in your life
Is the one staring back from the glass.

Some people may think you a straight-shootin' chum
And call you a wonderful guy,
But the man in the glass says you're only a bum,
If you can't look him straight in the eye.

He's the fellow to please, never mind all the rest,
For he's with you right up to the end.
And you've passed your most dangerous, difficult test
If the man in the glass is your friend.

You may fool the whole world down the pathway of life
And get pats on the back as you pass,
But your final reward will be heartache and tears
If you've cheated the man in the glass.

I started to cry. I was in my new house in Putney looking out of the window on to a floodlit church in my road and I felt an enormous surge of power going through me. Emotions were welling up inside of me. I felt a huge sense of loss and sadness but also a huge relief. I had given in. Booze had beaten me. I hadn't wanted to be an alcoholic. The tag did not sit well with me. I was a footballer, a winner. But I was the winner who had lost when it came to alcohol. And I felt strangely good to have given up the struggle and admitted that.

My account of how I came to accept I was an alcoholic and how I had some sort of inexplicable spiritual experience that gave me an incredible charge of hope is not one I have cared to tell many people until now. I thought I would sound like some fruitcake or a born-again religious nutcase, but it happened and I no longer worry about what people will think. It worked for me and the craving for alcohol left me immediately.

There was, too, an amazing symbolism to it. The weekend before, I had been in my old house in Emerson Park going through the shakes and all the shit that accompany the death rattle of active alcoholism. Now here I was on my own in my new house, experiencing the first days of the rest of my life. The common object was the bed, which had been moved over here. It was like the film *Bedknobs and Broomsticks*, come to think of it. My bed seemed to have been transported from the danger into the safety.

The next morning the doorbell rang. It was the vicar from the church at the end of the road. He had come to welcome me to the area and brought with him a bottle of champagne. Now, I can see the funny side of it. Then, it was confusing. What's all this? The church ... alcohol? I thanked him but after he had gone I threw it into the skip that was parked outside my new house. I couldn't bear the thought of booze in the place at that time.

So much of what was happening was confusing. I had been really nervous walking into that AA meeting the previous Friday in Fulham and I have to say I didn't really get much out of it. I felt very self-conscious and as I listened to people talking about how their lives were and how they had changed as a result of not drinking, staying away from booze by a simple method of one day at a time, I wondered if it really was for me. I felt more comfortable afterwards going for a cup of coffee with my friend Steve Jacobs, whom I bored rigid about Jane, the kids, therapists and treatment centres. Personally I dreaded going into a treatment centre. That would have been total humiliation for a winner. I couldn't accept that I was that ill anyway.

I couldn't get Jane out of my head. I thought if I could just mend the relationship, then things might get back to a more manageable state. Though I would be obsessed with her for a long time yet, I finally got the message from her that she did not want me any more when she told me that she had met someone else. That night as I drove along the Embankment, I threw my wedding ring into the Thames. Then I wrote the second of those letters to her, the more assertive but accepting one, the first draft of which ended up in the skip outside the house in Essex in which I was dumping a load of old stuff that had too many painful memories for me. That scrap of paper would be retrieved by someone for the *News of the World*.

Five days after my first AA meeting, I went to a second, Paul Merson taking me to one after training in St Albans. This one really spoke to me. Everything everyone said, about how painful and exhausting their lives had been with alcohol and how it was getting better gradually without it, I could only agree with. There was another Tony, an Arsenal supporter, and another bloke with three kids with whom I seemed to have a lot in common. 'You were nodding like one of those toy dogs,' Merse said to me with a smile after the meeting and I just couldn't help it. It was a relief to be somewhere I felt I belonged and no longer did I feel so alone.

The nice thing was that everyone spoke and nobody interrupted. People listened respectfully and calmly to each other. There was a peace about the room. I just knew I had to say something myself and a few minutes from the end, when there was a pause between speakers, I managed to blurt it out.

'My name is Tony,' I said, 'and I am an alcoholic.'

I talked quickly and briefly about how things had been and how I was determined to give this a try. Afterwards I felt elated. I had made a start and suddenly knew I was in the right place. That was a relief after my doubts about my first meeting. All of a sudden I was flying and knew that I was on the right path. They say that it helps if you can attend 90 AA meetings in the first 90 days of sobriety. It is not so much brainwashing as brain-cleaning. I think I went to 100.

Gradually the fog surrounding me cleared away and things began to look brighter. I came to have more insight into what had been going on with me. I came to understand how I had been gripped by a mental, physical and emotional illness that could be arrested if I did not drink alcohol – taking it that vital one day at a time. I began to see that I probably needed the rejection from Jane to spur me on, just as I had needed that rejection by England Schoolboys in my career as motivation. I sat on my sofa one night and a few answers came to me. The whole relationship with Jane had been for a purpose, to help me find myself. I had this sense that if I just kept doing what I was now doing, going to meetings and being honest with people about what I had been like, things would change – I would change – and that I need not pour booze down my throat again. It was all a great revelation and I just had to write it down quickly. It was also blind faith ... but it was faith.

I needed to get honest with the boys at work and I called them all together at London Colney on Friday 13 September 1996, four weeks after I stopped drinking. They told me later that they thought I was going to announce that I was the new manager, it being that time after Bruce Rioch and just before Arsène Wenger. During the time when Stewart Houston was the caretaker after George, a few of them called me 'boss' anyway because I was talking to him a lot about tactics and selection. 'Alright if I have a drink, boss?' Ray Parlour used to joke after a game.

Anyway, I simply announced to them that I had a drink

problem and that I was going to AA. 'I hope you will show me the same respect you gave Merse,' I added. It was all over in five minutes. 'I always thought you had bottle,' Ian Wright said. 'Now I know.' There were a few nervous laughs when he said it. Andy Linighan very touchingly said to me. 'You've cracked it, Tone, you've taken the first step.' And I had. The first of the Twelve Steps of Alcoholics Anonymous says: *We admitted we were powerless over alcohol and that our lives had become unmanageable.* Some of the boys may not have thought I was an alcoholic, like other people close to me, but the important thing was that I knew I was.

It got out in the papers the next day – you can never keep things quiet in football – but I didn't mind. I was relieved. There's a saying that secrets keep you sick. So after training that Saturday morning, Paul Merson and Steve Jacobs suggested that I face up to it and I duly agreed to see all the reporters milling about the car park at London Colney. I told them that I would give a statement to everyone together and for the first time I was assertive without being aggressive with the press. It felt good. As I drove away, the man from the *News of the World* was shouting figures at me as payment for my story, the sums seeming to go up as the window wound up. 'This is for me,' I told him. 'Not for money.'

That Sunday was difficult. I seemed to be suffering from an emotional hangover, a feeling of being drained by all the things that were happening to me. In fact, I felt a little bit sorry for myself reading all about me in the papers. There were also reporters doorstepping Jane at her new home nearby in Fulham. Like they say in AA, though, 'This too shall pass' and I got through another 24 hours without a drink.

My first game back after the knee operation and fitness work that I had been enduring was also horrific. It was in the reserves against Chelsea at Enfield's ground and there were only about 200 people there. I could hear every comment that was made and was sensitive to all of them. 'Want a drink today, Tone?' someone shouted. 'You've lost your bottle, you have, Adams,' came another. A little kid was standing near the touchline with a bottle of beer in his hands. 'Fancy a Bud?' he shouted.

Although it did feel good to be back playing and I got a real buzz from it, I was left afterwards feeling raw and vulnerable. I had always drunk and played football and without them there was an emptiness. My solution was to go to an AA meeting, as I often did after matches in those early days with all the emotions of playing bubbling inside me, and get it all off my chest. It disturbed me that I was having all sorts of feelings that I could no longer suppress with booze. Not that I could always get things off my chest at meetings. Sometimes I would feel too embarrassed to talk and it helped me to go to a meeting in Kensington especially for shy people where they reserved a section of time for those who had difficulties in speaking up. Again there was comfort in being around kindred spirits.

My emotions were all over the place for a while and anything sad or happy could make me cry. My honesty also gave me problems sometimes. I had just been given a new contract at Arsenal and one morning David Dein, the vice-chairman, asked me if I was OK. I think he expected me to be buzzing and grateful to him for my new deal but I just said, 'Actually, David, I'm not,' and proceeded to tell him what was wrong with me. I think he was a bit taken aback.

But I found the saying that the truth sets you free held good for me. No longer did I have to lie about my whereabouts or what I had been doing, covering up for my omissions or worrying about my drinking. I rang in a couple of times to say that I would not be in for training because I was feeling low and I needed to get to an AA meeting as my sobriety came first. The club, especially Gary Lewin and Pat Rice, were great, saying that I must do whatever I needed. I started to get back the honesty that alcohol had stolen from me. I started to let my barriers down and a conversation with my two sisters, Denise and Sandra, to explain what had happened to me was particularly liberating.

I found it difficult that October when I was not playing for England at Wembley against Poland and felt sad. So on the day of the game I went to a lunchtime meeting of AA in central London and talked about it. It did me a power of good and I knew that I needed at that time to be in that room rather than a dressing room.

By the time I was recalled for England, for the next game against Georgia in Tbilisi, I was feeling far more balanced and really beginning to relax into my sobriety. The day before the game, which we went on to win 2–0, it was announced that I would be captain in the absence through injury of Alan Shearer, Glenn Hoddle's preferred choice, and it was one of the most interesting, even enjoyable, press conferences I had attended. No longer did I feel I had anything to hide or be defensive about. There was nothing anyone could throw at me any more. Journalists had even stopped coming to my house to confront me about my latest drunken misdemeanour on the town. I told them that day in Georgia that I had thrown away the mask, that I was getting stronger by the day, and that for the first time I was feeling peaceful and content with myself. I found it an interesting experience and I think they did too.

I now had a blueprint for living, through the principles

of AA, which was working for me. All my life I had just existed on instinct, lurching from one situation to the next and reacting, often badly, to it. My therapist James had helped me identify that my problem was alcoholism and it was as if I finally had the rules and tools for life, and for dealing with it without booze, that I had been looking for for so long. Out of humiliation had come humility, my ego had been deflated and I acquired some self-worth, though it took me a while even to understand those terms. I remember when the penny dropped. 'Ah yes, ego. That's when I'm being flash. Self-worth, that's when I'm feeling good about myself.' It was like I was under new management.

My team-mates thought I was a bit of an oddball at times, I think. Paul Merson understood, because he had been in the programme of recovery for some time. I phoned him one day to apologise for having been talking about him behind his back at times and telling him some of the things I was saying, the names I had been calling him. 'I thought you were a bit of an arsehole, but I can see now what you were about,' I said, desperate to get it all off my chest. 'Tone,' he said good humouredly, 'There's a difference between honesty and brutal frankness.' He also pointed out that this was a match day and he didn't really need to be hearing this. The other players thought I was a recovery bore, some kind of David Icke, I think. I was so evangelical about this way of life that I was trying to give it to other people. Someone who knew me said, 'Tony, you didn't understand any of this for years. How can you expect them to?'

And it must have been difficult for them. They had known me as the social organiser and the leader, off the field as well as on. All of a sudden they had lost that figure. I couldn't go with them any more on their nights out. And for me, sometimes it hurt that they didn't invite me to a party. 'We didn't think you would enjoy it,' Ray Parlour said once. I told him that I would have liked to be able to make that decision. 'I can be shallow with the best of them,' I said to Steve Bould and he laughed. Intelligent man, Steve. They would also apologise for talking about booze in front of me.

One year at Paul Merson's gentlemen's evening at Highbury for his testimonial I remember being really smashed and losing track of time, thus turning up late to pick up Clare at a friend of Jane's in Islington. To make it up to Clare, I had paid £500 in the auction, ego rampant, for a giant teddy bear for her. How I got her back to Essex I'm not sure. No wonder she was frightened of me. Then, at Nigel Winterburn's evening the next year, Steve Bould was reminiscing about the Merse night, saying how pissed I had been and that I knocked over a table and banged my head on a door. 'Steve,' I said, 'I'm sorry I'm not going to be the source of your entertainment this time.' I was home by 11 pm ready for work the next day.

I got tired of doing things just to please other people and hope they liked me. It was time to do something for me and, in thinking of others, to do things properly. In the past I would always agree to do lots of charity work and some-times let people down. Now I decided to concentrate on one charity at the risk of upsetting the other 49. I was worried about what people said about me. I wanted to be seen as a nice bloke by everyone and for them to say nice things about me. But it got so tiring trying to keep everyone happy and losing myself in the middle of it all. It was at my own expense. Then my therapist said to me, 'Tony, what people say about you has got nothing to do with you,' and it made sense. What was important was that I was comfortable with what I said about me and I shouldn't waste time and energy worrying about what others said.

As my emotions were up and down, so was my game as a footballer. There was no guarantee what you were going to get. I could have been sent off – as I was at Newcastle, unluckily though it may have been in a tangle with Alan Shearer – or scored a goal, as I did against Tottenham with a volley. I was trying to be serene during a game, quiet and peaceful, as my new way of life taught, and I became very worried if I couldn't. I was still getting angry and nervous and if things had gone badly I would need to get on to the phone to a fellow AA member or go to a meeting. It was a healthy fix but I thought I needed to be perfectly healthy emotionally before I could play.

The boys must have found that difficult, too. No longer was I going round the dressing room shouting and bawling and winding everyone up. I was just taking responsibility for myself rather than the whole team and probably got a bit self-righteous. Then I was worried I was going too far the other way and that I was suppressing feelings that would eventually come out wrong on the field now and then, like taking someone out or saying something nasty to an opposing player.

At Derby in the last game of my first season sober, I was really angry, possibly because my ankle was hurting, and got sent off for two bad tackles early in the game. I nearly kicked the dressing room door off its hinge. It was meant to be that Paul Merson had come off injured 10 minutes earlier and he helped me through it. 'Come on, let's go and have a cup of tea and watch the game in the lounge,' he said. Once we would have been drinking something stronger than tea.

The next pre-season, we were in Switzerland and Arsène said during training that he wanted us to express ourselves. This airy-fairy lack of guidance annoyed me and I went to Pat Rice to complain. 'He hasn't got a clue,' I said. 'Matthew Upson wants to learn how to be a centre half, not about freedom of expression.' When I took out Nicolas Anelka in this free-for-all, Arsène pointed out to me that I was getting frustrated, which wound me up even more. I knew I needed an AA meeting and that night I found one in Geneva. I had drunk to extremes and now my early recovery was like that, too.

Soon after, I was playing for the reserves against Gillingham and one of their players nutmegged me. I was furious at this lack of respect, as I saw it. 'Don't mess with me. I've got 50 caps and you earn 50 quid a week,' I told him. Then I took him out, about chest high, but the ref let me off, probably because of who I was. It was frightening, like road rage. I could try and be calm but then it would all explode in one moment. And I thought I was not an angry man. But I can see now that my anger was like water; it had to come to the surface before it could evaporate.

People would say things to me, too. I expected all the abuse from the terracing, like 'Who drank all the beer?', and I became less sensitive to it. In fact, I think that is something football is good for – getting rid of anger – and my hope is that fans don't take it with them out of the stadiums. It was probably also the last thing people have on me and besides, it's better than being a donkey. On the field, mostly people either ignored it or were supportive, but I was shocked in a match against Coventry just after I sobered up when their player/manager Gordon Strachan was trying to wind me up by making the gesture of sinking a pint. I was furious and so was Steve Bould, who wanted to 'do' him. So did I, actually, but I had always done my best to keep myself in check on the field because, like when I took that first drink, I never knew where it would lead me if I lost my temper. Strachan took himself off before any revenge could be extracted, anyway.

I knew I had to address the situation, though, that I would not be comfortable with myself if I did not. I was still seething as I got dressed after the game and I marched straight to the Coventry dressing room, arriving just as Strachan was leaving. 'I need to have a word with you,' I said. 'Come into my office' he replied.

He closed the door behind us and before I could have a go at him, he told me that he had always admired me as a player and respected greatly what I had done. 'I'm very sorry,' he said. 'I don't know what came over me. Please accept my apologies.' I had wanted to hit him but he had taken the wind out of my sails. 'Right, well don't do it again,' was all I could say. When I got back to the dressing room the lads wanted to know what had happened. There was a time when I would have told them that I sorted him out. Now I simply said that I had accepted his apology. Less dramatic but more truthful.

I think gradually more balance came into my football. I realised that I didn't have to throw out the baby with the bath water and that not all of the old me had to be changed. I think the boys came to accept me as a more sensitive and thoughtful person whose contorted face and clenched fist on the field was just a mask and I think they still respected my ability as a player. They came to know, though, as I did, that I still felt the same intensity about the game but that I didn't need to go over the top. I could still be verbal, bossing people about.

'Have you given up all that encouraging before the

game, Tony?' Alan Smith asked me a while back. I said that I thought I was getting it back, that I realised it was an emotional game, not a quiet one, that it was part of me and that it helped me. I knew now, I added, why I was doing it, so that I wasn't going on to the pitch too wound up. He told me he was pleased, because it really helped him.

Off the field, I think I am 100 per cent better as a club captain in taking responsibility and organising all the events – like getting the players to do the record before the FA Cup Final and the fittings for the suits; whip-rounds for the staff who serve the meals on our coach – if not the piss-ups any more. It was my suggestion that we close the players' bar at Highbury for one trial season and have sandwiches and soft drinks on a table instead, and that there is no drinking on the coach, with which the boys went along.

I think I have been to the extremes of being intense, then laid-back, and now I have found what is best for me. I look now at the video of a League Cup semi-final we played against Crystal Palace and am shocked at my reaction when the referee awarded a penalty against us – chasing him, shouting and bawling, with my arms flailing. Then there was the time when we were 'miked up' for a TV documentary and I spent a lot of the time bellowing at the referee, David Elleray, and calling him a cheat. It did not make pretty viewing and is an uncomfortable reminder of the way I was.

I am comfortable with the way I play today. I can't suppress my emotions just to appear calm. I've done the 'big roar' part and the serenity bit and now I have the reality. It is a physical, spontaneous game and sometimes I will do and say things that may seem questionable in the heat of the moment, but I have to be true to me and my competitive nature. In a game at Blackburn when we were going for the '98 title, for example, I turned round and gave Remi Garde a real earful for letting his player in between us to score. I was pleased I did have a go – we were 4–0 up, so it showed my standards. Afterwards, in a less frantic atmosphere, I could apologise to Remi if I went over the top.

There is a time to talk the talk and another to walk the walk, I have discovered, and I think the lads are pleased to have some of the old me back, the right bits – because I did have good qualities, I've realised. It was just that booze turned me into a deceitful lager lout.

I was pleased, in the end, with the way I confronted the Gordon Strachan incident in a more mature way than I might have in the past and there were other issues I also needed to confront. Like my fear of flying and of heights. Now as a kid, I had loved going on aeroplanes and had no fear whatsoever. It was only as an adult that the apprehension crept in and I drank to overcome it, at least when I was able to. On outward trips before games with Arsenal, I would just have to endure the sweaty palms and panicky feelings. On one holiday flight, I wanted to get up and tell the pilot that he had to abort the take-off because I wasn't drunk enough yet. In the end I just sat there gripping the arm rests until I got another drink. So many times on planes I was shouting and singing and probably getting away with it because of who I was.

Anyway, they said in AA that alcohol had stunted my development and that I probably had an emotional age of about 17, so why should I not get back to feeling as fearless about being up in the air as I was then? In recovery I had met some new people, one of them called Dominic, who was into adventure sports, and he agreed to organise something for me. I decided I was going to do a parachute jump. And I decided I was not going to tell anyone at the club, as I was carrying a little ankle injury.

It was a beautiful sunny Sunday morning in April '97 when we drove down to the airfield near Salisbury in Dominic's open-top MG, the wind blowing through my hair and adding to the sense of freedom. Anxiety was also building up in me, though, and I was repeating in my head like a mantra the Serenity Prayer that AA has adopted:

God grant me the serenity to accept the things I cannot change, the courage to change the things I can and the wisdom to know the difference.

I was scared stiff, I had to admit. You got only a short period of instruction, watched a short video and before you knew it, you were in the back of this light aircraft. There were about 20 of us jumping, four for the first time, some on their own, some attached to an instructor, as I was. One girl took fright and wouldn't jump. I knew how she felt but suddenly someone shouted, 'Shut up and jump you wuss,' at me and suddenly I was out of the door clinging on to the instructor. I didn't mind the initial 120 miles per hour rush because I was concentrating hard, but then he pulled the ripcord and the exhilaration turned into stillness. I was suddenly powerless, dangling on a bit of string one mile up in the air. Oh my good God.

The instructor asked me if I wanted to go and look at Stonehenge. 'Sod Stonehenge,' I said. 'Just get me down.' He asked me if I wanted to operate the parachute's manoeuvring handles but I was worried that if I did and let them go, we would plummet to earth. I didn't know where to look. Everywhere served as a frightening reminder of where I was. He said that he could get me down quickly if he spun the 'chute so I asked him to spin it. When he did, I asked him to stop. It was making me ill. It took about two minutes to descend and finally we hit the ground, him falling on top of me. My ankle, the least of my worries, survived the impact unscathed.

Afterwards I felt elated with the sense of achievement. I phoned everyone I knew closely to tell them. It certainly gave me an insight into my character. Tony had always been in control and now he wasn't. There was a bigger, wider power at work in life. I was powerless over other people, places and things, something I tell myself when I fly these days, just accepting that what will be, will be. I told myself to get out of being the centre of every scenario. I had just been reading a book by Susan Jeffers and the title seemed appropriate: *Feel The Fear and Do It Anyway*.

In fact there is a section in the book that I have found very helpful in organising my own life. She suggested having nine compartments to your life, and filling them with the things that were important to you. At the centre for me was AA and in another compartment was my new home, which I decorated to my own taste and made comfortable for my children to come and stay. Then there were compartments for relationships, work, doing things for other people, and recreation, outdoors and indoors. The idea is that that if one area, or compartment, of your life goes wrong, it doesn't mean that your whole life has to. That was often how it seemed when I was drinking.

Outdoor recreation involved walking my dog, Harry the Dalmatian, on Putney Heath and playing golf, which had always been an excuse for a drink previously. I used to carry a bottle in my bag and would give up after nine holes if I wanted to get back to the bar. I have often thought that in recovery I would like to go back to Carlyon Bay, the hotel where I took the kids towards the end of my drinking, and play the golf course there. I have, in fact, been back to that club in Covent Garden where I was involved in a fight at around the same time and apologised to the manager.

With indoor recreation, I began to get involved in a variety of interests that had never occurred to me when I was drinking but then with drink I was just preoccupied all the time. I also met a new set of people and one of them was my new neighbour Amy, who became a friend. She was one of the people who introduced me to English literature, poetry in particular, and I seemed to have an affinity for it. It was a different experience to have a tutor rather than being one of 30 kids at school.

Because I was starting to experience things myself, because I was open-minded and impressionable, I could feel the emotions in poems and I enjoyed how the layers peeled away, as they were doing with me in my own life. The way Thomas Hardy lost his faith interested me, because I had just found some of my own. His poems became cynical, yearning like I was all those years. Then I began to read Keats and the Romantic poets, then Shakespeare. It occurred to me that I might even begin studying for an English literature O-level. I also started going to the theatre, which was an amazing experience, and going with people for coffee afterwards. It was a bit like the end of AA meetings when we would go to a coffee bar in the King's Road and I couldn't get enough of hearing people speak about recovery. I didn't want people to go home. One night I drank so much cappuccino that I couldn't sleep.

I also thought I would like to learn to play an instrument, because I love music and I can't sing, and at first the guitar appealed to me. The old me thought it might help me pull women, before it occurred to the new me that it might not be the right reason. Then the piano appealed to me, because from there, once I learned to read music, I could go on to play other instruments. I duly found a good tutor I could go to once a week and who takes me along at the right pace for me. It was also a good way of spending time with my daughter, as we share the lessons together. I only hope I don't break my fingers playing football.

Then I wanted to add a language to my education and Italian always sprang to mind. David Platt said it was an easy language to learn. But I had a base in French, one of the few subjects I took seriously in school. We had French guys at Arsenal and with a tutor at the club every day and a World Cup in the offing, it seemed like a good idea, though for my own self-esteem more than anything else. I wanted to prove to myself that I could do it, that I was not an idiot, and I was beginning to feel that I no longer was. Now I was doing things that I had only talked about in the pub. Actually, sometimes I said I would do things and had to go through with them when I didn't really want to just because I had been shouting my mouth off. I have also considered getting a place in France to stay in when I retire. With a piano in it, of course.

I also had to see if I was good at anything besides playing football. Like being a father. I had always provided for my kids but I hadn't really been there for them, nor considered their needs, nor talked to them properly. At first it was really difficult. My attention span was as short as theirs and for the first couple of months, I could only take them for a few hours before wanting them either to be quiet or go back to their mother. The turning point with them came that first summer after I got sober.

I decided to take them to Disneyworld in Paris, which I don't advise anyone who is struggling with their sobriety to do. During the days I would walk them round the theme park, take them on all the rides, get really stressed out and in the evening run up a huge phone bill calming myself down talking to fellow AA members while the nanny who came with us was taking care of them. After that I needed a proper holiday, though at least I had lasted longer than I had that time at the Magic Kingdom in Florida.

We came back to England for just a day before I took them to St Lucia and we were half an hour from the island on the plane when the captain announced we had to divert to Antigua as a thunderstorm had damaged the radio antenna. There at the airport we had a seven-hour wait while another plane was flown in and I had to endure all sorts of stress. It was my first holiday sober and I had combatted the fear of the flying without a drink. I was also getting echoes and memories of my holiday with Jane in the Caribbean in 1991. I had three children who just wanted their daddy all the time, and were annoying a lot of other people. They were all over me.

Even with a nanny to help out, I was feeling really tense and the only place open in this airport was … a bar. Everyone was drowning their sorrows so I went up to the bar, bought a packet of cigarettes and smoked four of them. They made me feel sick but at least I hadn't taken a drink. Then, though it was pouring with rain, I found a football and took the three kids outside on to a little patch of concrete where we all let off some steam and got drenched. I just let them go and it helped me as well. By giving in, yet again, I had been shown how things would work out. I thought afterwards that if I could get through that without a drink then I could get through anything.

Since that experience I have come to love looking after my kids as my attention span and tolerance levels have increased. I have an unconditional love for them and the certain knowledge these days that I will be there for them no matter what. Where I used to take them to social clubs and beer gardens, now I take them to all sorts of places in London, like circuses, cinemas and parks, like the Trocadero, places I had never been to before in 29 years of living near the city. Very early on in recovery, I took them on to Putney Heath for the afternoon and just got a rug and bundled up everything in it – soft drinks, crisps, all sorts of balls and toys. Then we just ran riot. It is great to know that Oliver and Amber are seeing a sober Dad. With Clare it was very important for me to tell her about my drinking and why I no longer drink, and she accepted it all very quickly.

I still have a lot of neuroses and progress to make through self-examination but I am loosening up and I am aware both of how I am feeling and what I am doing. I'm not Tony Adams the footballer, I am Tony Adams the human being and I take him into football, into playing the piano, into being a father. Into life.

Life is unbelievable. It is just astonishing how it has changed. It is great to be alive – as people say, AA also stands for Alive Again. It is said that the flower is beautiful when it opens and that's how I feel about myself. I am not suppressing anything with a substance any more. I used to think that a strong man was one who covered up what he was feeling. Now I can see that a strong man is one who is open to his feelings, be they happy or sad, confident or vulnerable.

If I am worried or upset, I go to a meeting and talk about it. At other times when I am in pain, I need to sit with myself and see the feeling through to get to understand it and learn what I am supposed to from the experience. I am in touch with me. I do many of the things I used to do but now I feel differently about them. And no longer do I run away or seek to escape the difficult things in life. AA also stands for Altered Attitudes. I do believe there is a spiritual solution for everything and I listen to all suggestions.

In the early days of recovery my head was messed up and obsessed by Jane. I'm sure, looking back, that was how it was meant to be because it took my mind off the drinking. Now I have a peace and calm, which was all I was ever seeking through a glass. Peace of mind, they say, is the handmaiden of inner freedom. I am a very lucky alcoholic. The compulsion to drink was taken from me that Friday 16 August 1996 at 5 pm. The desire to stay away from drink was given to me a week later.

AA has taught me so many things. I learned a definition of insanity that suited me and my behaviour: making the same mistake over and over again and expecting a different result. I have also learned that it is the first drink that does the damage; that it is alcoholism, not alcohol-wasm and that I will always be a recovering alcoholic, not a recovered alcoholic, who needs to keep going to meetings to maintain his spiritual well-being. Complacency has no part in recovery. It is a cunning, baffling and powerful disease and can lie in wait for you. One craziness of it was that I got a feeling one day that I had missed out on cocaine and heroin. I actually craved crack. And this was a sober man lying on his sofa one afternoon.

One drink, or shot of any substance, will lead me back to the madness, I know, and I just do not want it back. It really is Jekyll and Hyde stuff – which helps me understand that I was suffering from an illness, because I no longer do the things I used to under the influence. Today I know I am just a sick man trying to get well, not a bad man, as active alcoholics feel, trying to get good. This is about being a real person, not some goody-goody. I have learned, too, that where I did not have a choice before, as after Euro '96, that today I do. And that I can even be grateful to Gareth Southgate for helping me to reach the jumping-off point.

At that time, I did not feel I had another kick left in me. Today I am grateful for the reprieve that saw me in 1997/98 play some of the best football of my career. My frustration early on was because my anger came out as I was not physically right. Once I went to the South of France and got fit, mentally I could be positive again. The desire, confidence and self-assurance came back. I wanted to go back on to the pitch and impose myself on my striker, play off the front foot again.

Of course I still get anxious about my football but now I can accept anything that happens in the game; it is only a game. Once you have prepared properly and have a desire to do your best, there is nothing more you can do. It really is that simple. And I will never forget on the day we clinched the '98 title, the papers were full of the death of the actor Kevin Lloyd, alias Tosh Lines in *The Bill*, from alcoholism and the suicide of the former footballer Justin Fashanu.

That same day, my Dad gave an interview to one of the Sunday papers saying that he had watched me drinking and had to let me get on with it, to find my own path but that he had been there if I had asked for his help. The best thing, he added, is not that Tony has come back as a player but that he has come back as a person. It moved me a great deal.

It is hard for me to say if I am a better player now. Certainly I am more experienced and comfortable with my game and I do think people have recognised that I can play a bit, that I am more than a donkey – something that I can have a bit of a laugh about these days as I have even adopted one, called Dean, at a donkey sanctuary in Devon. I also enjoy my job more than I have done for a long time. Arsène was right in that talk we had; he had not seen the best of me. I think he did get to, though. Now I am often the first one into training despite probably having the worst journey, up from South-West London, and I have my own routine of stretching and power exercises. I do know that if you are going to survive at the top level of the game these days, with its pace and intensity, you can't drink anywhere near the way I used to.

What of the future? It's not something a recovering addict can speculate or project about, though he can plan. I would like to stay at Arsenal for the rest of my career if I can, in a romantic way, but in a realistic way as a professional, I have to say that it depends if they come up with the right deal or if another club comes in with one. I did think David O'Leary slightly spoiled his career by having an injury-plagued spell at Leeds in the end. Perhaps I could go for his appearance record and play for Arsenal into a third decade.

Arsène thinks I would make a good manager but I don't know. I do want to take my FIFA coaching badge when it can be fitted in and see how things progress from there. There are just so many social things I want to do, like going to the cinema and theatre, spending more time playing the piano, reading and travelling.

One thing that does interest me is working with young players at football clubs to talk to them about alcohol and their careers, to help them if they feel they need help. I have already spoken to the PFA about the prospect and they are keen when I finish playing to establish some kind of programme. In my case, it all happened how and when it was meant to happen – take the miracle that for some reason I put a seatbelt on that day in 1990 I crashed the car.

But I do believe firmly that there should have been some element of rehabilitation in prison, some introduction for someone like me who had been convicted of drink-driving to a life without alcohol. Perhaps I would still have been in denial at that time but at least the seed would have been sown earlier. Maybe I could do that with young players.

Before any of that, though, there was one thing I was especially looking forward to. I can still recall vividly what happened in 1990. In a way, what transpired when I went and spent a week drunk in Rhodes after being rejected by Bobby Robson showed how important a World Cup finals tournament was to me. This time I had a chance, and a chance to do it right. France '98 was beckoning.

TWELVE

A New World

Before I could follow the voice beckoning me to the promised land that was France '98, though, there was a long and winding road to be negotiated. This was England and English football, after all. It wouldn't be the same without a large measure of intrigue, would it? The World Cup finals would be dramatic and controversial enough, what with questions over Glenn Hoddle's strategy, then David Beckham's sending-off and the agony of another penalty shoot-out, but first we had to go through such ordeals as an intense qualifying match in Italy and a traumatic day in Spain when all would be stunned back home – as most of us were out there – by the omission from the squad for France of Paul Gascoigne.

I made my return to the England team after the admission of my alcoholism and my knee injury in the November of '96 against Georgia in Tbilisi, even being named captain in the absence of Alan Shearer. The comfortable, professional 2–0 win was one of only three qualifying games I was fit to play, however, the second being the return against Georgia, also a 2–0 win. Then came that epic night in Rome.

Having missed the first game against the Italians at Wembley, when we lost 1–0, I was keen to take part in this

314

one. Everything was riding on it. Italy had only drawn in Poland and Georgia – which I think showed how good our away performances had been, with the boys also having won 2–0 in Chorzow – and now we could win the group and qualify automatically without the need for a play-off, with a draw in the Olympic Stadium. Just a draw. It sounded simple enough, but it would be far from it.

I felt very serene and confident, though, right from the moment we got to our beautiful hotel complex, La Borghesiana, just outside the city. Each morning I sat under a tree reading *The Celestine Prophecy* by James Redfield, a book about meditation, human insight and spirituality. It was eerie, because I noticed Glenn Hoddle was reading it too.

Not that I saw eye to eye with him in the build-up to the match. Though Alan Shearer was still missing through injury, Glenn made Paul Ince captain, which I must admit surprised me. He had a gut feeling for Paul, he said, coming back to Italy where he had played his club football for Inter Milan the season before. Glenn said he wanted me just to concentrate on my own performance as I had been injured and was still feeling my way back. 'I think you're wrong,' I replied but I was in a good frame of mind and accepted his decision.

I have always felt I should be England captain, having proved over the years that I can lead a side, and I felt I had the respect of my peers, both at club and international level. I have to admit, though, that Glenn did have an interesting reason for naming Alan Shearer as his first choice. A striker who is captain, Glenn maintained to me, will win more penalties and free-kicks around the opposition penalty box. He is known to the referee, probably has his respect, and a defender only has to touch him for the ref to blow for a foul. It worked for Maradona, Glenn reasoned. I didn't agree with him, mind, because I still felt I had more to offer as a captain, but I went along with the decision. I felt privileged, anyway, just to be playing for my country and not being captain was certainly not going to affect my performances for the team. It was no time to dwell on perceived injustices. It was a time to be getting on with the job.

I think the press were more annoyed when it turned out that I wasn't captain, because I had been 'put up' before them for interview the day before and they assumed therefore that I would be. They were also upset at being told that Gareth Southgate and David Beckham were injury doubts for the game, which proved not to be the case. Glenn is a great believer that if he has the opposition's team sheet then he has an advantage, so he does not want the opposing coach to know our team. If that means not acknowledging the whole truth, then so be it, he feels. It can be difficult if you are a player, and some of us do not enjoy concealing things from the press, but Glenn has his way of doing things and he was the boss.

None of it got to me that week. The weather was wonderful, the location perfect and England had tremendous support for a big game, even if there would again be a minority of hooligans whom we could have done without. This was one of those days and nights I came into football for and I felt particularly proud to be English and playing for my country.

We put on a thoroughly controlled and professional performance. We were very solid and resilient, especially when Paul Ince had to go off for a spell of about 20 minutes with a head injury, and Gazza did exceptionally well. He was his usual bag of nerves before the game in the stadium where he used to play for Lazio, but as soon as he got out onto the pitch he was like his old self, wanting the ball and keeping it for us.

Gradually, as the game continued without a goal, the Italians became frustrated and they just didn't know where to go with the ball. I had, I think, a good game, if not the great one that some people were saying, because I didn't really have that much to do, so well did we steer the Italians away from the danger areas. We might even have won the game when Ian Wright hit a post late on, although I did have one dodgy moment immediately after that when the Italians came straight back down the field and I dived in on Alessandro Del Piero, who got in a cross for Christian Vieri. Everybody has told me that their heart stopped as his header flashed just past a post, but I was still composed. I always had this sense that it would be our night.

After that, expectations were naturally very high – when are they not with England? – but our build-up to France '98 was disappointing. I lost my unbeaten record on my appearances as captain when we were beaten 2–0 by Chile at Wembley, which was followed a month later by a 1–1 draw in Switzerland that I missed. Even a 3–0 win over Portugal was not that satisfactory as we looked very bitty. To be honest, I wasn't that focused that night – even though I had the ball in the net with a header for what should have been my fifth international goal on my 50th appearance, only for it to be disallowed for a push that the ref imagined. The chase for honours with Arsenal was coming to a head at the time and, I must confess, the following Saturday's match at Barnsley was more significant to me.

After hitting the Double heights, I actually felt quite flat and was also quite concerned about England's prospects for the finals when we assembled at Burnham Beeches on the

Monday following the FA Cup Final. It was probably just the space I was in at the time after all the emotion of my club season.

The work on the training ground at Bisham Abbey was very intense, so much so that a lot of the boys were going berserk, wondering why they were being put through all this at the end of a long season. Paul Ince, in particular, was fond of a moan now and then. I found myself just saying to the lads that some had already had a couple of weeks off and needed some fitness work. I just wanted to get it done, because I saw it as money in the bank that we might be needing to draw on sometime during the Finals. Still, the players were resentful about a lot of it and the coaches – John Gorman, Peter Taylor, Glenn Roeder and Ray Clemence, nice men all of them – had to work hard to keep everyone's enthusiasm going.

Most of the time we were doing two sessions a day, at ten in the morning and four in the afternoon, of about 90 minutes a time. We did a lot of technical ball work as well as stamina drills and some 11 versus 10, playing against a team that had had a man sent off and working on how to break them down. We also did a little on playing with 10 men against 11 – more significant, as it would turn out. Paul Durkin, England's World Cup referee, came in to work with us to demonstrate what was and wasn't an illegal tackle from behind, which helped us think more about our defending, and the need to stay on our feet. As the years have gone on, I have tried more and more to nip in ahead of strikers to take the ball, with the stricter rules about the tackle from the back, but even in the so-called bad old days when defenders found it fun to take the player from behind, George Graham was telling us to stand alongside the striker, ready to tackle ahead of him.

Off the training ground, there was all manner of other things going on, including drug-testing, with the maximum permitted eight players per game from the March onwards being tested, according to FA requirements, until all members of the potential squad had been done. We also had thorough check-ups from a dentist and a chiropodist, David Beckham's feet being the most in need of attention, perhaps because he insists on wearing new boots every other game.

The main issue, though, was diet. Glenn brought in the same biologist, Dr Yann Rougier, that Arsène Wenger uses for Arsenal. He duly gave us the same talk as I had had from him two years earlier, about the importance and value of dietary supplements such as Creatine, to which I personally do not object though there have been reports in the United States of people having died taking it. Those were extreme cases of individuals taking an overdose; if taken in moderation and under strict supervision, Creatine can be invaluable in physical conditioning. Were it mood-altering, for me that would be a different matter.

We were all blood-tested to determine which player needed which level of vitamins. Some needed more B1 than others, for example, while others required increased levels of iron. As for me, mostly I needed anti-inflammatory tablets for my ankle, which would ache with all the training work if I did not take them. The tablets would bother me long-term if I continued to take them, though. In fact, they can cause stomach ulcers, which is why I only ever used them in small doses and for short periods. If I felt that I had to keep taking them just to be able to play, I would have no hesitation in retiring. These days, I have too much respect for myself to damage my body.

In addition, we were lectured on food and the right

protein and carbohydrates to eat. Some of the boys were surprised by it all, especially the stretching that was designed to increase agility, but I was familiar with the methods from being at Arsenal. Glenn also gave us a lecture of his own at this time. 'I want you to think like World Champions, train like World Champions, do everything on and off the pitch like World Champions,' he said. Naturally enough, some of the boys had some fun with that and started posing. Glenn also mentioned that there would be only the odd time when players would be allowed the occasional beer.

The main problem was boredom and there was a lot of time spent on your own in your hotel room. Then, when the players came together, sometimes you could get on each other's nerves. Largely, players kept themselves to themselves, the younger ones more interested in everything that was going on. Rio Ferdinand, for example, I told to take note of everything, to watch and learn, ready for when his time came. The diversions were pool, table tennis and snooker. I made telephone calls and read the amazing new book I had started, *The Diving-Bell and the Butterfly* by Jean-Dominique Bauby, about a man with 'locked-in syndrome' who was so paralysed that he could move only his eyes. It was touching and fascinating and put things in perspective for me.

A squad of 30 had been named but with Jamie Redknapp and Ian Wright declaring themselves unfit it became a question of 28 being whittled down to 22. The Saturday match against Saudi Arabia, which was to be my last before the tournament proper, thus became like another school-boy trial and was almost inevitably a scrappy goalless draw. Then it was off to our training camp at the La Manga golf complex near Murcia, in southern Spain.

To me, it was a bit like a working holiday because it had been decided that I would not be risked in the games against Morocco and Belgium that had been organised in Casablanca, an hour and a half's plane journey from Murcia over to North Africa. I enjoyed the sun – in which my hair bleached with the help of lemon juice I applied to it – and the training on a beautiful pitch, but probably ended up more tired than the boys who played as I was working all week, whereas they got some time off around the games. We flew in and out to the matches, as practice for what we would be doing in France, though this time it was in and out on the day rather than in the day before. The idea was that if we came through that well enough, we would be all right for the real thing.

The games themselves were mainly dull affairs, with people again playing for their places – mostly Gazza, it would transpire, though we barely knew it then. The exciting Michael Owen confirmed himself in the squad with his first goal for England, becoming the youngest at 18 to score an international goal, with his winner against Morocco. The game against Belgium on the Friday night was a goalless non-event, after which Glenn told the press that he would be deciding on his 22 on the Sunday and going to the rooms of the six omitted players to let them down gently.

On the Saturday night, we were encouraged to socialise in the bar set aside at our hotel at La Manga, the Hyatt Regency, as it would be the last opportunity to let our hair down together before the Finals. I actually resented a bit what I saw as a contrived attempt to get everybody together. These days, I can go into a bar and have a coffee if I want to without worrying too much, but I don't like feeling that I am being told to. We called it the Blue Oyster bar, after the comical gay club of that name in the *Police Academy* film. Anyway, I did decide to go along for a little while with Paul Merson just to be sociable.

When we walked in, Gazza was on the karaoke machine, singing the old Elvis Presley song 'Wooden Heart', amongst other things. Nobody could get the microphone off him. There was a sadness in me for him as he was obviously worse the wear for drink. 'Come on Tone, give us a song, you boring bastard,' he shouted at me, but it just wasn't my scene any more. One part of me wanted to drag him out of there but that was not realistic. Instead, at about 11 pm, I just said to Merse, 'Come on, let's get away from this crap,' and we went and had a coffee and a sandwich somewhere else before bed. I was told that Ray Clemence and Peter Taylor broke up the party at about 1 am.

The next morning there was a notice on the board saying that Glenn had decided that he was going to talk to each player individually in his hotel room about the squad and his reasons for either picking them or leaving them out. A list of appointments was shown, beginning at 4 pm with David Seaman. Thereafter, they would be held every five minutes and I was one of the last, at 6.15 pm. Gazza's appointment was scheduled for 5.15 pm.

I suppose I could understand the strategy. Glenn really didn't know how best to do what was an agonising job and any alternative, such as waiting until we arrived home then phoning the unlucky six, was going to be just as difficult. Personally, I was all right with it because I was reasonably sure of my place, but for many people it was an excruciating experience and not one I believe they should have been subjected to. All day long there was speculation amongst us as to who would be the six left out.

Nobody at that stage really expected Gazza to be one of

them, although the evidence on and off the field was mounting against him. Most of us were playing golf that day, Gazza in a foursome with David Seaman, Ian Walker and Phil Neville. I didn't see him until four o'clock in the afternoon after we had both finished our separate rounds. He was sitting on a terrace at the hotel, trying to get himself together, I think. The word was that he had been drinking cans of lager – something to which he later admitted – that he had bought while on the golf course.

Seeing him in this state, Paul Merson and I persuaded him to go down to the swimming pool to try and freshen himself up for his meeting with Glenn. He was not in a good state of mind, self-doubt besetting him.

'I can't believe how it's come to this,' he said. 'I don't know if I can do it any more. I'm not going to go, am I, Tone? Am I going to go?'

At this point I still thought he was, but it was becoming easy to see how he might not be.

He steadied himself enough to go upstairs for his meeting at the appointed hour and John Gorman met him in the corridor, put an arm around him and forewarned him of the news Glenn was about to deliver, so Gazza was already upset when he heard it from the horse's mouth. It was all over in a minute apparently and, according to the reports that reached me down by the pool, Gazza went straight to his own room where he kicked out at the furniture, cutting his leg in the process. Within the hour, he and the other five dropped – Ian Walker, Phil Neville, Andy Hinchcliffe, Nicky Butt and Dion Dublin – were on their way to the airport for a private flight home. The only one that really surprised me was Phil, as we appeared short of defensive cover for Graeme Le Saux, but you just can't cover every position and eventuality.

With the Gazza shenanigans having interrupted the schedule, my meeting was put back to 6.30 pm. Glenn looked drained when I got there and I took a cup of coffee up to him. 'I thought you might need this,' I said, and he said he did. Our conversation lasted barely a couple of minutes. I told him I felt fit and was looking forward to the finals. He told me that I was part of the spine of his team along with David Seaman, Paul Ince and Alan Shearer and asked me, as an experienced player, to help him out if I saw anyone getting out of order.

Disruptions were clearly something that Glenn wanted to avoid. In that team meeting at Burnham Beeches, he had mentioned his own experiences in 1982 in Spain when two members of the party had diverted the focus of the campaign. Everyone assumed he meant the injured Kevin Keegan and Trevor Brooking.

Clearly Gazza would have been a diversion too. He was obviously not fit enough for the demands of a modern World Cup and though it was shocking to think that we would go without a player of his talent, Glenn was making the right decision, I'm sure. The way Gazza was that Sunday made it an easier decision for him. I think, though, it probably need never have got to this. As far as I am concerned, Gazza was an ill man and Glenn did not understand properly the illness of addiction even if he tried to deal with it in the best way he knew how.

Terry Venables might have got Gazza sober, might have coaxed the odd good performance out of him, but Glenn encouraging him to have a drink on the Sunday night was not the best thing for him – not that Gazza needed much encouragement. Really, the whole issue needed to be addressed sooner. Paul, I'm sure, now has an idea of what is wrong because I had sat next to him on the plane back from Casablanca after the Belgium match and shared my experiences with him, but until he realises that he needs to do something about it himself, there is not much anyone else can do.

At the time, he told me how he felt he had so many things weighing him down – like his relationship with his wife Sheryl and the worries of whether he would be able to perform again at a World Cup – that once he woke up that Sunday morning after a drinking session the night before, he was probably back in the pain again and felt he needed another anaesthetic. I've been there before myself. The smashing up of his hotel room showed the anger and self-loathing that we can feel. There was no dignity there.

All I know is that I am glad on that painful day I was a recovering alcoholic and not an active one because with everything the players had to go through, I probably would have got drunk myself, as I did when I was left out in 1990. I was fortunate now that I was secure in myself and in my place in the squad.

It is why I think I can understand what Teddy Sheringham did when the now-selected squad of 22 flew back on the Monday. We were told to keep a low profile and most of us just took advantage of the few days off before going to the finals to sort out details at home and be with our families. As a single man, though, Ted wanted to let his hair down, and he was pictured in a bar in the Algarve alongside a blonde and with a cigarette in his mouth. Whether he had been set up or not, it was a stupid thing to do and over the next few weeks, Paul Merson and I reminded him of that. We nicknamed him 'Charlie' after his 10-year-old son; Ted had had his hair cut short and after acting like him, now also looked a bit like him.

Glenn went to town on him as well and Ted was forced

into a public acknowledgement of his mistake. He was also 'rested' from the practice game we had arranged against the French Second Division team Caen on the day we flew out to France for the Finals, Michael Owen taking his place. I'm sure it was Glenn's way of instilling a bit of fear in the player, a bit like George Graham used to do, to put them in their place. It reminds a player who is boss and is no doubt designed to keep them on their toes and get a performance out of them in the next game. Soon, David Beckham had taken over from Ted as the player in the firing line.

We defeated Caen 1–0 with a goal by Paul Scholes – but David did not play well, looking jaded and constantly giving the ball away. In fact, David said himself that he was knackered. Then, three days before our opening game against Tunisia in Marseille, Glenn held a team meeting and announced the side, one without David in it, to most people's surprise despite recent events. Now I could see the reasons for it, but I don't think Glenn handled the situation particularly well, especially when he told the press a day or two after the match that David had not been fully focused. He had looked focused in training to me. Anyway, after the team meeting David asked to see Glenn, who replied: 'Not yet. In my own time.'

Again, as with Teddy, Glenn had his own agenda and though it was not the way I would have dealt with matters, perhaps it was his way of motivating David for the rest of the tournament. I simply thought David wasn't playing well and that should have been the reason given. There were some who thought it was to do with Darren Anderton playing right wing-back but it was never a choice between the two. With Gazza now gone, Glenn had earmarked David for a central midfield slot. As it proved, Becks being left out was a reasonable decision because we won the

Tunisia game comfortably and he probably benefited from the extra week's rest.

I was very nervous, more nervous than I could remember being for a game in years. You were not only carrying the expectations of the team but the whole country, and much as you were telling yourself that this was just another game, you knew it wasn't. 'This is the World Cup,' was the phrase that kept going through my head. I was also very aware that, as well as my Mum and Dad, my children were up in the stand at the Stade Velodrome watching their dad play in the biggest tournament in the game. I had agreed to Jane coming with them, after some discussion, as I felt they would want their Mum with them.

Personally I got off to a bad start as one of the Tunisians' nippy little strikers went round me, but I felt I grew into the game as the team did. Paul Scholes had two good chances, before we got the break we needed just before half-time when Alan Shearer headed home Graeme Le Saux's free-kick. I had my part to play in it, too, making a rehearsed dummy run that took their biggest defender with me.

After that, I couldn't see any way that we could lose the game and it simply became a question of whether we would add to our tally. Finally we did when Paul Scholes curled home a great shot to make it 2–0. Mission accomplished. The important thing in a tournament, as European Championships had taught me, was not to lose the opening game but we had gone one better by winning it, even if it was against a poor team. In fact, we should have won by four or five, but two goals were sufficient and had the added bonus of not raising expectancy levels too high.

We had heard all the disturbing stories about the lunatic fringe of the England support in Marseille – some doubtless true, some probably exaggerated with fans from other countries also involved – but it was a happy party which flew back to the airport at St Nazaire near our hotel at Escoublac, a village just outside the Brittany seaside resort of La Baule. My apprehension about flying was still with me, though I did become more used to it in taking something like 16 flights during our campaign through Morocco, Spain and France, but that night I even enjoyed being allowed to sit in the cockpit as our chartered plane landed.

Now we couldn't wait for the second game, against Romania, but that was another week away. Already we had had to endure five days between watching Brazil start the tournament against Scotland and our own first match, and again we spent a lot of time just watching football on television – no one team particularly impressed us – and training, often twice a day. The World Cup experience may come across as vivid and colourful on television, but to us it was a job of work and we felt very isolated much of the time and quite some way from the hub of the competition.

Some of the boys played a lot of golf but on the rock hard surface in Marseille, I had sustained blisters on my feet because I had worn long studs – an old-fashioned thing, as we defenders consider moulded studs a bit wimpish – so I needed to rest. I spent a lot of time watching videos on the big screen erected in the hotel, fortunate to get the latest releases like *Good Will Hunting* and *As Good As It Gets*, as well as reading. I read books about personal development and recovery from the illness of addiction by such people as Sam Keen and Bob Earll, along with a novel called *Drinking* by Caroline Knapp and the autobiography of the paralysed actor Christopher Reeve, which inspired great humility in me. We also had a room set aside with games in it and I spent some time playing pool against Rio

Ferdinand. Next to us, Michael Owen was usually thrashing Paul Merson on the video car driving machine.

We rarely left the complex, just for a walk on the beach and a few cappuccinos one day and to have a night out at a local restaurant. The players had separate rooms, with an adjoining kitchen, and it was helpful that Merse was next door to me. Each morning we got together to chat and read the thought for the day from a meditation book called *Day by Day*. All the waiting was a good test of my patience.

Before the Tunisia game, Glenn's team talk at our hotel at Marseille airport focused on the importance of discipline with a referee who was likely to enforce the letter of the law. This time, before Romania in Toulouse, Glenn talked a lot about set plays, and going into the penalty box believing that you were going to score a goal. Personally, I felt I didn't need to be told something like that. In fact, at this point in the tournament I have to be honest and say that a lot of what Glenn was doing and saying did not particularly impress me.

I thought he was quite nervous a lot of the time, which could be seen in the fact that he whistled a lot; not the sign of a man who is relaxed or serene, in my opinion. I also felt a little left out, in that Glenn would talk to Alan Shearer and no one else. Perhaps I was a little jealous, and I had to watch out for that, so I decided that I would not get involved in the internal politics of the squad but instead just get on with my own job, despite not agreeing with some of the tactics or the selections. Elsewhere we were seeing how things could go wrong, with Tino Asprilla walking out of the Colombia squad after arguing with the coach.

Glenn, I have to say, is an excellent technical coach and it was nice to hear him say to me after one training session how much my own game, my left foot in particular, had improved technically down the years. He did his best to make training sessions enjoyable and varied and there was a welcome emphasis on ball work and skills rather than just running. We even jogged with the ball at our feet, as the Brazilians do in training.

Sometimes, though, I felt that we were too regimented, treated like kids in fact, and expected to do too much in training. During a warm-down at the end of one session, Gareth Southgate turned an ankle and Glenn was furious with him. It was probably Gareth's own fault for staying out there himself, but even so we should all have been on the bus earlier. It was obvious that he would not be fit for the Romania game, but still he had to face the press and go through the motions of being 50–50 for the game, which I don't think he was happy about. I reminded Glenn at one point that he had told us to be honest, but he replied that there were times when you had to withhold the whole truth and press conferences could be one of those times.

So Gary Neville was the only change for the side to face Romania, with David Beckham again left out of the starting line-up. It was a game that a few people privately had bad feelings about. In fact, Glenn told us afterwards in the dressing room that he had a gut feeling we might well lose. We took it too easy, I think, and did not press the ball properly high in the field. The idea had been that players would get behind the ball, then pressure the man in possession when the opponents reached certain positions on the field. In the game itself we were getting behind the ball but not working when there. The Romanians were able to knock the ball around and put too much pressure on our defence. Up front, Alan Shearer was just not getting any service and was rendered ineffective, often unable to hold the ball up for us.

When they took the lead with Gheorghe Hagi spinning away from a throw-in to chip a ball over me for Viorel Moldovan to knock home, it was a sloppy moment. All season I had been playing in a back four where I was a marker and now I was caught in between two opponents in a three, sometimes expected to mark and sometimes to be the spare man. At this point, Gary Neville was supposed to take Moldovan but with it being his first game and after himself having played in a back four all season, he was caught out too wide. Gareth might have averted the danger, but who knows. I do know, though, that the Arsenal back four would probably not have conceded a goal like it and that Moldovan would have struggled to score one like it against us when he was at Coventry.

The introduction of David Beckham and Michael Owen was the lift we needed. David gave us a new enthusiasm and Michael that injection of phenomenal pace. Actually, from that point we could have buried them, but Michael's well-taken equaliser was enough for me. I looked at the fourth official holding up the board to show three minutes of added time and I thought that the draw would do for us, because at least in the early stages before their ageing legs went, the Romanians were a good side who passed the ball well and pulled you around a lot.

Then Dan Petrescu got the better of Graeme Le Saux inside the penalty area to slip the ball past David Seaman. We had lost 2–1; another sloppy mistake, a stunning defeat. When the final whistle blew I was actually relieved, though, believe it or not – relieved that this was not the third match and we'd blown our chances of qualification due to a last-minute goal but that we still had one more match to put things right. It was a very quiet, disappointed dressing room interrupted only by Glenn asking accusingly 'What were you doing?' to Graeme Le Saux – who had not had a great game, it has to be admitted – in the heat of the moment, for which Glenn later apologised.

Now Romania, who had beaten Colombia 1–0 in their opening match, were top of the group with six points and we were left needing a point from our last game against the Colombians just to qualify, let alone win the group. Like us, Colombia had three points but they had beaten Tunisia only 1–0 and had an inferior goal difference. Thankfully, this time there was only four days until the next match and we didn't have too much time to dwell on the defeat.

Instead we worked hard in training but there was still an edginess to some of the work, a creative tension you could say, which may have been what Glenn intended. One day the first team had been working on set plays, while the other eleven all sat watching. At the end of the session, Glenn began asking the substitutes what all the hand signals were for the various corner routines – near and far post, one hand up or two, that sort of thing. It was like a test, with Glenn the teacher. Anyway, nobody passed so Glenn insisted that the substitutes then go through the whole drill themselves. We in the first team quietly sloped off.

On another occasion, some of the boys were practising a free-kick routine where one player flips it back to David Beckham to volley, the idea being that sometimes it is easier to score from further out because of the ball's trajectory towards the goal. Becks was struggling to do it and Glenn, to the disquiet of the boys, said: 'Obviously you're not good enough to do that skill.'

We talked among ourselves about whether we would prefer to face Argentina or Croatia in the next round and there were pros and cons to both. The Argentina match would take place in the cool of the evening, we didn't think they were as good as they were being made out to be and the country's expectation levels would not be as high as if we were facing Croatia, who had a lot of English-style players and would be tough to play against, in the heat of an afternoon. Then again, most of us felt that the Croats weren't as strong right through the team as the Argentinians, who had been my tip to win the tournament.

That was all luxury talk, though. First we had to beat the Colombians in Lens, a game that we thought was always going to be the decisive one anyway, with it being rare that you have actually qualified after only two games in a World Cup. Glenn told us the team the day before, with, as expected, David Beckham returning in place of David Batty, and Michael Owen replacing Teddy Sheringham. There were stories that Alan Shearer had insisted on Michael playing, that senior players had advised Glenn to pick the pair, but Glenn was always his own man, never really approachable in that sense. We spoke tactically only once, and then after the Colombia game, about Paul Ince and we both agreed that we needed to get him further forward. My strategy with Paul was to keep encouraging and praising him all the time, to which he responded. The conversations Glenn had with Alan also seemed brief, if more regular.

Anyway, on form, Glenn had little choice but to pick David and Michael. Ted was feeling the effects of a long season and it would have been perverse not to include Michael, though I still thought Ted should have had a role to play in the tournament. There was still an element of uncertainty, with there being no guarantee that David wouldn't revert to his pre-tournament form, despite his undoubted class and enthusiasm, or that Michael would start a game the way he had finished the Romania match.

In his team talk before the game, Glenn told us to get our aggressive heads on. Now, I never actually felt that I could go up to Glenn and say, 'Look, this is what we need' because Glenn was always going to do things his own way, but that was exactly what I would have said that night. Get back behind the ball and then go to work, he emphasised, instead of letting them pass the ball. 'Push up, push up all the time,' he added. We followed Glenn's instructions to the letter and the Colombians, especially the likes of Carlos Valderrama, could never dwell on the ball as they like doing. Consequently our defence didn't have to work too hard and what I did have to do, I felt I did well. I really thought I was growing with the tournament.

We got off to a great start when another player who was getting stronger with each game, Darren Anderton, hit home an excellent shot. Then came David Beckham's free-kick, the best of the tournament. I was standing behind and just to one side of the 30-yard dipper but I could see that it was always going to find the net. It was a genuinely great goal of the sort you treasure in a big game with the pressure on and which David often scored in training.

After that, we were never in any danger and cruised through to the last 16. In the dressing room afterwards, all the coaching staff were on a high because they had been under a lot of pressure. After the Romania game, the mood had turned a bit at home and I think if we hadn't qualified the coaching staff in particular would have been pilloried. I did always think we would get through, though, and I was not getting carried away. I just acknowledged that we had done well enough and now had to knuckle down to the next challenge.

And we were quickly into it. After getting back from Lens in the early hours of a Saturday morning, we were flying to St Etienne on the Monday afternoon to play Argentina, Romania having won our group by drawing with Tunisia.

We had watched videos of the Argentinians against Japan, Jamaica and Croatia and they had not looked all that impressive, very beatable in fact, and especially vulnerable at set plays because they lacked height. The night before, we trained in the Geoffroy Guichard Stadium and I thought how English it was, nice and compact, and I was raring to go. I felt fit and excited, and aware of just what a big game this was, another of the sort I was in this job for. That is probably why I belted out the national anthem that night with such gusto.

It was a chance to pit myself against Gabriel Batistuta, who at that point was the competition's leading scorer, and Ariel Ortega – two of the best players in the world, and I really was relishing the challenge. In fact, I had to stop myself wanting to mark Batistuta all the time, because I really felt I could control him, and instead leave him to Sol Campbell so that I could be the spare man at the back. Ortega is just a fantastic player who makes quick, clever runs and can really hurt you with the ball.

We got off to the worst possible start when David Seaman brought down their captain Diego Simeone in the penalty area. Looking back I suppose it was a penalty, even though my knee-jerk reaction was to appeal to the referee. In fact, as the incident was happening I can remember thinking, 'What are you doing coming out there, Dave?' After Batistuta had converted the penalty, I don't remember worrying that we were behind because the game at this point was so frantic and I couldn't really think about anything.

Then, all of a sudden, we were level because Michael

Owen had used his pace to run at them and a defender had brushed him inside the box. Glenn had told us several times in the past that we should be professional and fall – but only if fouled and not to dive – rather than be prepared to stay up. It was something that other international teams did and we were not good at but had to start learning to do. Diving is quite another matter; as you would expect, being a defender it disgusts me. Anyway, going at that speed, Michael was always likely to get a penalty, and with Alan Shearer converting it, we were level. Phew.

The next thing we knew, it was 2–1 to us with Michael scoring a breathtaking goal, quite possibly one he will look back on as the moment that changed his life. It was the sort that Ian Wright has specialised in at club level, and probably the sort, too, that Michael himself has scored and will score again in the Premiership. Because it was on such a world-wide stage, though, it will go down as one of *the* great goals. It was a weird feeling for me as a defender watching the move unfold. When Michael received the ball from David Beckham in the centre circle, of course I was urging him on as he held off the first defender, Jose Chamot. Then I found myself watching the mess the last defender, Roberto Ayala, made of it, standing square on and flat-footed as Michael ran at him, allowing him to go to his right rather than forcing him left. Once the ball was on Michael's right foot, I could tell he was going to finish. What a moment it was when he did.

With a lead, I was confident that we would go on to win the game. In fact, it should have been all over when Paul Scholes was through on goal just before half-time but pulled the chance wide. Had that gone in, I really could have seen it being another game like the 4–1 win over Holland at Euro '96, one of our really great victories. 'Here we go then,' I remember thinking when Paul missed. 'Got to dig in now.'

I'm sure the Argentinians felt reprieved and, fair play to them, they came back at us with a magnificent equaliser, much as it pains me to acknowledge it. At the time I thought it was just bad defending when Javier Zanetti received the ball in space from their free-kick taken some 20 yards out by Juan Veron, but I have since watched it on television and realised how well worked it was. Zanetti actually started out on the right side of our wall, made his way along the back of it and received the ball with perfect timing before shooting left-footed past David. And Zanetti is right footed.

At the time I was ranting and raving, wondering how it had happened because I had never seen a goal quite like it. We always worked in training on set pieces, both attacking and defending, but this one was almost impossible to defend against because of the surprise element and the slickness with which the Argentinians brought it off. It never showed up on any of the videos of them we watched and I wonder if it wasn't just conceived spontaneously on the night.

From being in control of the game, from what should have been 3–1, we were suddenly level at 2–2 and back in the dressing room feeling a bit sorry for ourselves. Personally, I felt reasonably happy because we were in a better position than five minutes into the game. Glenn was doing his best to lift us. 'Come on, you are better than them,' he was telling us. I felt that though it was a bad time to give a goal away, we were getting stronger – I certainly felt that I was – and that we would go on to win the game. 'We're not going home yet, boys,' I shouted.

I didn't see the incident that changed everything only seven minutes into the second half.

I asked the referee, Kim Milton Nielsen – who was having a bad game, I thought – 'What did he do?' He replied that David had retaliated. I had seen the first foul, which was nasty, Simeone's knee going into Becks's back, but not the kick that David flicked back when he was on the ground. I have retaliated myself in a situation like that but it was impulsive, it has to be said, and the sending-off really set us back. Not that there was any time to dwell on it. We reshaped to 4–4–1 and I said to Gareth Southgate alongside me at the back that we had to push up and not defend too deep.

Even then, I thought we might have won it. But Michael Owen and Alan Shearer were forced to play too far apart now, with Glenn alternating them between wide on the right and in attack down the middle. I think we might have done better to leave Michael up front on his own and perhaps even take Alan off, though I could see why he was left on because of his ability to win corners and free-kicks and the possibility of grabbing a winner with his head from one of them.

The substitution in normal time of Paul Scholes by Paul Merson made sense because Merse's delivery from free-kicks is usually excellent, though he had put the wrong boots on and was having trouble keeping his footing. I was hoping that he might deliver the way he did for me in the '93 FA Cup semi-final against Tottenham, but it was not meant to be. Argentinian defenders, most of whom were playing in the Italian League, know how to mark you and nudge you out of your stride as you attack the ball. They also had the extra man.

I wasn't convinced by David Batty coming on for Darren Anderton, though. I know Glenn had a balancing act between wanting to win it in open play and maybe playing for penalties, but I think we would have been better off putting on another attacking player, as the back four was looking nice and solid anyway. I have always thought that Michael and Teddy Sheringham would be a good pair, Ted to link the play and feed Michael's runs.

Even then... I knew straightaway, though, that Sol Campbell's header home from a corner with a few minutes of normal time left would not be allowed because I was standing right next to the referee when Alan went up with the goalkeeper and was adjudged to have used an elbow. It was an almost comical moment, with Sol on the sidelines and three others celebrating the goal while the Argentinians went downfield from the free kick and almost scored. I was still desperately trying to get back when Darren Anderton made an amazing tackle to save the day.

And so to extra-time, with Glenn coming on to the field to get us all going again and we exchanged a high five. Now we were really flying.

Even then ... I did have one header go not too far wide and then David Batty should have put me in but I couldn't control a difficult pass and they almost went downfield and scored. We also thought we might have had a penalty when Chamot challenged Alan for a high ball and seemed to handle it. All the while, I could hear the drums of the England fans' band as they belted out that theme tune from 'The Great Escape' as the play moved from one end to the other. It was just a thrilling experience, a privilege to be part of it, and I believe I played one of the best games of my career.

Glenn was right when he said we were physically well prepared because our fitness level that night was immense and I was really proud of the way we had more than held on when the final whistle went after extra-time. We had not practised penalties in training though, except for Alan

Shearer, who always likes to. I wonder if there is anything that prepares you for the ordeal. However, I believe that they should have been rehearsed, especially after our Euro '96 experience, but nobody had suggested it at the end of training the previous day.

At this point, I just tried to keep the lads on their toes and keep them motivated.

'Come on, we're not going home,' I had kept repeating during extra-time.

'Enjoy it,' I said now to David Seaman.

'Yes, I'm looking forward to it,' he replied. But then the pressure isn't really on the goalkeepers, is it?

I also turned to Gareth Southgate and said, 'You start my book, Gareth, and I want you to end it by scoring a penalty this time.'

He just smiled. He was seventh in line, after Gary Neville and before me – ever the reluctant penalty-taker through ability rather than attitude, though afterwards I did momentarily feel a bit guilty that I hadn't stepped forward. Sol Campbell and finally David Seaman were the final two in our penalty line-up ... but it would not get that far.

Dave did strike the first blow, saving from Hernan Crespo, but Paul Ince then saw his shot saved by Carlos Roa. Michael Owen was the coolest person in the house, smiling all the way back to the centre circle after almost casually knocking in his shot off a post. The penalty count was 4–3 to them, with David Batty deputed to keep us in it.

'He's told me he's going to blast it straight down the middle,' Alan Shearer, who with Merse had also scored, said to me as Bats walked forward.

Instead he tried to place it and Roa saved again.

For a moment it didn't sink it. I just stood there. Then the realisation dawned. We were out of the tournament. I gave

Bats a look of mock disgust as he slowly made his way back to the centre circle, then a smile and an arm round the shoulder, as we all did. All that was left for us was to applaud the fans for their magnificent support. Marseille memories were eclipsed.

I was the first back to the dressing room where David Beckham was sitting alone.

'I'm so sorry, Tone,' he said.

'Don't apologise,' I said. 'It happens. I love you. Keep that chin up.'

In fact, there were no recriminations in the dressing room. I think all of us knew that but for the grace of God, there we could have gone. David knew what a huge mistake he had made and none of us was going to throw stones at him, no matter what our private thoughts were at that moment.

I actually thought he was very brave. He went through the pain, didn't go out and get drunk afterwards, but bore it all with quiet dignity. Once out in the compound near the team coach later on, he did have a cry when he met his mum. I wish I could have been like that in the past; done my crying there and then instead of going out drinking. Becks is a phenomenal man for one so young. Now, sadly, every professional footballer who goes to the World Cup knows the responsibility he carries and the vilification he can expect if something goes wrong. We have to get back to remembering that this is football, nothing more, and a team game too.

David Batty dealt with things in a different way after his penalty miss. There is a stubbornness inside him and he put on a brave mask, going out to do the interviews and saying, 'Well, I missed a penalty and I'm sorry but I'm not going to let it ruin my life.'

Glenn's reaction to the defeat really impressed me. At first you could see he was down and really shocked by events, but he went round to every squad member, thanking them for their efforts. Even with Martin Keown, for example, he said: 'I know you didn't take part, but thank you for everything you have done within the squad.' In those moments he revealed a human, caring side that made me very emotional. For that I was willing and able to forgive him the times when I believed him to have been wrong.

I had been the one who broke the silence. Everyone was really quiet, just wallowing in their disappointment, but it was not for me.

'We did well,' I said, going round and patting everyone on the head. 'Come on, let's have a shower and get out of here.'

Our team bus was next to the Argentinians who were jumping up and down and singing in celebration. It offended some of our boys as it looked as if they were gloating, but I didn't worry too much. I might have acted the same if we had won. At the end of the game I had gone round to each of the Argentinians and wished them luck for the next round because that's the way I would like to have been treated.

We got back to La Baule at about four in the morning and some of the boys headed straight for the bar, then to the golf course when dawn broke. I headed straight for bed. I was shattered, though I couldn't sleep. Within a few hours we were heading home on Concorde, which British Airways had sent for us and which inspired a bit of fear in me, given my feelings about flying but which I coped with. I certainly had no need then to go to my local pub, put my kit bag behind the bar and embark on a bender, for which I was grateful. I just bought myself a McDonald's on the way home and the next day picked up my kids and took them down to Brighton for the day.

I have strange, mixed feelings about my World Cup campaign. On the one hand, I was proud of my performance, on and off the field, and feel I did credit to myself and my country. I was able soberly to get myself physically, mentally and spiritually in the best order to try and win the greatest prize in the game. I was grateful for the whole marvellous experience, a feeling I have overlooked in the past. I showed patience and tolerance over a long six weeks even when I disagreed with Glenn, who redeemed himself in my eyes in many ways and showed himself a promising international coach.

In fact, I was sorry that I was not able to go on and have more games because I really think I could have shown that I was one of the best defenders in the tournament. As a team, I think we earned a lot of respect and were far from the laughing stock that some England sides of the recent past have been – all heart, but no brains.

When I watched Patrick Vieira and Emmanuel Petit combine to score France's third goal in the 3–0 defeat of Brazil in the Final – on a big-screen TV in Portugal, where I had gone on holiday with my Mum and Dad and children – I was genuinely moved and delighted for them; and also jealous, thinking that it could have been me. I resolved then to give them the 'We are not worthy' routine when we met up again for pre-season training.

England also discovered Michael Owen, a phenomenal talent, but he and we must be careful because there are so many pitfalls for him in the game, as I have experienced. I do have fears for him, just as I do for David Beckham. We have so much talent in this country if we don't destroy it, and now we are getting the knowledge and experience to complement it. As for myself, I don't know how much longer my international career will go on. I certainly don't want to hang around to hinder the progress of such good young players as Rio Ferdinand, but, on the other hand, I will continue to serve my country as long as I am required.

Now we come to the 'on the other hand' part of my view of our performance. In a way, the English are good at cheering people when they come close or fail and that concerns me, almost as much as, on those occasions when we do win something, we dismiss it by pointing out how weak the opposition must have been.

My views on winning have changed a lot, however. Today I am not just Tony Adams the footballer, I am Tony Adams the human being. I do my best every day in every walk of life and seek to treat myself and other people with respect. In that there is also victory. Winning on the field is sweet, of course, but in addition, as far as I am concerned, with each day that I do not take a drink, I will always be a winner.

Postscript

The brown envelope on the doormat inscribed with 'On Her Majesty's Service' looked a bit like a tax demand. The temptation was to bin it, but I knew I had better not. This wasn't the usual bill or junk mail. I opened it slowly. It was from the office of the Prime Minister. 'From the Honours Section, 10 Downing Street', it said. I had been awarded the MBE in the Queen's Birthday Honours List. On the football field, it would take someone pretty sizeable to knock me over. Now, a feather would have done the job.

In my cynical drinking days, I would have ridiculed the Honours list. I would have considered it a sham and a way of rewarding all the cronies in government. Probably there was some envy in me at that time. This morning at the end of May 1999, though, I felt very proud as I took in the contents of the letter.

I'm sure the honour was to do with my services to English football, for both Arsenal and the national team, but I would also like to think it was in some way linked to my recovery from alcoholism. To those struggling with the illness, it showed what can be done and that people are really willing to reward those who help themselves. I had been to prison for drink-driving. I had plumbed some degrading depths, taken there by the drinking. But I had been fortunate enough to find recovery and now I was a Member of the British Empire.

The July day when I went to Buckingham Palace to receive the award was a special, beautiful moment, even though I was nervous. It helped having my Mum and Dad there for company. The Queen seemed very well informed about football and asked me if I had managed to have a long enough rest this year. It was an impressive performance seeing that she had 130 people from all walks of life to deal with that morning, among them the snooker player Jimmy White.

It marked the climax of an astonishing and rewarding period after *Addicted* was first published. On the playing level, it was a strangely mixed year, with Arsenal coming so close to repeating the Double triumph of the previous season but ending up with nothing, and England undergoing a traumatic time. From a personal point of view, it was another period of change, growth and development that has furthered my recovery from my illness as I continue not to drink alcohol, one day at a time.

I have to say I did not feel very fresh or ready for a new season when I came back to Arsenal after the World Cup. The break I had was only about three weeks, which was just not enough for my body to recover properly. It was even worse for the French lads in the Arsenal team who played in the Final of the World Cup and the Dutch boys, who reached the semis, as they only had about a week of pre-season training. It explained a lot about Arsenal's inconsistent first half of the season, in my opinion.

Pre-season for me and my fellow England squad members David Seaman and Martin Keown – with the non-World Cup players away in Germany on tour – consisted of working with Arsène Wenger's French fitness trainer

Tiburce Darrou at Sopwell House for an hour each day on intense conditioning work.

Then it was straight into the Charity Shield. At first, we covered up the cracks reasonably well. The Manchester United players had their own World Cup hangover to deal with and we beat them well, 3–0, as we would do six weeks later at Highbury in the Premiership, when I scored what would prove to be my only league goal of the season, a header, naturally enough.

But while we could always get ourselves up for such big games, it was difficult at times to rouse ourselves as a team for games of lower profile. Personally, I was still feeling match-fit. The little blast of pre-season had been adequate to get me fit for a demanding start to the campaign, but, looking back, it was never going to last nine months. My back was also probably still benefiting from the anti-inflammatory tablets I had taken during France '98 and not having taken part in the latter stages of the tournament.

The week after the Manchester United game, we lost 1–0 at Sheffield Wednesday to slip as low as ninth in the Premiership table. At this point, the end of September, weariness and the pain of my back injury was starting to kick in with me. What should have been a rousing and enjoyable Champions' League campaign, with our home games at Wembley, developed instead into an anti-climax both personally and for the team.

Our first game in Lens was a travesty. We led through Marc Overmars and should have won by two or three, given the chances we had, but then conceded a goal in added time to drop two points. It was a deflating experience and we knew we had missed the chance of a flying start in our group, which also contained Panathinaikos of Greece and Dynamo Kiev, as we sought to qualify for the quarter-finals.

We got back on track with a 2–1 home win over Panathinaikos, in which I scored what was to prove my only other goal of the season, but I was beginning to feel pain in my lower back again. I knew I had to try and keep going, though, through what were big games to us. I survived against Dynamo Kiev at home, a game which we were a little fortunate to draw 1–1 although they only equalised late on.

Arsène Wenger could see I was struggling. He gave me a week off and offered me the option of going to the South of France for some warm-weather rehab work or to go to a health farm in Surrey for plenty of swimming and massage. I chose the latter, so I missed the 3–1 return defeat in Kiev, which seriously damaged our chances of qualifying, but I don't think I would have been much use to the team anyway.

The Lens game at home was a big one for us and we had to win to reach the last eight. I knew I had to give it a go but it was idiotic. By half time I was in agony. Now anyone who plays as long as I have is going to see some degeneration in their body, and the discs in the lower back were the vulnerable area for me. But this wasn't just degeneration. This was excruciating. A disc was actually bulging due to the inflammation.

Just trying to run was bringing tears to my eyes. As I sat down at half-time, Arsène didn't even have to ask. He saw the pain in my eyes. 'No more,' he simply said to me. I shook my head. 'No more,' I replied sadly. Lens pinched the game 1–0 and we were out. In our final group game in Athens, the makeshift side we put out did really well to beat Panathinaikos 3–1 to show what we could have achieved had we been fit and healthy as a squad, but overall the campaign was a let-down.

I felt that the European Cup had passed me by. My last had been in 1991 and we had messed that up then. It is the one big thing left to achieve for me at club level and I have to admit I really envied Manchester United when they went on to lift the trophy in that amazing Final against Bayern Munich.

I don't accept that we didn't have enough quality, or that our technique was not good enough. The timing was simply all wrong for me personally and for us as a club, and it was something we would have to address for the next campaign. 'Why do you always start slowly then come on strong?' someone asked me at the end of the season and I didn't have a ready answer. 'If you started better, you'd be uncatchable.' He had a point.

Thinking about it, injuries and suspensions proved that we needed a greater depth of squad next time round. In addition, we were simply not ready for Europe, but then we weren't the only ones. Juventus, with the Frenchmen Didier Deschamps and Zinedine Zidane, fell away against Manchester United; Marseille slumped in the Cup-Winners' Cup Final, in which Laurent Blanc performed poorly; and Marcel Desailly, I thought, ran out of steam along with Chelsea. If you were to look at the end of the season at the clubs around Europe who did well, Manchester United and Bayern chief among them, the common factor was they had few players who had contested the latter stages of the World Cup.

It might have been different if we could have clung on through the group stages because I know we would have been stronger in the spring. We also had to learn about discipline, I feel. We were without Manu Petit and Patrick Vieira due to suspensions for important games. I think their weariness around that time – and, yes, possibly getting carried away because they were World Champions – were big factors in some mistimed tackling. Around this time Manu talked about quitting the English game, but I think it was just frustration. We can all have rash outbursts when things aren't going our way.

From my own point of view, my body had packed up on me again. I had messed about with the injury instead of getting it sorted out the moment it recurred. As soon as I was under pressure, or got a bang on it, the disc inflamed. It was yet another lesson for me at my age of what my body can and can't stand. I had learned from the intense, quick pre-season that it needed longer to build up these days. Also, when you are carrying an injury, it means you don't train properly, which means your fitness goes, which means your form eventually deserts you and you don't do yourself justice.

The previous season, the problems had started in December and January. This time because of the World Cup, it was September/October and my back simply needed rest. It might have been different had I taken some time off in August, but we had so many important European games that it didn't seem feasible.

Now I had no choice. The week at the health farm had only postponed the problem. Now more drastic action was needed. I saw a specialist in Harley Street who recommended a cortisone injection in my back near the base of my spine. He spent a morning explaining it all to me and then I went to St Mary's Hospital in Paddington. There they gave me a general anaesthetic before injecting me, because they wanted me out completely so that they could locate the exact spot away from all the vital nerve areas without me flinching. I was in and out the same day.

After that, it was decided that I would have six weeks off,

divided into two weeks' rest, two of light training and two of full training and reserve matches before first-team action again. For the first week I simply rested at home, for the second I went to Palm Beach in Florida for some warm-weather recuperation.

There I wrote my Christmas cards on the beach, met up with an old football chum Gary Walker who now coaches schoolkids – Greg Norman's daughter being among his students – and took in a few AA meetings. It was a nice week, though I did have feelings of missing the action and even guilt, thinking I might be letting the lads down.

That grew when I saw that they had let in an unheard-of three goals and squandered a 2–0 lead at Aston Villa. It was the day I got back from Florida and I couldn't believe the final score. That night I was at the BBC Sports Personality of the Year event in London with David Seaman and a few of the other Arsenal lads, who seemed shell-shocked by the afternoon, recovering just enough to smile for the camera when we received the team award. I was flattered to have been nominated for the main award, which was won by some nice young lad called Michael Owen.

By and large the boys managed to stay in touch well with the leaders, ready for what was becoming our customary annual push after Christmas. They even went up to third with a 1–0 win at Charlton over the holiday period.

By then I was back in training and feeling ready to go back to work. I took my children, along with my mum and dad, to Center Parcs in Norfolk over the Christmas but travelled to London Colney to work out. Our new fitness conditioning coach Tony Colbert also lived quite near Center Parcs so we would have sessions on local school pitches as well. It was great being with the kids for the second Christmas in a row, but I had to tell them not to get used to it.

Mind you, I think they should. It is crazy in our country that we do not have a midwinter break with all the football we are expected to play these days. The Italians and Germans do. To be honest, I thought Bayern Munich would outlast United in the European Cup Final, but United gave it one last push and I was amazed where they got the energy from.

It is no surprise to me that we have not done that well at international level of late in view of the intensity of the crammed programme we are expected to fulfil. It will only get worse for the top clubs with the new Champions League format.

We do need to give the England manager a chance as well. More and more international dates are being pencilled in for June, such as our games against Sweden and Bulgaria, and we just don't give him or ourselves a decent opportunity of doing well. Our tired and uninspired performances in those games illustrated the point.

To get match-fit, I played in a reserve team game against Northampton in the second week of January. It was an eventful night. I got booked for a late tackle on their player/coach Kevin Wilson, the former Chelsea striker, who had been winding me up, and we lost 2–0. I was angry, which was good. It showed me I still had the desire to win and that it hurt me to lose. My pride was dented and that was good motivation. Afterwards, Nigel Winterburn, who had also played, remarked that he would pack up the game if he had to play at this level every week. I agreed with him. That was also motivation to get back in the first team.

My return was against Nottingham Forest and it was a good clean sheet as we won 1–0 at the City Ground. I felt very tired afterwards but my back held out and although I didn't have the strength yet to be on the top of my game, I felt I deserved my place back. I was a bit sad it was Steve

Bould who had to give way because he had done a good job, yet again, in the seven league games I missed.

I really felt that this was the starting point of the season. I said to the boys that they had done well, and it had been a good effort to keep us in touch at fourth place, but we really needed to push on now. The difference between also-rans and winners is this ability to step up an extra gear when the serious time of the season approaches. You drive and you drive and then drive some more. You have determination. To me, that was what separated us and Manchester United from Chelsea and Aston Villa who went off the boil too early.

A lot of people have looked at our season last year and this year and noted how we always come good in the second half of the campaign. They suggest that Arsène Wenger's training and dietary methods must have a lot to do with it. And they do have something to do with it. It is, of course, also down to good players and depth of squad, however, as well as injuries and suspensions, and above all to talent and mental attitude.

These days, footballers take a lot more out of our bodies and we need to replace that lost energy. Personally, I am okay with taking Creatine, the dietary supplement that is designed to bring toning and strength to the body. It is really just the equivalent of taking all the good nutritious parts of, say, an apple, or a potato, and concentrating them in one substance. It comes in powdered form and is taken mixed with a drink, of orange juice in our case.

Believe me, if I thought it was in any way damaging, mood-changing or addictive, I would not take it. But I have spoken at length with the nutritonist and been given all the facts. Having been reassured about any long-term effects, I feel it is an aid to my profession. It is all strictly monitored and taken only in moderation.

Of course, I wouldn't take it at all if I wasn't an athlete. I am happy to take vitamins and minerals that are natural. After all, I give my kids Vitamin C and my mum gave me vitamin tablets when I was a kid. Mind you, Arsène also believes in these caffeine tablets that are supposed to improve concentration and stamina, but I don't take them because they give me the runs.

In turn, Arsène would probably not approve of me having fish and chips at home on a Friday night if we're not in a hotel, or getting a McDonald's on the way home from a game with the kids. But it's about balance, not getting fanatical about things. Otherwise my diet is very healthy these days – banana and soya milk on my cereal for breakfast, no milk or sugar in my tea, toast with hardly any butter. And I have pasta every day for lunch.

I would also like to think that our return to a winning run had a little to do with me coming back fit and healthy. We beat Chelsea 1–0 at home in a big match in which personally I didn't play that well, although the team did, and soon after we got a 1–1 draw at Old Trafford against Manchester United. Nicolas Anelka was in his purple patch – he had scored twice against England for France at Wembley just before – and we really needed to hold on after his opening goal. We just couldn't, however.

This time, United had learned a lot of lessons from the previous season when they peaked too soon. They may not have got off to the flier of the previous season but they were well in touch and, like us, had recognised that, come January, it was time to get serious. The depth of their squad helped, with Alex Ferguson able to rotate it frequently.

We had an amazing struggle with them in the semi-final of the FA Cup. It was touch and go which of us got to the Final and, in fact, which of us did the Double again.

We had had an interesting Cup run, to say the least. I sat out the 4–2 win at Preston in the third round, when the boys came back from 2–0 down, and after the 2–1 win at Wolves, I was rested and missed the fifth round tie against Sheffield United at Highbury. I missed that incident as well.

I had left early to avoid the traffic and was probably on Putney Heath walking the dog when Nwankwo Kanu – who proved to be an excellent signing for us – ran on to Ray Parlour's throw-in that was supposed to have gone back to Sheffield United after one of their players had been treated for an injury. In fact, I didn't see the incident for another fortnight, though I heard plenty about it back in training on the Monday for a game that, amid the uproar of Marc Overmars turning home Kanu's pass, the FA had decided should be replayed on the Wednesday in accordance with an offer from Arsène Wenger.

Poor Kanu, who had only been playing football in England for a month, was baffled by the whole situation, although he came to realise what he had done, and to feel sorry for it. There was plenty of mickey-taking. I asked Marc Overmars what he thought he was doing and he said that he had just lost concentration. When he saw the game going on, he said, he reacted instinctively. 'I understand, Marc,' I said. 'I know you like to float in and out of games.' He smiled.

I returned for the replay, which we also won 2–1 in rather less frantic circumstances, and then we secured a late win over Derby in the quarter-final, with Kanu this time the goalscoring hero. After that it was United. The first game at Villa Park, which ended goalless, was not an especially good one, but the replay more than made up for it.

I suppose I have come to look back with some gratitude at having taken part in such a memorable game, although at the time I was simply a loser and that stuck in my throat. It was, as many people have said, a fitting way to mark the end of FA Cup replays, with ties due to be settled on the night from the following season.

I must say, incidentally, that I was shocked at the end of the season when United said they would not be entering the FA Cup the following year because of their commitment to the new World Club Championship in Brazil. Their attitude was an insult to a great competition, in my opinion.

Success in football goes in cycles, as United manager Alex Ferguson knows only too well. After all, winning the FA Cup in 1990 baled him out when it looked as if he might lose his job. Brian Clough, who has never won it, could also tell them how much the competition means. Who knows, in another ten years United might see the Cup as a lifeline.

They have enough resources to enter some sort of team – even if it is only their youngsters, who would love the experience – and I don't believe they should be allowed to get away with such an arrogant attitude. The game must take a stand against the biggest clubs dictating terms, otherwise it will crumble. If United persist with their approach, they should be granted their wish…then never allowed back in the competition.

The game was a lot more open than the previous Sunday, because we all knew there would have to be a winner on the night. When David Beckham opened the scoring from about 25 yards out, I suppose I could have got a bit closer to him but with David Seaman behind us, we have never really worried about people letting fly from that distance. Becks is a world-class striker of the ball though, no doubt.

After that, we might not have got back in it, to be honest, but for Roy Keane's sending off. Then Dennis Bergkamp scored with a deflected shot and all of a sudden we had a big chance. United had a few of their own to win it, but when Gary Neville brought down Ray Parlour in the last minute of normal time, I thought we were through. I couldn't really believe it when we hardly deserved to be still in the game.

But Peter Schmeichel saved Dennis's penalty and the momentum was with United in extra-time, even though they only had ten men. I didn't expect Ryan Giggs to keep going and going when he got the ball for their winner, but then he had come on as a substitute and his legs were fresher. I think I expected one of us to stop him. But he got past Lee Dixon and Martin Keown and I couldn't get there in time before he struck home what was a wonder goal. At least it had taken something special to beat us.

What pleased me was the way I accepted defeat. Once upon a time when I was an active – rather than recovering – alcoholic, I might have behaved like an idiot and wound up the opposition. This time I didn't need to do that and neither did I need to run to the bottle to suppress the feelings of disappointment.

All I could do in the end was accept defeat with dignity and treat people the way I would wish to be treated. I stood at the entrance to the United dressing room and shook their hands one by one. Teddy Sheringham wanted to swap shirts. Mostly I felt sorry for Dennis, who had missed Wembley the previous year, and the younger players. Dennis was very low and apologetic afterwards.

People might have expected our morale to be low after that but instead it redoubled our determination to win the Premiership. We could still have done it, perhaps should have, even going into that last fortnight of the season.

I believed that if we won three and drew the other of our last four games, we would retain the title with 79 points. We duly beat Derby, then had a tremendous 3–1 win at

Tottenham when I felt on top of my game – and it was a feature of the season for me that I played my best football away from the live TV cameras.

I'm sure it was meant to be like that. Last year, as exemplified by the goal against Everton that helped secure the title, was all meant to be played out in full view. This year, it was right for me not to get public attention, just to step out of the limelight and acknowledge to myself, rather than needing the accolades of others, that I had done well.

Going into the final week, I still felt that a draw and a win from the away game at Leeds and the home game against Aston Villa – meaning those 79 points – would be enough, even though United were in pole position, level on points but top because of their better goal difference. I just had the feeling they would drop points somewhere along the line in their two games against Blackburn and Spurs.

We had to get at least a point at Leeds, preferably three because I was doubly certain that 81 points would win the title. And we had our moments – though not enough of them. We were fortunate to survive after Martin Keown conceded a first half penalty but finally we capitulated when Jimmy Floyd Hasselbaink got between me and Nelson Vivas to head home.

With United drawing 0–0 at Blackburn the next night, it just went to show what might still have been achieved. There was still a feeling that we could win it, but when it goes out of your hands, you do sense that it may not be meant to be. It was certainly a different atmosphere at Highbury on the final day of the season from twelve months ago, when anticipation dominated anxiety. We did our bit in beating Aston Villa, but United did theirs too despite a glimmer of hope when Spurs went a goal up before United fought back to win 2–1.

Actually, come to think about it, our season wasn't all that different. We performed excitingly at times, like the 6–1 win at Middlesbrough, followed by the 5–1 win over Wimbledon, and conceded only 17 league goals. We had finished with 78 points, the same as last season. We had been one penalty kick away from the FA Cup Final, in which we would again have faced Newcastle.

But then again, it may not have been good for Tony Adams to have won a double Double. Sometimes things are fated to happen, so that you learn from them.

What was I supposed to learn? Perhaps it was the incentive I, and the team, needed to motivate us to come back for another battle with Manchester United – or whoever else was at the top – the following season. I could have accepted another Double, to be sure, but learning to accept disappointment is part of the growth. I had learned to win sober and now I needed to learn to lose sober.

I learned that I could still perform at the highest level and that I had at least two more good seasons left in me if I took care of my body. I received some criticism for pulling out of England's end-of-season Euro 2000 qualifiers against Sweden and Bulgaria, but it had to be done if I was going to be available for any play-off that might materialise, and even the finals in Holland and Belgium. At least, I had to be thinking along those lines.

My body was telling me that I needed a six-week break if I was going to be playing England internationals – if selected – in the autumn and a demanding Champions League campaign as well as the Premiership and other club games. If I tried to manage on just three weeks' rest as last year, then I felt certain that my back would pack up on me somewhere along the line.

It was not a great season for me at international level, nor for the England team for that matter. After the euphoria of the World Cup, everyone thought it would be a simple task to qualify for Euro 2000 because we were a super team all of a sudden. That wasn't reality, however. Sweden, whom we faced that September, were a good outfit. Yes, we should have done better than a 2–1 defeat but two mistakes can cost dearly at the top level.

We dominated the first 20 minutes and Alan Shearer's goal from a free kick was deserved. Then Andreas Andersson's shot bumbled in off me and David Seaman, and Johann Mjallby got in ahead of Dave to nod home after the ball had spooned up off Paul Scholes. After that, I missed games against Bulgaria, Luxembourg and the Czech Republic through injury and so I didn't see Glenn Hoddle from the Sweden week before his departure as manager.

Now it was no secret that I had never felt totally comfortable with Glenn, his selections and his tactics. It was seen when I had my say about the World Cup campaign. Indeed, after the Sweden game we were both set in front of the press to show some kind of unity in a gesture which I thought was contrived and unnecessary.

I had set aside my differences with him about the way we played, though, and conformed to what he wanted, as a player ultimately must with a manager. I was striking up some kind of relationship and working for him to the best of my abilities. It was very different from what came before with Terry Venables, when I was completely in tune with the way he wanted to play.

But for all that, I saw no reason for Glenn to go. I couldn't see what all the fuss was about in his comments about disabled people. I'm sure he meant no harm. He is a very spiritual man and I didn't see anything in him that was cruel to anybody. He wouldn't hurt a fly. His words did, it seems, but that was just the interpretation put on them, which he could do nothing about.

I thought he could have defended himself a little better once all the furore erupted, but then other people had different agendas and in the end I think the press and the FA wanted him out. It looked like the last straw after some previous controversies. I maintain that the job came too soon for Glenn, that he was still learning the game, but I do think he will make a good manager one day if and when he decides to come back.

No doubt it was a shock both to him and others, but I try to stay away from this shock mentality and keep life and football in perspective. Far more shocking, and sad, to me was the death through cancer of my counsellor James's wife. And if you asked Glenn the most painful experience of the past year for him, I am sure he would say it was dealing with the break-up of his marriage and the effect of that on his children.

Glenn will surely learn and grow through it all because he is the type of person who believes in growth through change. In that, I am with him. It was quite simply that in footballing matters we didn't always see eye to eye.

After he departed, we had Howard Wilkinson in charge for a couple of weeks around a friendly against France, a match for which he chose Seaman, Dixon, Keown and Adams. His only mistake, in fact, was in omitting Nigel Winterburn, and the depleted Arsenal defence let in another Arsenal player, Nicolas Anelka, for two goals. We joked afterwards that we had played Nicolas back into form for the Championship run-in.

I made my own views known publicly, that I would have liked Terry Venables back, but I think it was always likely that the FA were looking at Kevin Keegan. The FA's acting chief executive, David Davies, who had taken over after a spell of blood-letting that saw the chairman Keith Wiseman and Graham Kelly depart, came round the team hotel the week of the French match and asked senior internationals what they thought of Keegan.

It seemed simple to me. There is no doubt to me that we have gone backwards since the Venables era, and if we are not careful we will slip behind the rest of the world again when it looked as if we were getting back up there with them. We had to get back to footballing matters and he, I believed, was the best coach I had worked with, leaving aside any baggage about business dealings or politics within the FA.

We were on the right track with Terry having Bryan Robson as part of his backroom staff, grooming him for the job. Maybe we'll see that with David Platt having got his first taste of coaching with one of the England age-group teams. I would like to see Bryan Robson involved again, maybe after Kevin. But then, as a simple player, what do I know?

It is becoming a problem now, all this stuff outside of football. Glenn learned the hard way, this lesson of not sticking to football. In the end, it became hysterical, front page stuff, with even Tony Blair getting involved. I think if I ever go into management I will make sure that I stick to issues such as whether I pick Alan Shearer or not. I don't think, to be honest, that the public is much interested in anything other than the manager getting the team to play well.

I told David Davies that I had no experience of Kevin Keegan, though Alan Shearer, having worked with him at Newcastle, said he was good. I do wish Kevin well, and I will continue to be available to him if selected because I love playing for England and want to do so again.

My early experience of Kevin was limited to a couple of days before England's match against Poland – which the boys won well 3–1 as a prelude to a disappointing 1–1 draw in Bulgaria – before a recurrence of the back injury sent me home. He kept things very simple, trying not to clutter the players with too much information, and tried to make everything very upbeat, very positive. He is a lovely guy. I hope his methods work and his motivational personality is enough.

I know today that my personality is enough, that I am enough. When I was drinking, there was this sense of inadequacy in me, that I was somehow flawed or deficient as a human being, but as I continue my recovery, I can see that I am as I am supposed to be.

I think I have become more balanced emotionally. There was a time when I would experience sadness, fear, anger and joy all in one morning. It was an emotional roller-coaster. Now I think I've mellowed a little. I have experienced many things sober for the first time and now second time around I am repeating them with more confidence.

For the first time since I was Young Player of the Year in 1987, I went to the PFA dinner and it was something I wanted to do sober. Once there, I was asked by Gordon Taylor, the chief executive, if I would pick up the Young Player award on behalf of Nicolas Anelka, who had not turned up. I agreed. It was interesting doing that, like I was being told something, being given the opportunity to make amends for the embarrassing drunken acceptance speech I made those twelve years ago.

The football has been wonderful. I am a different player these days. I obviously don't have the raw enthusiasm of a

19 or 20-year-old any more but I have an experience and maturity to replace it. Enthusiasm, in fact, can get you into trouble if you rush into situations. I used to go to ground even if the situation was 90 per cent in favour of the attacker. And I used to get cramp all the time with all the nervous energy I had.

There was a time when I thought I was invincible. I remember once talking to the Chelsea chairman Ken Bates when I was young and he was saying that I needed pensions and investments to take care of myself. I wondered what the hell he was on about. I didn't need all that. I felt then like I would go on for ever.

I feel that now I will go on for at least two more years. As long as I rest properly and prepare properly, I can still play a lot of games a season. It is trying to play injured, or trying to cram in too many games, that causes me problems. Rest means I am fighting fit.

It is why I had no hesitation in accepting medical advice in the summer that I should have an operation on a double hernia rather than soldier on, even though it would mean I would miss the first four weeks of the season. I know my body pretty well these days. And mentally I am strong still.

Going into the 1999/2000 season, I thought the Arsenal back four of Dixon, Keown, Adams and Winterburn had at least another year in it; you don't jettison the best defensive record in any European league just because of age. The signs were there, though, that time was running out.

Breaking up was hard to do when it came to my old friend Steve Bould moving on to Sunderland, but it was only right to give him better prospects of regular first-team football in the twilight of his career. I'm going to miss Steve, but good luck to him. In addition, there was even more competition for Lee, with Oleg Luzhny being signed from

Dynamo Kiev, and Nigel, with Silvinho arriving from Corinthians of Brazil as a left-sided player.

After our reserve full-back Jason Crowe was sold to Portsmouth in July, Arsène Wenger did receive some criticism for not giving young English players a chance. This is a thorny issue. It is certainly a far cry from the days of George Graham, who always gave home-grown youth its head, but it will always boil down to the manager's decision and whether he considers a player good enough, irrespective of nationality.

The summer of '99 was also notable for the Nicolas Anelka transfer saga. For me it had little effect in the pre-season build-up simply because he wasn't at the club and therefore we were not basing our training routines and tactics around him. I would have liked him to stay with the club because he is lightning quick and a talented player of the sort Arsenal Football Club needs, but if he chose to play elsewhere and felt he had to move on, then so be it.

I think he was unhappy in London and it must be difficult for such a young man to live abroad. I'm not sure how I would have coped going to Paris as an 18-year-old. Nicolas certainly doesn't have the ego of an 18-year-old Tony Adams, though. In fact, he is a shy character but not as surly as portrayed. Sometimes he smiles, sometimes he doesn't. We're all different.

At times, though, I don't think he helped himself, because he did isolate and go into his shell. He was also too worried about the press, giving interviews solely to French journalists only to see them translated, sometimes erroneously, in the English press.

Away from football, I have remained involved with Alcoholics Anonymous. People sometimes think that once you stop drinking, all your troubles stop. Well, the big, central problem does stop but then you are left with a living problem that continually needs attention and it is important for me to go to meetings at least twice a week, more often sometimes. I am a recovering alcoholic, never a recovered alcoholic.

I need to be reminded that it's a daily programme and a daily reprieve from the illness. For instance, coming back from Arsenal's post-season trip to Malaysia and Thailand, I was sat next to Gilles Grimandi, who was drinking a glass of wine. It smelt very good. It went through my head: 'I'll just have one glass. It will be OK.' But it won't. For a person like me, one is too many, one hundred not enough. And if I hadn't spent that time in the AA programme, hadn't found a power greater than me in my life, I might have taken a drink on that plane journey.

I keep going to the meetings because I need to remain around like-minded, right-minded people. I need to remain healthy, emotionally and mentally, and AA is the best place for me to do that. Those who do get complacent and stop going are the ones who end up back in trouble.

I have had loads and loads of people asking for help, which is wonderful. I would think I answer ten letters a week that Arsenal receive from people who want to know more about alcoholism. I just try to point them in the right direction. I have also been into Pentonville Prison to talk to recovering addicts there, which was an amazing experience. They seemed to appreciate my telling them how it is possible to come back from such an episode in one's life.

When I think of my own time in jail, and the loneliness and fear involved, I am full of admiration for guys who try to recover when they are just left with themselves, their feelings and four walls. I have become involved with an organisation called RAPT – the Recovering Addicts Prison Trust.

So many crimes in this country that fill our jails – like accidents that happen and fill our casualty units – are alcohol-related, and if we could do something about that we would save money and the time of staff involved so that they could treat other cases. Not to mention improve the lives of many unhappy people.

It was the year that my divorce finally came through. I am now very comfortable living on my own. I've also got to know my children Clare, Amber and Oliver better. They are very demanding and seem to go through all the emotions that I'm experiencing myself. Fancy that.

For a few months, I did enjoy a relationship with the model Caprice, whom I met when I appeared on the Ian Wright show. She is a lovely woman. It is very difficult trying to sustain a relationship, though, when both people have demanding professions. You just can't devote the time and energy that is needed to nurture the partnership. We remain good friends, though. As is said, you can have different relationships with the same person but the first person I need to have a relationship with is me. It is probably not until I get to know me properly that I feel I will be able to sustain a relationship with a woman. I'm still trying to get balance, to counter the mood swings I feel around people.

Life is always interesting these days. I became involved in sponsoring a play being put on by a friend at the Edinburgh Festival, for example. It is not always marvellous, however. When I feel down, I think that maybe a new girlfriend or maybe changing football clubs will make me feel better. But I know that this is an inside job – that I have to look within me for the answers, not expect other people, places or things to provide them.

I can't see myself today swopping sobriety for getting

drunk, though a recovering alcoholic can never get complacent about that. I have a wonderful life. The insanity, the fear, the paranoia have been replaced by the reality and joy of living. It is nice to win medals, and to be awarded medals, whether they're from the Queen or my local AA meeting where they honour the length of your sobriety. It's particularly good as well to be able to give myself a medal.

The Twelve Steps of Alcoholics Anonymous

1. We admitted we were powerless over alcohol – that our lives had become unmanageable.
2. Came to believe that a Power greater than ourselves could restore us to sanity.
3. Made a decision to turn our will and our lives over to the care of God *as we understood him*.
4. Made a searching and fearless moral inventory of ourselves.
5. Admitted to God, to ourselves, and to another human being the exact nature of our wrongs.
6. Were entirely ready to have God remove all those defects of character.
7. Humbly asked Him to remove our shortcomings.
8. Made a list of all persons we had harmed, and became willing to make amends to them all.
9. Made direct amends to such people wherever possible, except when to do so would injure them or others.
10. Continued to take personal inventory, and when we were wrong, promptly admitted it.
11. Sought through prayer and meditation to improve our conscious contact with God, *as we understood Him*, praying only for knowledge of His will for us and the power to carry that out.

12. Having had a spiritual awakening as the result of these steps, we tried to carry this message to alcoholics, and to practise these principles in all our affairs.

© *AA World Services Inc. Reprinted with permission.*

Anyone seeking help for a drinking problem can ring Alcoholics Anonymous on (01904) 644 026 between the hours of 9 am and 5 pm, from where they will be put in touch with a local 24-hour hotline.

Career Statistics

Tony Alexander Adams

Born: Romford, Essex, 10 October 1966
Parents: Alex and Caroline, sisters Denise and Sandra
Height: 6ft 3in (1.90m)
Weight: 13st 9lb (86kg)
School: Eastbrook Comprehensive, Dagenham

Junior Football
Romford Royals, Gidea Park Royals, Dagenham United
(and West Ham, Orient and Fulham on trial as a schoolboy)

Professional Football
Joined Arsenal as an associated schoolboy in November 1990, as an apprentice in April 1983 and as a professional on 30 January 1984.

Club Record
Appearances + as substitute (goals) as at end of 1998/99 season in major domestic and European competition

League: 443 + 4(31)
FA Cup: 46 + 1(5)
League Cup: 58 +1(5)

European Cup (including Champions League): 8(1)
Cup-Winners' Cup 16(2)
UEFA Cup: 3(–)

International Record
England Full: 57(4)
England 'B': 4(1)
England Under-21: 5(1)
England Youth: 18

Major Club Honours
Arsenal FC captain since March 1988
English Premier League Championship winner: 1998
English League Div One Championship winner: 1989, 1991
English FA Cup winner: 1993, 1998
English League Cup winner: 1987, 1993
European Cup-Winners' Cup winner: 1994

Major International Honours
Debut: for England v Spain, 18 February 1987, Bernabeu
    Stadium (won 4–2)
Captain of country for first time: England v Romania,
    12 October 1994, Wembley (drew 1–1)
World Cup Finals squad member: 1998
European Nations' Championship Finals squad member:
    1988, 1996

Other Honours
PFA Young Player of the Year: 1987
Awarded MBE in Queen's Birthday Honours List: 1999

Index